English for a
New Generation

English for a New Generation

Hans P. Guth

Professor of English
California State University, San Jose

McGraw-Hill Book Company

New York
St. Louis
San Francisco
Düsseldorf
Johannesburg
Kuala Lumpur
London
Mexico
Montreal
New Delhi
Panama
Rio de Janeiro
Singapore
Sydney
Toronto

English for a
New Generation

2 3 4 5 6 7 8 9 0 D O D O 7 9 8 7 6

This book was set in Times Roman by Black Dot, Inc.
The editors were Robert C. Morgan, Phyllis T. Dulan, and Linda Richmond;
the designer was Anne Canevari Green;
and the production supervisor was Joan M. Oppenheimer.
The printer and binder was R. R. Donnelley & Sons Company.

Library of Congress Cataloging in Publication Data

Guth, Hans Paul, 1926–
  English for a new generation.

  1. English philology—Study and teaching.
I. Title.
PE65.G8   420'.7'1173   73–767
ISBN 0-07-025241-6

Acknowledgments

Every care has been taken to trace the ownership and to locate the copyright holder of every selection
included. If any errors or omissions have accidentally occurred, they will be corrected in subsequent
printings, provided notification is sent to the publisher.

I am indebted to the following for permission to reprint copyrighted material:

Atheneum Publishers for permission to quote from *The Persecution and Assassination of Jean-Paul
Marat as Performed by the Inmates of the Asylum of Charenton under the Direction of the Mar-
quis De Sade* by Peter Weiss. Copyright © 1965 by John Calder Ltd. Originally published in
German under the title *Die Verfolgung und Ermordung Jean Paul Marats Dargestellt Durch Die
Schauspielgruppe des Hospizes zu Charenton Unter Anleitung des Herrn de Sade,* copyright ©
1964 by Suhrkamp Verlag, Frankfurt am Main. All rights reserved. Reprinted by permission of
Atheneum Publishers.

Beacon Press for permission to quote from James Baldwin, *Notes of a Native Son*, copyright © 1955 by James Baldwin, reprinted by permission of Beacon Press.

Sterling A. Brown for permission to reprint "Sister Lou" from *Southern Road* (Harcourt Brace Jovanovich, Inc.) 1932. Copyright of the author. Reprinted by permission of the author.

California English Journal for permission to reprint "Roller Coaster" by Linda Blueford from *California English Journal*, January, 1969. For "The Unknown Student" written by a ninth grade class in collaboration with their teacher, Paul Cummins, from *California English Journal*, April, 1969.

Chilmark Press, Inc. for permission to reprint "Vergissmeinicht" by Ketih Douglas from *Selected Poems*, edited and with an introduction by Ted Hughes. Copyright 1964 by Marie J. Douglas; introduction copyright 1964 by Ted Hughes.

The Dial Press for permission to quote from *Die, Nigger, Die!* by H. Rap Brown. Copyright © 1969 by Lynne Brown. Reprinted by permission of the publisher, The Dial Press.

Mrs. Shirley Graham DuBois for permission to use an excerpt from W. E. B. DuBois, *The Souls of Black Folk*.

S. Fischer Verlag for permission to use excerpts from *Die Farm in den Grunen Bergen* by Alice Herdan-Zuckmayer. © S. Fischer Verlag GmbH, Frankfurt am Main 1968.

Harcourt Brace Jovanovich, Inc., for permission to reprint E. E. Cummings, "Buffalo Bill's." Copyright, 1923, 1951, by E. E. Cummings. Reprinted from his volume *Poems 1923–1954* by permission of Harcourt Brace Jovanovich, Inc. From "Prayers of Steel" from *Cornhuskers* by Carl Sandburg, copyright, 1918, by Holt, Rinehart and Winston, Inc.; copyright, 1946, by Carl Sandburg. Reprinted by permission of Harcourt Brace Jovanovich, Inc. From William Saroyan, "The Hummingbird That Lived Through Winter" from *My Kind of Crazy, Wonderful People*. Reprinted by permission of Harcourt Brace Jovanovich, Inc.

Harper & Row, Publishers, Inc., for permission to use excerpts from pp. 89–91 of *An Empty Spoon* by Sunny Decker. Copyright © 1969 by Sunny Decker. By permission of Harper & Row, Publishers, Inc.

Hayden Book Company, Inc., for permission to use excerpts from Ken Macrorie, *Uptaught*.

Hill and Wang, Inc., for permission to reprint Sam Cornish, "One-Eyed Black Man in Nebraska." Reprinted by permission of Hill and Wang, a division of Farrar, Straus & Giroux, Inc., from *Natural Process* edited by Ted Wilentz and Tom Weatherly. Copyright © 1970 by Hill and Wang, Inc.

Holt, Rinehart and Winston, Inc., for permission to reprint "Stopping By Woods On A Snowy Evening" from *The Poetry of Robert Frost* edited by Edward Connery Lathem. Copyright 1923, © 1969 by Holt, Rinehart and Winston, Inc. Copyright 1951 by Robert Frost. Reprinted by permission of Holt, Rinehart and Winston, Inc.

Alfred A. Knopf, Inc., for permission to reprint Langston Hughes, "Bound No'th Blues." Copyright 1927 by Alfred A. Knopf, Inc., and renewed 1955 by Langston Hughes. From *Selected Poems*, by Langston Hughes. Reprinted by permission of Alfred A. Knopf, Inc.

Harold Matson Company, Inc., for permission to use an excerpt from Ray Bradbury, *August 2026*. Copyright 1950 by Ray Bradbury, reprinted by permission of the Harold Matson Company, Inc.

National Council of Teachers of English for permission to quote from Hans P. Guth, "English as a Many-Splendored Thing" from the April, 1972 *English Journal;* Hans P. Guth, "The Politics of Rhetoric" from the February, 1972 *College Composition and Communication.* From articles in *Language, Linguistics, and School Programs, College English,* and *English Journal.* All reprinted by permission of the National Council of Teachers of English.

New Directions Publishing Corporation for permission to reprint Bob Kaufman, "Benediction." Bob Kaufman, *Solitudes Crowded With Loneliness.* Copyright © 1961 by Bob Kaufman. Reprinted by permission of New Directions Publishing Corporation. Ezra Pound, "Hugh Selwyn Mauberley, V." Ezra Pound, *Personae.* Copyright 1926 by Ezra Pound. Reprinted by permission of New Directions Publishing Corporation.

The New York Review of Books for permission to use an excerpt from Herbert Kohl, *Teaching the "Unteachable."* Reprinted with permission from *The New York Review of Books.* Copyright © 1967 Herbert Kohl.

The New Yorker Magazine, Inc., for permission to reprint Jon Swan, "The Opening." Reprinted by permission; © 1960 The New Yorker Magazine, Inc.

Harold Ober Associates for permission to reprint Langston Hughes, "The Ballad of the Landlord," from *Montage of a Dream Deferred.* Reprinted by permission of Harold Ober Associates Incorporated. Copyright 1951 by Langston Hughes. Arna Bontemps, "A Black Man Talks of Reaping," from *Personals.* Reprinted by permission of Harold Ober Associates Incorporated. Copyright © 1963 by Arna Bontemps.

October House, Inc., for permission to reprint "Frederick Douglass" by Robert Hayden from *Selected Poems.* Copyright © 1966 by Robert Hayden. Reprinted by permission of October House, Inc.

Prentice-Hall, Inc., for permission to use an excerpt from the book *Up the Down Staircase* by Bel Kaufman. © 1964 by Bel Kaufman. Published by Prentice-Hall, Inc., Englewood Cliffs, N.J.

Random House, Inc., for permission to use an excerpt from "Two Soldiers" from *Collected Stories* by William Faulkner. Reprinted by permission of Random House, Inc. From Karl Shapiro, "Auto Wreck." Copyright 1942, renewed 1970 by Karl Shapiro. From *Poems 1940-1953,* by Karl Shapiro. Reprinted by permission of Random House, Inc.

Tim Reynolds for permission to reprint his poem "A Hell of a Day" from *Poets of Today* edited by Walter Lowenfels.

Scorpion Press for permission to reprint Edwin Brock, "Five Ways to Kill a Man." Reprinted by permission of the publisher, Scorpion Press.

Scott, Foresman for permission to use excerpts from Porter G. Perrin, *Writer's Guide and Index to English,* first edition, copyright 1942. Reprinted by permission of Scott, Foresman.

Third Story Music, Inc., for permission to reprint Tim Buckley, "Goodbye and Hello." © 1968 Third Story Music, Inc. All Rights Reserved.

The Urban Review for permission to reprint excerpts from Wayne A. O'Neil's review of Roberts English series, from *The Urban Review,* a publication of the Center for Urban Education.

The Viking Press, Inc., for permission to reprint excerpts from *The Crucible* by Arthur Miller. Copyright 1952, 1953 by Arthur Miller. All rights reserved. Reprinted by permission of The Viking Press, Inc. From "Flight" from *The Long Valley* by John Steinbeck. Copyright 1938, © 1966 by John Steinbeck. Reprinted by permission of The Viking Press, Inc.

Contents

Preface

This is a book about what English teachers should know and what they should do. Many different people teach English, and many conflicting interests absorb their attention. This book is an attempt to define the common core of English as a subject and to sketch out the most basic responsibilities and commitments that English teachers share. In order to do so, the book addresses itself to five major needs:

(1) As English teachers, we need a definition of English as the central part of every student's *general education.* Life as we know it has an ever-present verbal dimension. Language is everywhere part of our human environment. Language is our basic medium of communication and human interaction, of self-expression and personal growth. As teachers of language and literature, we try to help students become more articulate, more aware, more responsive. We try to help them function more fully as human beings.

(2) We need a workable *synthesis of current theory* in the major scholarly disciplines that help shape our subject. English as we teach it today is the result of major movements and countermovements in research, criticism, and scholarship. Teachers have to be able to sift and put to use the contributions of linguists, critics, historical scholars, and other experts in major related fields.

(3) As teachers, we have to bridge the gap between *subject matter and method.* New materials, new theories, new ideas—how do they affect our day-to-day work in the classroom? How do they affect what teachers and students do? We have to relate the what and the how, theory and practical application.

(4) We have to learn how to bridge the gap between the teacher's standards and the *student's performance.* We have to learn how to do less testing, judging, and correcting and more activating, catalyzing, in-

spiring. To teach English means to mobilize the student's resources, to unlock their creative potential. We have to learn how to open up conventional structures and routines to bring about fuller involvement, fuller participation by our students.

(5) We need to see English in its larger *social and cultural context*. American English is a common bond in a pluralistic society. The literature we teach mirrors and helps shape the common values, confusions, and unsolved problems of our culture. How we teach language and literature is related to who we are as people, how we relate to cultural minorities, and where we look for roots in a common past.

This book is based in part on my earlier *English Today and Tomorrow* (Prentice-Hall, Inc., 1964). Some of the material on major current trends first appeared in articles in the *English Journal, California English Journal,* and *College Composition and Communication.* For permission to reproduce sample materials, I am indebted to the publishers of my high school and college textbooks: McGraw-Hill Book Company (*American English Today,* 1970) and Wadsworth Publishing Company, Inc. (*Words and Ideas,* 1972). I am especially grateful to teachers who have let me see and use writing produced by their students: Gabriele Rico, formerly of Camden High School, San Jose; LaVerne Gonzalez and Paula Backscheider, of Purdue University; and Joseph Garcia, of Francisco Junior High School, San Francisco. I wish to thank the many teachers who over the years have listened to me think out loud, and who have in return shared with me their problems, enthusiasms, and rewards.

Hans P. Guth

English for a
New Generation

An Agenda
for English Teachers

The Need for Synthesis—The Positive Approach—The Rediscovery of the Student—The Relevance of English

English as a subject in school and college deals with the student's understanding and use of language. English teachers, if they are successful, keep alive the student's interest in language and develop his control over its resources. They deal with what language does for (and sometimes to) people. They deal with the practical uses of language, with language as self-expression, with language as imaginative experience. They deal with how language serves business and leisure, individual and society.

To teach English with confidence and a sense of direction, we need a coherent view of what English is today as a subject in high school and the early years of college. People who teach English vary greatly in background, interests, and philosophy. But they share a basic commitment. They have common responsibilities and common problems. To find common ground, teachers need answers to four major questions:

(1) What kind of new or updated *subject matter* provides the content of a "New English"? How much do English teachers need to know about the workings of language, the process of communication, the dynamics of literature?

(2) What kind of *teacher* does it take to make new programs and new materials work? How can the teacher develop a positive, modern approach that stresses the resources of language, the rewards for the effective speaker and writer, the satisfactions to be derived from literature?

(3) What is the role of the *student* in today's English classroom? How can we put the emphasis on the student's potential? How can we have him participate actively in the process of discovery? How can we convince him that his use of language, or his experience of literature, is a personal thing, playing a large role in how he defines his identity?

(4) What is the role of English in the larger context of the students' lives and of our common *culture?* What is the meaning of English to alienated middle-class youth, embittered young blacks, students from Spanish-speaking minorities? What definition of American English, and of our literary heritage, does justice to the cultural pluralism of our society?

THE NEED FOR SYNTHESIS

As a minimum requirement, we expect English teachers to deal with language and literature with some degree of technical competence. They have to be able to look at language and literature as something "out there," to be studied objectively and systematically. They need an understanding of language as a system—as a code that works when recurrent elements are combined in patterns according to built-in rules. They need an understanding of variations in usage—of how and why people "say it (and write it) differently," and how and why other people react to such differences in usage as they do. They need an understanding of the purposes and processes of communication—of how words inform, judge, admonish, beckon, incite; of what gives spoken and written discourse substance, structure, and style. They need an understanding of the workings of imaginative literature—of how a whale becomes a symbol, and a rose a simile; of how characterization and plot and style furnish their clues to the intentions of an author.

What we require of English teachers is that they be knowledgeable about what they daily work with: words and sentences, paragraphs and metaphors, poems and plays and stories. Though English has a strong human dimension, it also has a technical base. Though English is in some ways like marriage counseling, where attitudes are as important as physical facts, it is in other ways like botany or engineering, where good intentions are not enough.

English teachers, in other words, need a grounding in some of the relevant subject-matter disciplines: linguistics, rhetoric, literary criticism, literary history. But what they need equally is the ability to see the facts and theories of these specialties as part of a larger whole. Teachers need a sense of how different parts of their knowledge, and their skill, hang together. They need a feeling for how different parts of their subject mesh. They need to be able to build on what they have done in the past, and to look forward to what they have planned for the future. Whether dealing with the new and provocative or with the tried and true, they have to be able to feel: "This is organically related to what I, as an English teacher, am trying to do."

The need for synthesis has always been strong in a subject that ranges from a study of the vowels in *merry, marry,* and *Mary* to the search for the something in Hamlet's soul.

> O'er which his melancholy sits on brood.

But the need is especially strong in several major areas where recent decades have brought new content into our programs. Thus we ask, How compatible are the language materials English teachers have adapted from different major schools of modern *linguistics?* The earlier "structural" linguist was stubborn in his insistence on concrete "surface" fact, on the tangible signals that make language work. He asked us to approach language, not with ready-made definitions and preconceptions, but with an open eye for what in fact makes the difference in pairs like the following:

> He had repaired the faucet.
> He had the faucet repaired.

> The physician studied burns.
> The physician's study burned.

> Who do you think this is, John?
> Who do you think this is—John?

The later "transformational" linguist shifted our attention to the hypothetical processes that generate the surface product. He made us stipulate, in the underlying "deep" structure, the source sentences from which more sophisticated structures were derived:

John mowed the lawn.
His uncle was cranky.
Something annoyed his uncle.

He then took us through the steps leading to the finished product:

John's mowing the lawn annoyed his cranky uncle.

Today we ask, What kind of information about the signaling system, and about the underlying processes, can best give our students an understanding of how language works? What kind of theoretical framework is most likely to "pay off" when we try to help students develop their own sentence repertory? What, from the teacher's point of view, is most instructive and most usable in the work of the scholarly traditionalists, with their strong sense of how our language developed historically; of the structural grammarians, with their respect for unexpected, contradictory linguistic fact; and of the transformationalists, with their pursuit of the hidden mechanisms that make language work?

In the related area of English *usage,* where are we now, thirty or forty years after teachers first started to bring the traditional rules for "good English" into harmony with the facts of educated usage? How successful have linguists been in their battle against artificial rules for *shall* and *will,* and *can* and *may?* What do we do today with the tremendous amount of "objective" information that the advocates of a liberal approach to usage collected about the actual uses of *reason is because, like I said,* and *these kind of potatoes?* How aware are we today of the human and social implications of any large-scale attempt to teach a prestige dialect, no matter how realistically defined? What is our attitude toward the natural speech patterns of children outside the mainstream of affluent, suburban, middle-class America? Assuming that we can agree on the goals of instruction in standard English usage, do we have workable methods for achieving these goals?

In the teaching of *composition,* how have the last few decades changed our view of what meaningful communication is and how it is produced? The new programs and textbooks of a decade ago showed a serious concern with the structure and style of prose. The "revival of rhetoric" led English teachers to take writing seriously—not as a pretext for testing the student's ability to avoid "common errors," but as an opportunity to put together a structured composition, to communicate with a reader. Students studied common rhetorical forms: the process theme, the theme of classification, the theme of comparison and contrast. They studied the elements that shape a writer's style: figurative language, point of view. But imperceptibly, the focus shifted from the analysis of the finished product to the *process* of composition—the student's question inevitably being: How do *I* produce anything remotely like the orderly patterns exhibited in your sample essays and your model themes? Teachers learned to make allowance for *pre*writing—the preliminary stage of observation, incubation, immersing oneself in the subject. They learned to stress the central task of bringing a subject under control, of *working out* a pattern of organization that would do justice to the material. Writing became the process of thinking the matter through, of making up one's mind. And here, trying to involve the student in writing as a creative process, teachers inevitably discovered the central role of motive, of purpose. Today, we ask first of all what it takes to *get* students to write— to use writing as a means of authentic self-expression, of coming to terms with their experience. We try to make students see that writing is "for real" as a means of human interaction—as a vehicle of controversy, of protest, of manipulation. We try to make students see writing as one facet of a broader range of creative expression, with fruitful parallels with oral discourse and nonverbal media.

In the teaching of *literature,* our teaching materials of ten or twenty years ago reflected a turning away from conventional literary history. Teachers rejected a perfunctory piety toward classics that too often remained remote, truncated, unquestioned, unexamined. They gave up a historical approach that in practice meant too many snippets from too many minor authors. Instead, the ideal literary experience became the honest, firsthand reading of selected pieces of true literary value. As far as possible, biographical and historical hearsay was kept from distorting the reader's response. The "New Criticism," dominant in the forties and fifties, encouraged close, formal analysis of a few selected texts. The emphasis was on the way the writer made language serve his special purposes—his use of metaphor, simile, irony, symbol, allusion, paradox, ambiguity. Teachers were encouraged to ask their students not just "What does this writer say?" but above all "How does he say it?"

In recent years, the pendulum has swung back from a technical preoccupation with form to a strong emphasis on theme—on the human and social meaning of literature. Today, we present literature to our students first of all as an interpretation of life—as a record of youth and age, hope and disappointment, effort and defeat, love and hate. We turn to writers because they have something to say—about the condition of man, about social barriers to individual aspiration, about the disasters of war. We look in the work of great writers for eloquence, for the "truly written word." We try to teach literary history so that it illuminates the great themes that have shaped our cultural tradition. We try to make students more responsive to the *language* of literature so that they will be more responsive to the *meanings* of literature.

Subject-matter competence in English is more than the ability to deal with isolated chunks of information. It requires some sense of what makes facts and concepts and skills significant, and how they fit in. It helps us decide what is worth preserving in our traditional ways, and what is counterproductive or obsolete. It helps us decide what in today's ferment points toward progress, and what is fad, whim, hot air.

THE POSITIVE APPROACH

Though drawing from diverse sources, the movements feeding new content into English have by and large been headed for a common goal: *They have made possible a positive modern approach to a subject that had traditionally been treated in too negative a fashion.* Much of the debate over new content was really a struggle over the spirit in which English should be taught. What had defeated the "old" English was its negative attitude toward language as it is used every day. Students knew the English teacher first and last as the policeman of the language. An English teacher was someone who would interrupt people in midsentence to say *"Whom—not who!"* or *"As—not like."* The student who was asked to write his heart out on the topic of the day soon discovered the real purpose of the assignment: to provide the opportunity for an error count, to give the teacher yet another chance to write in the margin *sp, frag, agr, ref, rep, CS,* and *ww.* While little attention was paid to the student writer's opinion on war, women, or juvenile delinquency, much attention was lavished on his alleged misuses of the comma. Teachers who thought of themselves as committed to humanistic values turned out to be preoccupied with the most mechanical aspect of their subject. They were forever measuring inadequate reality against a set of arbitrary, ritualistic rules.

No matter how dedicated individual teachers might be, they were ultimately defeated by a basic orientation that put the emphasis not on where language succeeds but on where language fails. For generations of students, English dealt not with how communication works but with how communication breaks down. No matter how constructive or encouraging the approach of individual teachers, they were part of a larger system operating on the assumption: "The student does things wrong; it is our job to set him right." Students knew in their bones that "English is where you make mistakes."

English teachers have had to learn to start on a different foot. A positive modern approach to English puts the emphasis on what language is and *what language can do.* English is concerned with the resources of language, the power of words, the student's language potential. Language and literature have a tremendous inherent interest that is for us to exploit. They offer powerful intrinsic rewards that are for us to make available to our students. Language is a fascinating, rich, and glorious thing. English as a subject lives up to its potential when the student begins to feel some of that fascination. The student must get a sense of personal satisfaction out of what he is doing. An English class is successful when students emerge from it feeling "That was good—good to know, good to feel, good to do."

Whatever we teach in detail, our basic message as teachers of English is simple: *Language works.* If we have something to say, there is something to say it with. Man is not meant to be deaf and dumb. He communicates. Whatever else we do, we try to keep before our students the example of people—young and old, amateur and professional, living or dead—who have the gift of words. Our basic source material in English classes is always the living example of people able to say what is on their minds:

Nature made ferns for pure leaves, to show what she could do in that line. (Henry David Thoreau)

All electric appliances, far from being labor-saving devices, are new forms of work, decentralized and made available to everybody. (Marshall McLuhan)

It requires enormous intelligence, innate or acquired by cultivation, to discharge the full responsibilities of managing a household; doing its endlessly repetitive work without deadening the mind; bringing up children, restraining, encouraging and helping them; being a companion and helpmeet to one's husband, helpfully and intelligently interested in his work; and being, at the same time, able to take on his duties and responsibilities if she must, as thousands of women have had to. (Dorothy Thompson)

The living use of language is not a simple printing out of information. A basic part of our job is to give our students a sense of the full *range* of what language does. Words do our bidding in a variety of vital ways. Thus, language does not just inform. It *interprets;* it clarifies. It helps us find our way. It sheds light; it brings things into focus. It serves the basic need that makes us turn to someone who says, "Let me explain":

What the American young do know, being themselves pushed around, itemized and processed, is that they have a right to a say in what affects them. They believe in democracy, which they have to call "participatory democracy," to distinguish it from double-talk democracy. . . . they want the opportunity to be responsible, to initiate and decide, instead of being mere personnel. (Paul Goodman)

Disobedience is a long step beyond dissent. In this country, at least in theory, no one denies the right of any person to differ with the government, or his right to express that difference in speech, in the press, by petition, or or in an assembly. But civil disobedience, by definition, involves a deliberate punishable breach of a legal duty. However much they differ in other respects, both passive and violent resisters intentionally violate the law. (Charles E. Wyzanski)

At the same time, the message of language does not exist in a vacuum; in various ways, it reveals and disguises its source. Language *expresses personality*. It is part of who we are. Words reflect the way people think and feel. We become individuals as we begin to use language in a way that is true to ourselves. In authentic language, we hear a living human voice; we recognize a person who is in some ways unlike any other:

I wear my hat as I please indoors or out. (Walt Whitman)

I always go to sea as a sailor, because they make a point of paying me for my trouble, whereas they never pay passengers a single penny that I ever heard of. (Herman Melville)

Better be a nettle in the side of your friend than his echo. (Ralph Waldo Emerson)

To do good is noble; to teach others to do good is nobler, and no trouble. (Mark Twain)

And if on the one hand language expresses the person, it on the other hand *reaches out toward others*. We use language to make others take notice, to make them pay attention. We share our sorrows, our triumphs, our fears:

As I walk down the hard sidewalk, the sunlight is behind me, and I stare blindly into my dark shadow. A group of people pass me talking happily among themselves. It seems as if they are in a moving box, and I can see the walls. I smile, but there are no windows to see me through. A gusty cold wind blows and has crept into my mind. A dark concrete building looms ominously above me. No lights, no colors, just gray unfinished concrete. My mind is cold; I feel the hollowness, the hurt, but cannot rid myself of these bitter feelings. (Student theme)

Language bears witness. It draws us in; it makes us feel part of the larger human community. We find it hard to feel neutral, to stand aside, when a writer who used to suffer from a speech defect tells us what it means to be a handicapped child in a "normal" world:

> The word was my agony. The word that for others was so effortless and so neutral, so unburdened, so simple, so exact, I had first to meditate in advance, to see if I could make it, like a plumber fitting together odd lengths and shapes of pipe. I was always preparing words I could speak, storing them away, choosing between them. And often, when the word did come from my mouth in its great and terrible birth, quailing and bleeding as if forced through a thornbush, I would not be able to look the others in the face, and would walk out in silence, the infinitely echoing silence behind my back, to say it all cleanly back to myself as I walked in the streets.—Alfred Kazin, *A Walker in the City*

The writer who bears true witness has the power to make us say with Walt Whitman: "I was one of them; I was there":

> I and two Negro acquaintances, all of us well past thirty, and looking it, were in the bar of Chicago's O'Hare Airport several months ago, and the bartender refused to serve us, because, he said, we looked too young. It took a vast amount of patience not to strangle him, and great insistence and some luck to get the manager, who defended his bartender on the ground that he was "new" and had not yet, presumably, learned how to distinguish between a Negro boy of twenty and a Negro "boy" of thirty-seven.—James Baldwin, *The Fire Next Time*

Finally, language is not merely a tool that serves us in our lives; it is part of the drama of life itself. Words *feed our need for color, rhythm, and excitement.* They keep alive our sense of wonder; they appeal to our capacity for laughter. They create for us a universe in which we live more fully, and see more intensely, than in our nonverbal lives:

> I was born in a large Welsh town at the beginning of the Great War—an ugly, lovely town (or so it was and is to me) crawling, sprawling by a long and splendid curving shore where truant boys and sandfield boys and old men from nowhere beachcombed, idled and paddled, watched the dock-bound ships or the ships steaming away into wonder and India, magic and China, countries bright with oranges and loud with lions. —Dylan Thomas, *Quite Early One Morning*

> The garden sprinklers whirled up in golden founts, filling the soft morning air with scatterings of brightness. The water pelted windowpanes, running

down the charred west side where the house had been burned evenly free
of its white paint. The entire west face of the house was black, save for
five places. Here the silhouette in paint of a man mowing a lawn. Here, as
in a photograph, a woman bent to pick flowers. Still farther over, their images
burned on wood in one titanic instant, a small boy, hands flung into the air;
higher up, the image of a thrown ball, and opposite him a girl, hands raised
to catch a ball which never came down.—Ray Bradbury, *The Martian Chronicles*

English teachers readily respond to definitions of their subject in
positive or even inspirational terms. Yet they have found it difficult to
implement a positive approach in their daily work with language. They
have found it hard to overcome ingrained habits: They had become used
to teaching diction in order to get at words *misused*, to teaching coherence
in order to get at the *lack* thereof in the student's writing. They have to
develop habits of the opposite kind—making sure that the prevailing
slant of all language activities be *constructive*. Thus, doing exercises
once meant "finding the mistake" in a sentence that to the unspoiled ear
of the student was in itself a mistake:

Had we known of your desire to go with us, we most certainly would of
invited you to join our party.

Neither Harriet nor Claire was completely convinced by Joan's insisting
that it was them who were to blame.

Today, doing exercises means doing productive things with language,
putting something together rather than tearing it apart. Thus, we look
for *sentence-building* exercises that show, not how a writer gets trapped,
but how he manages to be articulate, how he loads a sentence with freight.
We look for "muscle-building" exercises that make a student feed simple
parts into a larger structure:

Five Statements:	The astronaut entered the capsule.
	The astronaut was *a boy*.
	The astronaut was *Russian*.
	The astronaut was *handsome*.
	His entrance was *quick*.
One Statement:	The *handsome Russian boy* astronaut *quickly* entered the capsule.

Statement:	The hall burned to the ground.
Added Source:	The hall was *a "fireproof" multimillion dollar structure*.
Result:	The hall, *a fireproof multimillion dollar structure*, burned to the ground.

Statement:	The police found the murder weapon.
Added Source:	The murder weapon was *an Italian mail-order rifle.*
Result:	The police found the murder weapon, *an Italian mail-order rifle.*

Again, a large part of our repertory used to be *horrible* examples. Today, we look for examples of how things are done right. When we teach the adjective, we quote Mark Twain, who put the adjective to good use, and who once called a person he disliked a "middle-aged, long, slim, bony, smooth-shaven, horse-faced, ignorant, stingy, malicious, snarling, fault-hunting, mote-magnifying tyrant." When we teach verbals, we turn to writers who use verbals well:

> Zurito, *sitting on his horse, walking him toward the scene, not missing any detail,* scowled.

> Manuel, *leaning against the barrera, watching the bull,* waved his hand and the gypsy ran out, *trailing his cape.*

> Manuel, *facing the bull, having turned with him each charge,* offered the cape with his two hands.

> (Ernest Hemingway)

When we teach figurative language, we no longer concentrate on the mixed metaphor, the inept metaphor, the extravagant metaphor, the trite metaphor. Instead, we concentrate on what figurative language can do:

> Putting the hubcap back on the rim is *like putting an undersized lid on an oversized jar.*

> The candidate *surfed* to the speaker's table on a nice *wave of applause.*

> Cornelia's voice *staggered and bumped like a cart in a bad road.* (Katherine Anne Porter)

> She would look for dark spots in his character and *drill away at them as relentlessly as a dentist at a cavity.* (Mary McCarthy)

> He lay down in his shirt and breeches on the bed and blew out the candle. Heat *stood in the room like an enemy.* (Graham Greene)

Just as we look for a positive slant in the materials we bring to our students, we look for what is promising in what our students bring to class. We look for interests and habits that an English teacher can relate to and build on. Anyone who listens to children knows how language-conscious and verbally oriented they are. Their favorite jokes and stories revolve around a *play on words,* the repetition of a catchy phrase, the

repetition of a familiar verbal pattern. For the adolescent, much that for
the jaded adult has become trite is still fresh and entertaining. The adolescent delights in the discovery that language is not always businesslike,
responsible, admonitory. He prefers the casual, colloquial style to the
self-important, pompous style (and takes delight in mimicking the latter).
He has a weakness for outrageous puns and other ways of playing games
with language. Students with allegedly "low verbal aptitude" will expend
loving care in constructing something like the following:

> In a small town in the USA there came a day when the town ran out of funds.
> They didn't have enough money to run the schools, pay the teachers, or run
> the libraries. The town called a large meeting. What could they do? They
> already had tax on cigarettes, luxury, sales tax, alcohol, property, income,
> etc. One gentleman stood up and said, "It's time to get down to the brass
> tax."

In their eagerness to stamp out "immature" informality and ex-
travagance, English teachers have in the past banished from their classrooms much of what gives language life, sparkle, human interest. Today
we try to keep alive in the students' use of language the very elements
that make the difference between sparkling, spontaneous, living language
and gray, homogenized committee prose.

Most basically, we are learning that resourcefulness, inventiveness,
and articulateness are more essential to the effective use of language than
is a narrow conventionality. Where we used to wince at the slanginess of
children's playground speech, today we take heart at the inventiveness
investigators discovered in the following small sample of insults used by
English schoolchildren:

> bats, baby, barmy, crackers, crackpot, daffy, dippy, dizzy, dope, dotty,
> goofy, ninny, nitwit, nutty, potty, cracked, cuckoo, loco, nuts; "he's not all
> there," "he's out of his wagon," "he's off his rocker," "he's off his chump,"
> "has a screw loose," "is a bit touched," "a bit wrong in the head," "half
> baked," "a stupe"; clown, fathead, mutt, muggins, oaf, "a bit of a twerp,"
> "a silly goop," "a proper Charlie"; thickhead, "a head full of lead," "bone
> from the knees up," dimwit, dullard, dunderpate, numbskull, "a brainless
> chump," pea-brain

We are beginning to see that a pretentious, excessive formality is as
much, or more, a danger to honest talk as an excessive informality ("I
sincerely believe that the government should *divulge* more on the subject
of socialism and its *cohorts*, because its *impetus* has reached a frightening
momentum"). We are beginning to admit that a truly effective speaker

and writer never removes himself entirely from the *common idiom,* from the leavening informality of everyday talk:

> A sturdy lad from New Hampshire or Vermont, who in turn tries all the professions, who *teams it, farms it, peddles,* keeps a school, preaches, edits a newspaper, goes to Congress, buys a township, and so forth, in successive years, and always *like a cat falls on his feet,* is worth a hundred of these *city dolls.* (Ralph Waldo Emerson)

> There was a broad streak of mischief in Mencken. He was forever *cooking up* imaginary organizations, having *fake* handbills printed, inventing exercises in pure nonsense. (Philip M. Wagner)

> To reject the book because of the immaturity of the author and the *bugs* in the logic is to throw away a bottle of good wine because it contains bits of the cork. (E. B. White)

We are beginning to see that verbal humor is one of the signs of life in language—that there is hope for a writer who responds to verbal nuances, echoes, and doubletakes:

> I enjoyed the riding school thoroughly, and *got on—and off—*as well as most. (Winston Churchill)

> I was gratified to be able to answer promptly, and I did. I said I didn't know. (Mark Twain)

> Bear it like a man, even if you feel it like an ass. (George Bernard Shaw)

> A major television network last night premiered the only new live music-and-dance program of the season. . . . A word should be said about the dancers. The word is "appalling." (Newspaper column)

> People who should know tell us that during the Paleolithic Age man's store of knowledge doubled every 100,000 years, give or take a month or two. Even then it didn't amount to much. Man learned to build fires, say, and then in another 100,000 years he learned to put fires out. That sort of thing. (Patrick Butler)

One major barrier to a positive approach to our subject is the traditional division between *ordinary* language use ("grammar," "composition," "expository prose") and literary, *creative* language use ("literature," "creative writing"). The former was often treated as the unwanted poor relation of her more glamorous and seductive sister. Teachers taught language and composition in a grimly businesslike spirit, putting them in front of their students as hurdles to be cleared before they could be admitted to the glories of literature. This split has served neither language nor literature: It has caused us to drain the poetry from our work with ordinary language; and it has cut our work with literature loose from its moorings in common language and common experience.

The poet uses *more* of language; the novelist and the playwright respond *more fully* to experience. This is exactly what we try to accomplish in teaching our students English: to have *them* use the full resources of their language, to have *them* respond more fully to the world around them. No one should teach composition who is not aware of the creative, imaginative element in the best expository prose. No one should teach poetry who does not respond to the poetic element in the verbal play of children. Whether we teach language, or composition, or literature, we deal with the same basic questions: How people use words, how language charts experience, how dialogue reflects human interaction. These are the questions that give English as a subject its fundamental positive attraction and human value.

THE REDISCOVERY OF THE STUDENT

A teacher must be able to reach his students. When a teacher is committed to his subject, excited by its challenges, the question remains whether he can share that excitement with his students. If there is a common denominator in current educational reform in America, it is the rediscovery of the student in the back row—more often than not alienated, defiant or apathetic, "turned off," just barely polite. Today's "romantic" critics of American education, whatever their specific diagnoses and remedies for our educational ills, insist on a basic truth: Teachers must be interested in children. People who ultimately cannot genuinely like children would be better off in some other calling. A teacher of adolescents should be someone who, whether sentimentally or not, loves young people. A teacher should be someone who can appreciate children's energy and spirit—"the brightness of children's faces when they are hard at their games, the vivacity of their voices, the swiftness of their invention, the accuracy of their observations." He should treasure the "gay intelligence" of childhood, which education must not be allowed to destroy. Insofar as possible, he should encourage growth through "immediate and intrinsic" rewards inherent in the learning activities themselves. He should have students develop a "sense of the skills and the varieties of behavior that lead to greater pleasure, greater security."[1]

True teachers do not merely move prepackaged goods off the shelf. They do not turn out a product according to specifications. One of their most basic objectives is to make the student *actively participate* in learning. One of the most important things a successful student learns is to carry his own weight, to make his own contribution. An essential part of our task as teachers is to break through the crust of apathy, indifference, and dull routine. We try to keep alive the student's spontaneity and creativity. We try to foster student initiative and student response. We try to move from a narrowly teacher-controlled pattern toward *interaction* in a more open, more student-centered classroom.

Ideally, to make something new his own, the student participates in its discovery, tries it out in practice, tests it in new contexts, learns from the trials and errors of his fellow learners. The teacher, in turn, gets "involved." He brings in his own experience and commitment; he *listens* as well as talks; he respects students as people; he learns from their confusions and rebellions, their triumphs and mistakes.

The requirement for active participation in fundamental ways shapes daily classroom routine. Put in the most elementary terms, there must be things for the student to do. There must be things for students to get involved in and become intrigued by. There must be *activities* that stimulate their initiative, that provide scope for the exercise of their imagination. Thus, when we present the subject-verb skeleton of the simple sentence, we catch ourselves early in the hour, lest we provide all the explanations and all the examples ready-made. Instead, we early say to the student: "Your turn." We let the student explore the full range of the "intransitive" verbs that fit into the "Birds fly" pattern. We ask him to find other single words that fit into the identical slot:

What do birds do? They _____. (They fly. They chirp. They tweet. They hop. They flutter. They soar. They swoop. They dive. They nest. They brood. They migrate. They depart. They return.)

What do angry people do? They _____. (They shout. They frown. They glare. They argue. They fume. They sulk. They boo. They hiss. They rebel. They demonstrate. They riot. They organize. They petition. They march. They protest.)

What do happy people do? They _____. (They smile. They whistle. They hum. They dance. They skip. They grin. They smirk. They dawdle. They relax. They sing. They wander. They roam. They chortle. They chuckle. They guffaw.)

What do students do? They _____. (They work. They play. They study. They read. They write. They groan. They complain. They doze. They cram. They pass. They fail. They experiment. They bluff. They flatter. They conform. They learn. They graduate.)

Whenever possible, we put the student through his paces. When we talk about the way modifiers build up a barebones sentence, we have the student write open-ended practice exercises that show the process in action:

The cowboy rode.
The *tired* cowboy rode *into town.*
The cowboy, *a famous outlaw,* rode *slowly into the sunset.*
The cowboy, *a lean-jawed matinee idol in an $800 suit,* rode *onto the set.*

The man approached the gate.
The man *in the convertible* approached the gate *at high speed.*
The man *in the shabby coat* approached the gate *at the end of the park.*
The man *with the kangaroo* approached the gate *at the end of the park in a devil-may-care mood.*

As we become more ambitious, we increasingly involve the student in the discovery of the actual structures that our examples illustrate and our exercises implement. There is all the difference in the world between a rule that the student found ready-made on a printed sheet and one that he discovered as something actually functioning in observable reality. This is the strength of the **inductive** pattern that proceeds from the raw data to generalizations, conclusions, "rules": The student begins to see that ideas are anchored in reality; that abstractions are ultimately derived from and tested against experience. Again and again, to give our students a sense of basic mechanisms at work in language, we can start from actual samples of language in use. Here, for example, are some actual samples of the kind of pidgin widely spoken by school children in Hawaii:

Today, one man almost went run me over in the crosswalk.

I going to tell Mommy you went do that.

Ugly dat one!

Hurry up! We going home. You no like go or what?

"Daddy, where you?" "I stay here."

Yesterday she like go leech one ride from Dennis but Dennis no like give her one.

He been work too hard.

Fast, man, them guys going.

I been go downtown shopping.

My car went broke down. You can give me ride?

What are some of the things here that students would notice? What conclusions could they draw about how this dialect "works"? One thing we are bound to notice is how *went* is used in these sentences: It does not seem related to *go* in the sense of coming and going. "He *went* run me over," "you *went* do that"—the *went* here seems to come in simply as a signal that this is not happening now; it already happened. It happened *in the past*. *Went* is a past signal; it is used as if it were an auxiliary that says "not now but in the past." There is a similar use of *going* to signal future: "I *going* tell Mommy." And in fact there is a similar use of *been* to signal "perfect"—something in the past whose effects are *presently* felt: "He *been* work too hard"—and he's *now* tired. We thus get the following scheme:

> *Past:* One man *went* run me over.
> You *went* do that.
> My car *went* broke down.
> *Future:* I *going* to tell Mommy.
> *Perfect:* He *been* work too hard.
> I *been* go downtown shopping.

We can contrast this simplified system of tense auxiliaries with the "mixed" system of standard English. We use auxiliaries for future and perfect ("He *will* listen," "She *has* left"). But we use inflections, that is, changes in the form of the word itself, to show past (ask-*asked;* listen-*listened;* bring-*brought;* know-*knew*).

This kind of inductive exploration reinforces a basic lesson: The basic rules for how language works are not something we invent. We *discover* them in the way language works. A similar inductive approach can shape the teaching of composition when we put the emphasis on actual *models* of effective writing. Instead of laying down abstract principles about the paragraph, we can present an actual living paragraph and look for what holds it together:

> When he was done shaking hands with me, the Judge smoothed back his thick, black mane, cut off square at the collar, like a senator's, put one hand in his pocket, played with the half-dozen emblems and charms on his watch chain with the other, teetered from his heels to his toes two or three times, lifted his head, smiled at me like I was the biggest pleasure he'd had in years, and drew a great, deep breath, like he was about to start an oration. I'd seen him go through all that when all he finally said was, "How-do-you-do?" to some lady he wasn't sure he hadn't met before. *The Judge had a lot of public manner.*—Walter Van Tilburg Clark, *The Ox-Bow Incident*

As we look at the details in this paragraph, we discover that they all point in the same direction; they all funnel into the same overall point— the big show the judge puts on in "meeting the public." This paragraph, in other words, "is going somewhere"—it has purpose; it has direction. There is indeed a "topic sentence" that sums up the point about the judge's public manner. But in this paragraph it appears at the end. The pattern is something like "Let me show you what I mean first; then I'll spell it out for you in so many words." We can contrast this pattern with the more common one that follows the opposite strategy: "I'll first *tell* you what I am getting at and then *show* you what I mean by practice." Again, the student here comes upon basic principles, not as arbitrary rulings laid down by teachers, but as something live, functional, part of how writing "really works."

The need for active participation by the student is equally strong in all major areas of English. When we teach poems, we have to show that people are not related to poetry as mere passive consumers: Poetry is first of all something people *do*. Music is not living music unless people play, hum, sing, dance, improvise. Literature is not living literature unless students have a chance to "get into it"—to act it out, to parody it, to improvise their own. When we talk about Aesop's beast fables, we are not talking about dusty exhibits in the literature museum. As a living form, they serve for edification and entertainment all around us—in political persuasion, in advertising:

The Seal and the Sandwiches

A picnicking seal, the family lunch tucked under one flipper, stood teetering dangerously at the brink of a steep cliff when his young son approached. "Daddy," piped the pup, "Mother says either come away from the edge or give me the sandwiches!"
Moral: It is well to know which side your bread is buttered on.

When we deal with Aesopian fables, students should feel: "I want to try one of those!" When we read E. E. Cumming's "Portrait" of blue-eyed Buffalo Bill, who "used to ride a water-smooth silver stallion," our students should want to do a similar portrait of someone more recently "defunct," who meant something—perturbing, inspirational, or ironic—in *their* lives. When we read Edgar Lee Masters' poetic epitaphs about the people of Spoon River, we want our students to get into the spirit of the thing. We want *them* to pretend that they are among the Lucinda Matlocks and Ann Rutledges "who sleep beneath these weeds." This is what the two junior high school students did who wrote the following poems:

My Epitaph (1)

Born by the banks of the Ohio,
This Hoosier set out for places unknown,
Found HER some years later,
Made her his wife and mother of two,
Sent the boys thru school,
Watched them grown up in what seemed like a short time,
Retired to the mountains and easy living,
Then, his dear one left him for eternity,
This is the epitaph
    of a long, weary, and happy life.

My Epitaph (2)

Out of me unworthy, and unknown,
The vibrations of the theater grew.
"With malice toward none and charity for all,"
Out of me came hit after hit,
Shining with youth and talent.
I am "John Fitzpatrick" who sleeps beneath these weeds,
Beloved in life by theatergoers;
Wedded to the stage, not through pull,
But through years of hard work.
"The show must go on!"[2]

To get a feeling for what literature is all about, students need frequent opportunity to read, pin up, edit, publish, anthologize *their own writing.* They need to learn that a poem is not dead letters on a page. It is something cherished and fussed over by a lonely individual; presented with trepidation and yet with secret pride; received, if the author is lucky, by someone who appreciates, who understands.

The emphasis on student participation thus conditions in basic ways what we do everyday in the classroom. But it also at the same time in basic ways affects our view of our long-range goals. Up to a point, like teachers in other subjects, we can measure our success by the student's ability to retain and apply information, to perform limited tasks. We can feel that our instruction has "taken" if the student has learned to spell difficult words, write sentences that contain an appositive, distinguish a literal from the figurative use of the same word. As long as these are our goals, we can accept a definition of "individualized instruction" that turns to prepackaged, general-purpose materials but selects them to fit an individual's needs or level of achievement—using these materials to bring him up to general norms.

But to teach English ultimately means to rely on, to bring in, and to do justice to the individual in more basic ways. First, true speech and writing are in essence an individual response. Though we may neglect this element in simulated practice runs, true language is something that the individual *wants to say*. True use of language means that the student becomes involved in the actual give-and-take of communication: A question arises that deserves an answer. A charge is made that calls for a reply. A misstatement is circulated that cries out for correction. A problem exists that desperately needs solution. A solution is offered that seems pitifully inadequate. Our "writing situations," our assignments, are no good unless somewhere the student learns what it means to feel: "There is something I want to say. I want you to listen while I set the record straight. Listen to me!" This is where the student becomes a genuine participant in the **dialectic** of assertion and response. Something strikes a spark, and the individual *talks back*. This is why we explore issues. This is why we involve the student in what has been thought and said; this is why we play the devil's advocate—all so that we may trigger in the student the unpredictable, authentic response.

Second, the test of competence in English is ultimately the *free choice of means*. It is true that much of the time we demonstrate *possibilities*. We show our students what has worked for other speakers and writers. But ultimately a competent speaker or writer has to make his own choices. Writing on a subject like censorship, the *individual* must decide whether to treat the subject seriously or satirically. He can move on a high plane, describing the processes by which, ideally, information is exchanged and responsible opinions are formed in a free society. Or he can move on a much lower plane, documenting the obtuseness, the presumption of the actual bumbling censor, who makes the author change his "damn" to "darn," his "My God" to "My gosh." Again, the individual writer has to decide whether to be conciliatory or aggressive. He may want to be reasonable, find common ground in shared assumptions, appeal to all men of goodwill. Or he may be losing his patience and decide to confront and contest, to drive the beast from its lair.

A paper like the following cannot be "normed." It cannot be programed or checked off against a list of objectives. The student who wrote it has discovered how to use language in self-directed, purposeful fashion. She uses language to focus on something that matters. She speaks out in such a way that she will be heard. She uses words as an honest expression of her own experience.

Prejudice

Prejudice, a word only the white man himself can create. Since I am black, and have been conditioned to act, think, react, dream, and live in a world of blackness, this inhumane word causes a hard knot to form within me. "Prejudice," I was born with and have lived with so long. However, before I continue, may I express to the reader that I realize prejudices are not limited to the black man alone. But I have lived so long with this word, I sometimes think so.

The white man's dictionary defines the word as being an irrational attitude of hostility directed against an individual, race, or group of people for their supposed characteristics. However the black man would define the word as "life itself." For only the white man in his world of computers, electronic devices, and the space race could enforce such a barbaric ritual, that would last for over a century. Such progress is not for me.

Prejudice is a gigantic monster that has many sizes and shapes. It may start in kindergarten with the youngster. The mind of a child wouldn't stop to think about why he went to an all black school. Or why the school was situated in an all black neighborhood. Or why busing wasn't extended to those that wanted to go elsewhere. But as the child would grow older and more experienced he would ask why. But there would be no reply. Who could tell him it was meant to be this way, because he was "different." Who would even have the heart to tell him how or why he was different. No one could or would. Prejudice has been with me since my family was the second black family in my neighborhood ten years ago. To have a petition sent around so that your family has to move is a feeling that I will never forget or forgive. The feeling of prejudice has been like my shadow in high school. It made me fill with hate when black girls were cut from cheerleading and pom-pom girls on first screening. The reason was, they had no rhythm.

Prejudice will always go hand in hand with the black child, even growing into manhood with him. And then it will mature and ripen like an old man, and die with him. However he will even be haunted in the grave, for he will be buried in a "black area" within the cemetery. I must conclude that "prejudice" is a companion of mine. As long as the white man is here to enforce its conditions, it shall always be with me.[3]

THE RELEVANCE OF ENGLISH

Ultimately, like other school subjects, English derives its significance from its relation to life outside the classroom. We study language because language everywhere plays a central role in human experience. We study metaphor, irony, and symbol in order to see how literature reflects, interprets, and in turn shapes life. The specialist tends to get absorbed in the internal workings of language as a system, in the forms and textures of literature as a special way of saying. As teachers, however, we ask how an increased technical understanding of language and literature can help us to promote their human uses.

As English teachers, our basic responsibility is to deal with *living language*—with language in the full context in the life of the individual and of society. How students talk, and what they write, has a great deal to do with who they are. How people use language has something to do with their cultural background, their social group, their private history as individuals, their personal aspirations and commitments. What literature we teach, and how we teach it, depend on how we see literature as part of our larger culture. It depends on how we define our cultural heritage.

Language, in our society, as in others, serves as a *social indicator*. How people talk correlates with where people live, what educational opportunities they enjoy, what their job prospects are. It is true that greater mobility and the mass media have produced in this country, earlier and more thoroughly than in comparable modern societies, a standard national language subject to only minor regional variations. What language differences there are seldom serve as a barrier to communication. But they do serve as a reflection, and partly as a cause, of social status.

English teachers have generally preferred to believe that "good English" was good and superior in itself, independent of the class structure and the political system in which it played a role. But in fact the language of the school is establishment English—the "educated" English of the white-collar worker in the schools, in administration, in business. Standard English is school English, office English, media English. It contrasts with the nonstandard English of the blue-collar American that for millions is shop English, neighborhood English, "down home" English. What we call "nonstandard" is actually the true folk speech of the great majority. It is a kind of English that is not squeamish about *ain't, he don't, like I said,* and *you was.* It is hospitable to the folksy idiom *(seeing as how, hadn't ought to, all the further, used to could).* It is hospitable to traces of regional dialect in pronunciation and vocabulary *(cain't, Foist Street).*

What we call standard English is basically the prestige dialect of an educated elite. This elite makes its living in jobs that involve much consumption and manipulation of words. How we describe this prestige dialect, what value we place on it, to whom we teach it and how, and with what success—these questions all have a strong social and political dimension. Having neglected this social dimension in the past, English teachers were ill-prepared for charges that their definition of good English serves the privileged to the disadvantage of the deprived; that their correcting of the speech of disadvantaged children does not really help them toward social mobility but is just another way of robbing them of dignity and pride. According to their radical critics, English teachers were serving the established system by instilling notions of inferiority in the underprivileged, the neglected, the exploited.

As English teachers became aware of the social relevance of their work with standard usage, basic realignments became necessary. *In the past, English teachers had typically taught too artificial a version of educated English.* They had thus broadened, rather than helped to bridge, the division between the educated elite and ordinary people. English teachers had played down the great body of grammar and vocabulary that nonstandard and standard English share. They had magnified minor differences, sometimes acting as if "irregardless" and "don't have none" were on the same level of concern as the sinking of the *Lusitania.* Today, we teach standard English in a more businesslike fashion. We present it as basically a variety of our common language, following certain special conventions, used everywhere as a public medium, indispensable to the ambitious and helpful to others. We try to make disadvantaged students see standard English not as a threat to their identity but as an opportunity for branching out, an opening up of possibilities.

As our definition of standard English becomes more realistic and viable, we try to relate it more organically to the language systems of our students. We are learning to *listen* to the language of our students before we try to improve on it. We are becoming intrigued by how and why nonstandard dialects differ from the prestige dialect. We are increasingly turning to linguists who explore the language mechanisms of the more clearly "different" social dialects:

> The lower income Negro child has learned to speak; he has acquired a formally structured linguistic system. However, the child's linguistic system interferes with his learning when he is placed in a middle-class school system which fails to give validity to his language. Our schools punish the child when he says or reads "he sit" for "he sits." But, in the dialect, there is no obligatory "-s" in the third person singular. Again, we presume that he is ignorant and unable to understand concepts when if we teach the rhyming concept in reading, he replies that han' ("hand") rhymes with "man." When we tell him that he is wrong, we confuse him, for he was right: han' and man do in fact rhyme in his speech.[4]

. . . what is usually termed a double subject is actually a sentence type found in other languages, the topic/comment sentence. That is, the sentence is constructed by first announcing the topic, and then a comment is made about this topic, this comment usually featuring a pronoun in its subject slot. Thus, **my brother, he go to college** would be exactly equivalent to the standard "my brother goes to college," and **the chicken, it got out of the coop** would express "the chicken got out of the coop."[5]

We have to develop an interest in the actual natural speech patterns of our students *before* we can deal with basic questions of method and motivation. We have to be able to give our students a sense of *where* their habitual speech patterns contrast with standard forms.

As English teachers, we are learning to ask: "What is out there?" before we administer our well-intentioned medicines. As a result, we are slowly breaking away from the old stereotype of the teacher—"educated," sensitive, refined—surrounded by, but isolated from, "careless," "sloppy," ignorant, and vulgar common people. We are rediscovering the forgotten men of the traditional English curriculum. Thus, we are rediscovering the *bilingual American.* In the heyday of unhyphenated Americanism, he by and large attracted attention in the classroom only when his catastrophic "wrasslings" with the English language provided innocent amusement for the natives ("Shaksbeer you metchink with Dante? *Shaksbeer?* Mein Gott!"). But for millions of bilingual, bicultural Americans, linguistic and cultural **pluralism** was a way of life. For millions of Americans, to be American has always meant to function in a common culture while retaining, in varying degrees, the ways, the accents, and the memories of a different ethnic past. A definition of American English and American culture cannot amount to much if it does not do justice to the pervading role of the ethnic American in American life.

In the past, the immigrant's children (and grandchildren) succeeded in school at least partly on the basis of how quickly and how thoroughly they could leave the immigrant's America behind. Today, we are rediscovering ethnic minorities too isolated, too native, or too homogeneous to allow for speedy dispersal and integration. We are discovering thousands of Spanish-speaking (or Chinese-speaking) children who have been left in a limbo between two languages and two cultures.

Finally, we are rediscovering the black American, who for years was the invisible man in our textbooks and our programs. We see young black people trying to establish their true identity, nursing rebellion and hatred and contempt in their hearts for a callous white society, alienated from its ideals that they see daily betrayed, turning against its culture

that seems to deny them their own. We make futile gestures of concilia-
tion as black Americans begin to feel, with Eldridge Cleaver

> that the past is no forbidden vista upon which we dare not look, out of a
> phantom fear of being, as the wife of Lot, turned into pillars of salt. Rather
> the past is an omniscient mirror: we gaze and see reflected there ourselves
> and each other—what we used to be, what we are today, how we got this
> way, and what we are becoming.

As teachers, we are groping to define a role for ourselves in relation to
black men and women dedicated to the "enormous task of rejuvenating
and reclaiming the shattered psyches and culture of the black people."[6]

English teachers cannot escape the social relevance of their subject
because language patterns help establish group identity. Language is not
merely a tool of communication; it serves as password, as shibboleth.
It works as a device for "ingrouping" and "outgrouping." But even when
we shift attention from language as group marker to language as tool,
the social relevance of English, though often neglected, remains para-
mount.

Language is the medium of social and political interaction. Language
reflects and in turn helps shape the terms on which people live together
in society. When we refer to a woman as a "broad" or to a boy as a
"punk," we may be half-kidding, but we are at the same time helping
to box them in, to restrict their breathing space. Prejudice works in part
through the *language* of prejudice: *Polack, wop, Jap, nigger.* Whether
we call a policeman a "police officer," a "cop," or a "pig" is not just a
matter of style. It reflects the role we define for ourselves in the social
and political world in which we live. When we keep shouting "fascist!"
or "Commie!" we are hastening the day when the voice of the bully will
prevail in the land.

Language does not merely mirror political and social reality; it is
in many ways involved in how that reality changes and takes a turn for the
better or for the worse. When we want to realize our aspirations, when we
want to make our purposes prevail, we rally behind people who can articulate what we want, what we feel:

> Official war propaganda, with its disgusting hypocrisy and self-righteous-
> ness, tends to make thinking people sympathize with the enemy. (George
> Orwell)

> The price the immigrants paid to get into America was that they had to be-
> come Americans. (LeRoi Jones)

> The glorification of one race and the consequent debasement of another—

or others—always has been and always will be a recipe for murder. (James Baldwin)

But just as often we feel the weight of words carrying ideas that are *not* our own. We feel the power of words for good or evil—threatening words, inflaming words, inspiring words, spiteful words:

Business is business.
A woman's place is in the home.
We don't serve Negroes here.
Some of my best friends are Jews.
You can't trust anybody over thirty.
Fight poverty—get a job.
Political power grows from the barrel of a gun.
Make love, not war.

The fate of individuals and of movements can be decided by their encounter with potent words: *loyalty, un-American, miscegenation, credibility gap, perversion, exploitation, racism, pollution.*

Traditionally, linguists and literary critics have concerned themselves too little with language as a social medium. One reason is that the scholar cannot long study language in society without endangering his prized neutrality, his privileged position above the din of battle. He may be able to reduce this danger by avoiding the more obvious invitations to partisanship: A study of the language of advertising is likely to tell us little about businessmen, and about the wants and daydreams of their customers, if it is conducted from a narrow, antibusiness point of view. A study of the strategies of persuasion is likely to be misleading if we always analyze the political propaganda of our opponents, never that of our own side. Even so, a study of how words do our bidding sooner or later brings into play basic commitments.

What we teach about the way men use language in society reflects assumptions about what that society is or should be. Thus, we are not just teaching style when we discuss with our students the way the catchwords of the moment bring into play, each in turn, a whole set of ready-made attitudes and associations:

law and order
crime in the streets
centralized federal bureaucracy
white power structure
military-industrial complex
law-abiding citizen

alien ideologies
hard-core pornography
guilt by association
police brutality

Each of these is likely to cause a more or less *automatic* reaction; it thus suits the closed mind. The future citizen can here learn how his capacity for fair judgment is dulled by the prepackaged phrase; he can learn how a conditioned reflex takes the place of an honest look at a situation. No one is for "crime in the streets," or for "police brutality," and a negative set of mind is already produced before we start asking what actually went on in what street.

When we talk about the way clichés and stereotypes channel our thinking, we proceed from the assumption that it is possible and desirable for the individual to have an opinion and that that opinion should be based on something other than habit, class allegiance, indoctrination, or the "historic moment." In a world where the first virtue in nation, church, or party has often been conformity, assent, we are stipulating the meritorious quality of independent thinking, of dissent. In a world that has often prized allegiance, solidarity, efficiency, we are opting for the right of private judgment. This choice may seem to us basically an intellectual commitment, but it is also a *political* choice, with far-reaching implications for the relation between the individual and society.

Our English classrooms offer our society one of its best chances to demonstrate what is meant by "open discussion" and the "public dialogue." This is the point of involving our students in situations where there really *are* two sides (not just a right one and a wrong one). This is why we expose them to writers that give the devil his due, who can present the arguments of the other side fairly, expose their weaknesses, and yet learn from them in the process. This is why we involve our students in plays where there is a true wrestling of opposites—plays where the spokesman of the author's view may carry the day, but where the dissenters have good lines. Thus, in Peter Weiss's *Marat/Sade,* the thesis is that there can be no better future for mankind without a fundamental restructuring of society; that a better world will rise from the ashes of the old. But the other side has its say, in words that are hard to forget:

Now, Marat,
now I can see
where it leads,
this revolution:

to a sickening of the individual
to a slow fading into uniformity
to the decay of the power of judgment
to the denial of self
to a weakness unto death
   subject to a state
whose structure is unattainably
   far above all
and beyond attack
I therefore am turning back
I have no more ties with anyone . . .
I secede from the Union
I merely observe
I am not involved
I watch, and I ponder what I watch.
I am alone
When I go
I want to leave no record,
   no trace.[7]

Again, we involve our students in the dialectic of thesis and antithesis, of *pro and con,* because of an intellectual belief that truth is more likely to be truth when it emerges from the contest of alternatives than when it is announced from on high. But again these intellectual habits have social and political relevance. They reflect our belief that in society at large the contest of pro and con can be and shall be more than mere window dressing or an excuse for inaction.

As we move on from the language of social intercourse, and of the "public dialogue," to imaginative literature, the questions we ask about social and political relevance have to be answered in the larger context of the general *human* relevance of literature. Literature can make us more aware of the world in which we live; it can seize on what is most significant and bring it into focus. It can help answer the questions of the young about the kind of world into which they were born. It can help us imagine the future and understand the past. But at the same time literature does not merely hold a mirror up to reality. It plays off what is real against what is perhaps possible. It judges and rejects reality; it remolds the world until it more nearly satisfies the heart's desire. To the grim truth, it creates a counterpoint of human aspiration. When we look in literature for social and political relevance, we have to remember that the poet, the playwright, or the novelist has *shaped* reality in accordance with human purposes.

Truly relevant literature concerns itself, not with the zigs and zags of the party line, but with some of the basic issues in human relations that determine our individual and collective fate. It has a documentary quality that makes us say "That is the way it was; that is the way it is; that is the way it will be." It engages more than our intellectual attention— it engages our capacity to feel, to identify, to judge. It makes us share in the writer's scorn and elation, in his feelings of solidarity and alienation.

Basic to every English teacher's job is the task of convincing students of the power of literature to illuminate human experience. We do so in part by bringing the testimony of imaginative writers to bear on the great questions that agitate us as a nation. Thus, we turn to poems like Keith Douglas's "Forgetmenot" to bring into focus the murderous ironies of war:

> Three weeks gone and the combatants gone,
> returning over the nightmare ground
> we found the place again, and found
> the soldier sprawling in the sun.
>
> The frowning barrel of his gun
> overshadowing. As we came on
> that day, he hit my tank with one
> like the entry of a demon.
>
> Look. Here in the gunpit spoil
> the dishonoured picture of his girl
> who has put: *Steffi. Vergissmeinicht*
> in a copybook gothic script.
>
> We see him almost with content
> abased, and seeming to have paid
> and mocked at by his own equipment
> that's hard and good when he's decayed.
>
> But she would weep to see to-day
> how on his skin the swart flies move;
> the dust upon the paper eye
> And the burst stomach like a cave.
>
> For here the lover and killer are mingled
> who had one body and one heart.
> And death who had the soldier singled
> has done the lover mortal hurt.[8]

We turn to poems like Helene Johnson's "Sonnet to a Negro in Harlem" to give our students a feeling for what is involved in the search for black identity and black pride:

You are disdainful and magnificent—
Your perfect body and your pompous gait,
Your dark eyes flashing solemnly with hate,
Small wonder that you are incompetent
To imitate those whom you so despise—
Your shoulders towering high above the throng,
Your head thrown back in rich, barbaric song,
Palm trees and mangoes stretched before your eyes.
Let others toil and sweat for labor's sake
And wring from grasping hands their meed of gold.
Why urge ahead your supercilious feet?
Scorn will efface each footprint that you make.
I love your laughter arrogant and bold.
You are too splendid for this city street.[9]

We turn to a play like Arthur Miller's *The Crucible* to probe the problems of conscience faced by men and women in a society where loyalty to established truth is placed above loyalty to people, where "justice" has become a cancer destroying the community, where faith and law have turned into bloody weapons of self-destruction:

PROCTOR. I have three children—how may I teach them to walk like men in the world, and I sold my friends?
DANFORTH. You have not sold your friends—
PROCTOR. Beguile me not! I blacken all of them when this is nailed to the church the very day they hang for silence!
DANFORTH. Mr. Proctor, I must have good and legal proof that you—
PROCTOR. You are the high court, your word is good enough! Tell them I confessed myself; say Proctor broke his knees and wept like a woman; say what you will, but my name cannot—
DANFORTH [*with suspicion*]. It is the same, is it not? If I report it or you sign to it?
PROCTOR [*he knows it is insane*]. No, it is not the same! What others say and what I sign to is not the same!
DANFORTH. Why? Do you mean to deny this confession when you are free?
PROCTOR. I mean to deny nothing!
DANFORTH. Then explain to me, Mr. Proctor, why you will not let—
PROCTOR [*with a cry of his whole soul*]. Because it is my name! Because I cannot have another in my life! Because I lie and sign myself to lies! Because I am not worth the dust on the feet of them that hang! How may I live without my name? I have given you my soul; leave me my name![10]

English teachers are everywhere becoming more fully aware of the larger human and social context in which they work. As they become involved in the larger implications of what they teach, there is a danger that their subject will lose its identity, its common center. But in the past the *opposite* danger has often been more real: English as a subject has too often been good for, and good in, only the English classroom. Good English has to be more than just the language of English teachers. Composition has to be more than a ritual conducted only in English classrooms. Literature has to be more than books assigned that otherwise nobody would read. An English teacher must convince his students that language is everywhere part of their world. He must show them that their ways of using language are part of who they are. He must show them that literature bears witness to how people live and to how they are trying to shape their lives.

FOOTNOTES

[1]George Dennison, "An Environment to Grow In," *Saturday Review*, Oct. 18, 1969, 74–76.

[2]Poems by students of Mrs. Gabriele Rico, San Jose, Calif.

[3]Student paper by Deborah Foster, from *Writers of Tomorrow* (Purdue University, Oct. 30, 1970), p. 13.

[4]Stephen S. Baratz and Joan C. Baratz, "Negro Ghetto Children and Urban Education: A Cultural Solution," *The Florida FL Reporter* (Spring/Summer 1969), 14.

[5]Beryl Loftman Bailey, "Language and Communicative Styles of Afro-American Children in the United States," *The Florida FL Reporter* (Spring/Summer 1969), 153.

[6]Eldridge Cleaver, *Soul on Ice* (New York: McGraw-Hill Book Company, 1968), pp. 99, 207.

[7]Peter Weiss, *The Persecution and Assassination of Jean-Paul Marat* (Frankfurt: Suhrkamp, 1964), pp. 71–72.

[8]Keith Douglas, "Vergissmeinicht," from *Collected Poems* (London: Editions Poetry).

[9]Helene Johnson, "Sonnet to a Negro in Harlem," in Arna Bontemps, ed., *American Negro Poetry* (New York: Hill and Wang, Inc., 1963), p. 102.

[10]Arthur Miller, *The Crucible* (New York: Bantam Books, Inc., 1959), pp. 137–138.

FOR FURTHER STUDY

A. Critical observers in the sixties and seventies have published many candid portraits of *actual schools.* Find a candid "capsule portrait" of a school as seen from an English teacher's point of view: Kenneth Eble, "Among School Children," *English Education,* 1 (Fall 1969), 18–28; George Miller, "The Blackboard Bungle," *College Composition and Communication,* 21 (May 1970), 157–162; or a more recent article in the same vein. Write a similar camera eye report on a school you have visited or observed.

B. In recent years, many voices have protested against too narrow a *definition of English as a subject.* Study one of the following articles, or a more recent article in a similar vein. How convincing are the author's arguments? Support or take issue with the author's central position: Charles Weingartner, "Semantics: What and Why," *English Journal,* 58 (November 1969), 1214–1219; Claudene D. Atkinson, "A New Approach: Drama in the Classroom," *English Journal,* 60 (October 1971), 947–951, 956; Robert Kirk, "English and the Arts," *English Journal,* 56 (February 1967), 229–234; Sheila Schwartz, "Science Fiction: Bridge Between the Two Cultures," *English Journal,* 60 (November 1971), 1043–1051; Helen Foley, "To Sing the Street: Using a Community Film Program to Teach Composition," *English Journal,* 60 (November 1971), 1101–1108; Neil Postman, "Linguistics and the Pursuit of Relevance," *English Journal,* 56 (November 1967), 1160–1165.

C. Study the treatment of one of the following topics in three or four *current language textbooks* intended for use in school or college: figurative language, connotation, slang. How, and how well, is the subject treated? What is the tone? What is the point?

D. The following statements deal with issues that concern English teachers. How do you react to each statement, and why? What examples, evidence, or arguments would you present pro or con? How would you formulate *your own position* on what is involved? You may want to select one of these for more detailed investigation.

1. One finds in current American all the characters and tendencies that marked the rich English of Shakespeare's time—an eager borrowing of neologisms from other languages, a bold and often very ingenious use of metaphor, and a fine disdain of the barricades separating the parts of speech. The making of new words is not carried on only, or even principally, to fill gaps in the vocabulary; indeed, one may well agree with Captain Hall that "there are words enough already." It is carried on because there survives in the American something that seems to have faded out of the Englishman: an innocent joy in word-making for its own sake, a voluptuous delight in the vigor and elasticity of the language.

—H. L. Mencken, *The American Language*

2.   The essence of language is symbolic, not signific; we use it first and most vitally to formulate and hold ideas in our own minds. Conception, not social control, is its first and foremost benefit. . . . Watch a young child that is just learning to speak play with a toy; he says the name of the object, e.g.: "Horsey! horsey! horsey!" over and over again, looks at the object, moves it, always saying the name to himself or to the world at large. It is quite a time before he talks to anyone in particular; he talks first of all to himself. This is his way of forming and fixing the *conception* of the object in his mind, and around this conception all his knowledge of it grows. *Names* are the essence of language; for the *name* is what abstracts the conception of the horse from the horse itself, and lets the mere idea recur at the speaking of the name. . . . The baby uses a word long before he *asks for* the object; when he wants his horsey he is likely to cry and fret, because he is reacting to an actual environment, not forming ideas. He uses the animal language of *signs* for his wants; talking is still a purely symbolic process—its practical value has not really impressed him yet.

—Suzanne K. Langer, *The Lord of Creation*

3.   The most important social process taking place in the high school is learning to be an American. But so much of learning to be an American is learning not to let your individuality become a nuisance. We conceive our country as having achieved a position of leadership and dominance by carefully subordinating personal and ethnic disparity to the interests of teamwork in a colossal technical and administrative enterprise. For us, conformity is a moral mandate. When we insist on taking a personal stand and bucking the system, we feel not only anxious, but guilty as well. . . . We conform, but not primarily (as is supposed) because of fear and alienation. There is a strong positive element in our conformity; we do not merely huddle together in little smug or frightened clusters. One has only to watch a committee at work to see that consensus is regarded as a good thing in itself, and intransigence a bad one. The members are eager to accept one another's point of view; awkward data are dismissed, not cynically, but as an act of public spirit. The old joke about a statesman needing the ability to rise above principle turns out to be no joke.

—Edgar Z. Friedenberg, *The Vanishing Adolescent*

4.   On opening day I entered the room . . . and said the usual: "Every student in this class who stays with the program will write at least one paper that knocks out the other students. Most will write several that deserve publication on campus.

"You will write, and your papers will be read around this table. The class is designed to move you from success to success. For the first month neither you nor I will talk about anything weak in the papers. Only the strong places. I will reproduce sentences or passages I think are strong and you will say why you like a passage, or just that you like it and don't know why. If you are not moved by the writing, you will say nothing.

"Keep your papers in one folder. I will not grade them until the end of the semester. In the meantime you will be getting more responses to your work than you ever got from a grade. Good writing will be reproduced and read. And praised. Later in the semester we will comment on weaknesses as well as strengths.

If at any time you feel desperate for a grade, because Dad has promised you a new car if you get a B or you need a grade for application to Harvard Law School, bring the folder and I will give it a grade as of the moment."

—Ken Macrorie, *Uptaught*

5. Teachers usually try too hard to interpret their pupil's work. If a child writes about violence he is looked upon as expressing violent impulses that are "really" within him. If he writes about loneliness his teacher tries to provide him with companionship. This usual view of writing condescendingly implies that the child is incapable of literary exploration. Worse, it implies he is as humorless as the adults who assume responsibility for his education. I have laughed, cried, been duped, outraged, and sometimes bored by what my pupils have written—and I have told them this. Their effort to understand themselves and the things around them demands no less.

—Herbert Kohl, *Teaching the "Unteachable"*

6. . . . the libelous little rag as the first edition was, . . . became a literary magazine in which the students defied convention instead of authority. Frankly, i feel that underground papers are put out by the intelligent child who lacks challenge or is too lazy to accept the everyday challenge. Too many advisers are concerned with winning a national award rather than letting the students publish a newspaper. Our girls elect journalism. They design, lay out, and write the annual and newspaper. That is, they do since I took over. I let them try what they want. If they are in error, what has been lost? I assure you, nothing is lost other than a small prop under my vanity.

—quoted in the *California English Journal*

Linguistics and English Grammar

Three Ways to Look at Language—The Attack on Traditional Grammar—Linguistics: The First Wave—Transformational Grammar: Theory and Application—Psycholinguistics, Tagmemics, and After—Linguistics and the Student

Our basic job is to make the resources of English more fully available to our students. We want our students to become aware of what language can do. We want to widen their range of choice. We want to help them tap their unused potential. We work with words in order to help them make words their own that at first were mere "big words." We work with sentences to make them use the full resources of the English sentence.

Grammar is the most concrete and technical part of our work with the student's linguistic resources. Grammar deals with how words work together in sentences. When we work with grammar in the classroom, we deal with the very stuff that language is made of. We try to have our students become intrigued by what makes language work. We try to show them the resources of language put to use. Through exposure, imitation, and practice, we try to have them acquire a broader, more confident command of the technical resources of their mother tongue.

For technical information about language, we turn to linguistics. Linguistics is the systematic study of how language functions. *It concentrates on the internal workings of language as a system, as a code.* Different movements in modern linguistics have stressed different aspects of language; they differ in their methods and results. Today, English teachers no longer look to the linguist for one final truth about language. Instead, they are learning how to learn from linguists without taking sides among competing systems of analysis.

The controversies and rapid shifts in the linguist's camp have often prevented English teachers from asking the basic questions: What have we learned from English linguistics *over the years?* What are the *lasting* contributions that linguists have made to the way we teach English? What are the aspects of the linguist's work that have proved most *stimulating and productive* in the classroom?

Linguists have successfully challenged much in our teaching that was negative or merely conventional. They have opened up a world of new materials and new ideas for us to draw on. However, they have by and large left to teachers the task of putting such materials to work in coherent and productive programs. Putting the emphasis on the technical analysis of language, linguists have by and large neglected its larger social and cultural context and its meaningful, purposeful use in speech and writing. An English teacher must learn how to put linguistics to *use*. He must learn how to put it in its rightful place as a *part*—the most technical part—of his work with language.

THREE WAYS TO LOOK AT LANGUAGE

English teachers have learned what they know about language from several major sources. These differ in their historical background and underlying philosophy. At least three major schools of thought have helped determine how we look at language: the school tradition of the "rules of grammar," nineteenth-century historical linguistics, and modern linguistics in its various forms.

The school tradition of handbooks and workbooks goes back to a **normative** eighteenth-century view committed to safeguarding "correct" English against the corruptions of ignorant popular speech. Eighteenth-century grammarians looked in language for the clear and unambiguous light of universal Reason. Their age, with Alexander Pope, saw in nature

One clear, unchanged, and universal light.

They tended to assume that language (as well as literature) was subject to rules that represented "nature methodized." Grammar became a means of eliminating from language what was illogical, confused, vague, inconsistent, or superfluous. From current speech—idiomatic, "irregular," subject to arbitrary shifts in usage—grammarians appealed to underlying principles more lasting, more simple and elegant, fit for educated conversation and rational discussion. Following the neoclassical bent of the age, they found the purest embodiment of universal, rational principles in the revered authors of "learned Greece" and "immortal Rome." Thus, eighteenth-century grammarians like James Harris and James Buchanan assumed the existence of a **universal grammar** embodied in its purest state in the Greek and Latin of classical literature.

Until recent times, English instruction in the schools carried on the struggle for a more correct kind of English that embodied logical thinking and the unchanging "rules of grammar." Very early, however, language scholarship and the school tradition had parted company. The romantic revival of interest in the native (nonclassical) heritage had brought about a strong emphasis on the historical study of the native language. What had earlier been considered the barbarous dialects of peoples lacking the true light of classical culture was now considered the authentic medium of national tradition. Emphasis in language study shifted from correction to restoration and rediscovery. As architects built colleges and post offices in a style copied from fourteenth-century cathedrals, professors taught their students to read *Beowulf* in the original and to know the different versions of a word in several Anglo-Saxon dialects.

Study of the vernacular, of the "folk-speech," in its older forms provided the basis of nineteenth-century **philology**. As practiced by the philologist, language scholarship in the universities meant above all **historical linguistics**. Students studied the Old English of the *Beowulf* epic, the Middle English of Chaucer. They came to see English as the descendant of a Germanic language brought to England from the continent, close cousin of German, Danish, and Dutch. They traced some of the basic vocabulary and grammar of English to a more remote Indo-European parent language, common ancestor of Russian, Latin, Greek, and the great majority of modern European languages. They pondered, for instance, relationships like the following:

Sanskrit	Greek	Latin	German	English
pitār-	patēr	pater	Vater	father
mātr	mētēr	mater	Mutter	mother
bhratār-	phratēr	frater	Bruder	brother
srd	kardia	cord-	Herz	heart
yuga	zygon	jugum	Joch	yoke[1]

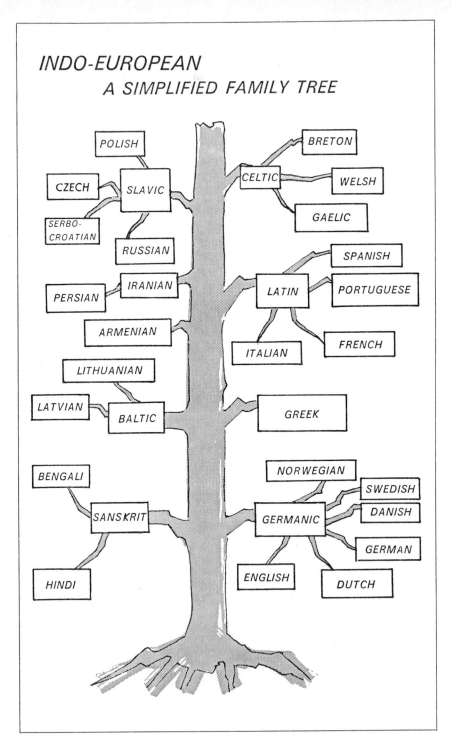

Closer to home, they showed how modern English was shaped by major outside influences: the medieval French of the Norman conquerors, the Latin and Greek of churchmen and scholars.

From the historical linguist, students learned two essential conditions of fruitful work. First, they learned to respect the stubborn *facts*—before they embarked on speculation, on the construction of elegant theories. Second, they learned to ascertain the *workings* of language—before they tried to tinker with it, to set up guidelines for improvement.

Historical study makes us see language as something that *grew*. Current English preserves, in fossilized form, remnants of earlier ways of doing things—like the plural ending of *oxen* and *children*, or the past forms in *sing—sang, ring—rang*. English spelling makes a certain amount *irreg. verbs* of sense when seen as a record of an earlier stage of the language. Thus, the spelling of *knight* and *light* reminds us that once these words were close to German *Knecht* and *Licht*.

Facts such as these make us tolerant of the diversity of language—its interesting byways, its apparent contradictions. Our pronoun system, for instance, is not something deliberately constructed, consistent, and efficient, like the Morse code. Rather, it is the result of confused shifts and historical accidents. From the speech of Scandinavian settlers, English took over the pronoun forms *they, them,* and *their*. These blended easily into a system that already had other forms beginning with *th: this, that. They, them,* and *their* gradually supplanted the older forms.

It took a long time before the old forms were finally displaced, nay, the dative *hem* still survives in the form *'em* ("take 'em"), which is now by people ignorant of the history of the language taken to be a shortened *them; her* "their" is the only form for the possessive of the plural found in Chaucer (who says *they* in the nominative) and there are two or three instances in Shakespeare.[2] *It is 'they ! !*

Though fact-oriented, the historical linguist was not satisfied with merely accumulating bit-facts, like a botanist forever collecting specimens without placing them in an overall scheme. Early, linguists began to look in language for laws similar to those at work in physics. They looked for laws that would explain a great mass of at first bewildering and contradictory facts, and that could be discovered *in those facts*. Nineteenth-century philologists discovered such laws in the sound changes marking important stages in the history of major Indo-European languages: "Grimm's law" summed up systematic sound changes that helped set apart the early versions of English and German from their Indo-European relatives. The *p* that is kept in Latin *pater* has changed to *f* in *father*.

The *t* in Latin *tres* has become *th* in English *three*. The *g* in Latin *genus* is *k* in English *kin*. *Father* ultimately derives from the same word as the Latin borrowings *paternal* and *patriot; foot* derives from the same word as *pedestrian* and *pedicure*. Shifts such as these affected literally thousands of words. The great vowel shift in the fifteenth century changed the vowel sounds in thousands of English words. In Chaucer's time, *came* was closer to our modern *calm, see* to *say, mine* to *mean, mouse* to *moose*. In the fifteenth century, these vowels went through a massive shift toward their modern English values.

This search for *system*, for the underlying principles, has remained strong in linguistic scholarship to our day. It has become stronger than ever in recent work. Thus, we find recent studies of the sound structure of modern English charting such patterns as the change from /aɪ/ (as in *dime*) to /ɪ/ (as in *dim*). We see this change in pairs like

divine—divinity
reptile—reptilian
ignite—ignition
expedite—expedition
contrite—contrition

We then have the investigator explain how apparent exceptions—like *right-righteous*—follow rules of their own. Typically, the linguist triumphs when he can show "a surprising degree of organization underlying what appears superficially to be a chaotic arrangement of data." He can thus identify with the tradition of modern science, marked, in Whitehead's words, by the "union of passionate interest in the detailed facts with equal devotion to abstract generalization."[3]

In the twentieth century, the emphasis in language scholarship shifted from historical study to the study of contemporary languages in their current form. Unlike much nineteenth-century philology, modern linguistics concerned itself with languages such as those of the American Indian, *outside the Indo-European language family*. Here the investigator found himself confronted with radically new and different linguistic structures. He was thus forced to forego familiar categories and preconceptions. Furthermore, he typically worked with unrecorded spoken languages. He was thus forced to deal directly with the sounds of *speech* —instead of approaching a language through written records. In the work of the linguistic anthropologist, the emphasis was on obtaining an accurate description of an unknown or little-known language in its spoken form.

The anthropological linguist approached English in the same spirit as he had the language of the Eskimo and the Navaho. He asked English teachers to approach English without preconceptions, as though it were the language of a newly discovered tribe. He asked them to describe as accurately as possible the recurrent structures and forms they encountered there. In the resulting **structural linguistics,** the premium was on observable fact—so that teachers could disentangle fact from linguistic folklore and the conventional say-so of textbook authors. Many of the familiar rules and arguments of the school tradition were thus shown to be at odds with English as it actually existed as a living language.

Inevitably, an ambitious second generation of modern linguists rebelled against a literal-minded commitment to observable, demonstrable fact. They found their elders' scepticism toward theory too narrow and confining. Linguists like Noam Chomsky and R. B. Lees, and their numerous disciples, rejected the "down-to-the-surface" linguistics of the followers of Leonard Bloomfield and Charles C. Fries. The new **generative or transformational** grammarians were no longer content to analyze language-after-the-fact, to record and classify structures found in actual examples of current speech. Instead, they attempted to reconstruct the *processes* by which the observable structures had been produced. In doing so, they reopened basic questions of theory about language and language learning.

To understand today's programs and instructional materials dealing with current English, the teacher needs an understanding of three major factors: (1) the modern reappraisal, and often drastic revision, of the school tradition, (2) the lasting contribution of the first wave of applied English linguistics, and (3) the pervading influence of transformational theory and practice. No matter what particular "mix" a set of materials presents, these are the three forces that have shaped our thinking about modern English and modern English grammar.

THE ATTACK ON TRADITIONAL GRAMMAR

Whatever else English teachers did in the classroom, they were traditionally expected to teach grammar—how words work together in a sentence. To do so, they spent much time sorting out words into major grammatical categories. These were the **parts of speech:** noun, pronoun, verb, adjective, adverb, conjunction, preposition, and interjection. They then proceeded to label the many kinds of combinations into which these parts of speech could enter: phrases (short word groups without a subject and verb of their own) and clauses (potentially, sentences of their own with a subject and verb, but, in practice, often subsentences in a larger combined unit). "Parsing"—labeling the words and word groups in a sentence in accordance with the traditional system of school grammar —played a major role in the education of untold numbers of children.

Both the content and the spirit of traditional instruction in grammar were challenged in fundamental ways by the revolution in language scholarship brought about by modern linguistics. Applied English linguistics brought with it new terms and procedures but above all a new attitude. The traditional teacher had treated grammar as if it had been created on the eighth day. It was something known and settled. There was no need to ask: Where do we *start* if we wish to develop a system of grammar? What procedures will work; what criteria are reliable? Linguists set out to convince teachers of exactly this need for starting from the foundations. They relied on two familiar arguments: The classifications of the school grammar were modeled on the traditional grammars of Latin and Greek and *did not really fit* the facts of current English. The definitions of the school grammar appealed to meaning and were inherently *ambiguous*.

Historically, an improvised "Latinizing" grammar was widely adopted when schoolmasters in the different European countries began to line up the grammar of the vernacular in a system parallel to that of the Latin grammar then primarily taught:

> The chief language taught was Latin; the first and in many cases the only grammar with which scholars came into contact was Latin grammar. No wonder therefore that grammar and Latin grammar came in the minds of most people to be synonyms. Latin grammar played an enormous role in the schools, to the exclusion of many subjects (the pupil's own native language, science, history, etc.) which we are now beginning to think more essential for the education of the young. The traditional term for "secondary school" was in England "grammar school" and in Denmark *latinskole,* and the reason for both expressions was obviously the same.[4]

When the business of the schools was to teach the classical languages, the adoption of a Latinizing grammar for the student's native language was a simple matter of pedagogical expediency. Even today, as Harold Whitehall observed, the resulting "traditional" grammar "does something to allow the student to move smoothly into the study of such morphological languages" as Latin, Greek, or German.[5]

Nevertheless, traditional grammar suffered from a major drawback: The Latin framework provided a poor fit for the modern languages to which it was applied. The *farther* a modern language had moved away from the original Indo-European grammatical system, the harder it became to fit modern facts into an ancient frame. Discussing the noun, the traditional grammarian was thinking of the Latin system of **cases**— with the noun changing its *form* depending on whether it was used as subject, object, possessive, and the like:

nominative	(subject form)	*vir*	the *man*
genitive	(possessive)	*viri*	the *man's*
dative	(indirect object)	*viro*	(for) the *man*
accusative	(object form)	*virum*	the *man*
ablative	(instrumental)	*viro*	(by) the *man*

The basic difficulty here is that the English noun no longer has any "cases": Where a Latin noun had four or five different forms for different slots in a sentence, the plain form of the English noun serves as an *all-purpose* form. Only a possessive form survives as a kind of linguistic fossil; and its use is optional (the *cat's* whiskers, or the whiskers *of the cat*). Prepositions (*of, for, to, by, with*) now do the work that special case forms did in Latin. The English noun still uses special forms for *number (bird—birds; man—men)*, but it no longer uses such special "inflected" forms for case.

Similar problems resulted when Latinizing grammarians set up a paradigm (a listing of all possible forms) for the English verb. "I *shall (will)* leave" was declared the English future tense, parallel to Latin *amabo*, "I shall love." But "I *am going to* leave" is more commonly used, and would thus seem to have just as good a claim to the future tense label. And if we list forms with *will* and *would*, are we also going to list forms with other "modal auxiliaries": "I *may* leave," "I *must* leave," "I *ought to* leave"? Again, English relies heavily on **function words** (here, auxiliaries) where Latin relied heavily on different forms of the main verb.

The objection to the "declensions" and "conjugations" of a full-fledged traditional grammar were well summed up by the Danish grammarian Jespersen:

> Latin was a language with a wealth of flexional forms, and in describing other languages the same categories as were found in Latin were applied as a matter of course, even where there was nothing in these other languages which really corresponded to what was found in Latin. In English and Danish grammars paradigms of noun declension were given with such cases as accusative, dative and ablative, in spite of the fact that no separate forms for these cases had existed for centuries. All languages were indiscriminately saddled with the elaborate Latin system of tenses and moods in the verbs, and by means of such Procrustean methods the actual facts of many languages were distorted and misrepresented.[6]

On the one hand, traditional grammar was haunted by linguistic ghosts, by the shadows of forgotten ancestors. On the other hand, it slighted features for which Latin (and Greek) had no exact precedent, and thus no ready-made terms and categories. Thus, from the linguist's

*also —
frog & comp. sent —*

point of view, the first major drawback of the traditional grammar was that it fitted English into a foreign mold.

The second major objection to traditional grammar focused attention on its definitions of the parts of speech. Generations of school children had repeated that the noun is the "name of a person, place, thing, or idea" and that a verb "expresses action." These meaning-based definitions turned out to be oversimplified and ambiguous. The word *walk* in some way refers to or "expresses" action in both of the following sentences:

> He had *to walk.*
> He went *for a walk.*

But in the first sentence, *walk* is a verb (the infinitive form, signaled by the infinitive-marker *to*). In the second sentence, *walk* is a noun (preceded by the article *a* and serving as the object of the preposition *for*). It is true that the verb to *thieve* "expresses action," but so does the noun *theft.* The very word *action* is itself a noun. Maybe noun and verb "express action" in different ways. But if so, the traditional textbooks were unable to pinpoint the difference. Apparently, even teachers using the traditional formulas actually distinguished nouns and verbs by other means.

Increasingly, teachers found modern grammarians rejecting familiar **notional**—that is, meaning-based—definitions. For decades, teachers had defined the sentence as a unit expressing "a complete thought." But "complete thought" also turned out to be a rubber concept. "He won't answer" is a complete sentence, but it is not really a complete thought without a *previous* sentence that tells us who *he* is. "He won't" is also a complete sentence, but the thought is not complete without an activity specified in an earlier statement. Thus, the traditional definition is too vague for practical purposes. It provides no concrete clue for sorting out the sentences and nonsentences in a list like

1. He won't.
2. Because I'm not hungry.
3. For the lights were low.
4. Until next Wednesday then.
5. That does it.
6. A remarkable recovery!
7. Who has always helped us in our hour of need.
8. Who has always helped us in our hour of need?

Conventionally, we would want to call 1, 3, 5, and 8 "complete sentences." But the thoughts they express are not any more or any less complete than those in the remaining examples. What really guides our

choice are other criteria: In a complete sentence, we look for a subject
and a predicate. We make sure the resulting statement is not made incomplete by a subordinator like *because* or a relative pronoun like *who*
or *which*. (A subordinator would make us look for a "main clause" to
hook the statement onto.) Note that 4 and 6 are also complete utterances,
though not sentences in the conventional sense. We might call them "nonsentences," or "permissible fragments," or "predicationless sentences."

Disillusioned with the traditional definitions, many linguists abandoned all attempts at semantic, meaning-based classifications. They
looked for concrete and tangible grammatical signals instead. When we
try to set up major grammatical categories, the most important of these
signals are position (word order) and inflection (word form). We can
graphically demonstrate the importance of word order by using **test
frames**: "The _____ gave a _____ to the _____." The words
filling the blanks, regardless of their meaning, belong to the same category.
As their *position* shows, they are nouns. The words that fit here fit in
after "noun-markers" (or **determiners**) like *a, an,* and *the; this, that,* and
these; my, his, and *your.* Nouns fill such typical slots in the sentence as
subject of verb, or object of verb, or preposition. Here is a test frame for
adjectives: "The evening was rather _____ but had a very_____
ending." Most true adjectives fit in after **intensifiers** like *very* or *rather.*
Adjectives appear after linking verbs or between a determiner and its
noun.

Inflection, or word form, supplies us with further tests for categories
such as these. Many nouns (though not all) have special inflected forms
for the plural or for the possessive: *boy, boy's, boys; man, man's, men,
mens'; child, child's, children, children's.* Verbs typically take the *-s*
ending for the third person singular of the present tense: *asks, meets,
talks, organizes.* They typically have special inflected forms to show the
difference between present and past: *ask—asked, meet—met, bring—
brought.* Some English verbs have preserved as many as five different
inflected forms: *break—breaks—broke—broken—breaking.*

For a time, linguists studiously avoided all meaning-based description and relied rigorously on structural and formal tests. As Charles
Fries said,

> Structures do signal meanings, it is true, and these meanings must be de-
> scribed. But the meanings cannot serve successfully to identify and dis-
> tinguish the structures.

Again:

> In describing the results of the analysis, only verifiable physical terms of
> form, of arrangement, and of distribution are necessary. Whenever descrip-

tive statements must depart from such formal matters, the fact is evidence of unsolved problems.[7]

In the short run, this structuralist suspicion of appeals to meaning made much grammatical description impossibly difficult. It is hard to give students a feeling for what the subject of a sentence is if we have to stick to strictly structural criteria. The most tangible structural signal is agreement between subject and verb: "The bird *sings*. The birds *sing*." The subject is the noun that *changes along with the verb* from singular to plural. But for the past, and for many auxiliaries, English no longer has distinctive singular and plural forms: "The bird *sang*." Word order is a rough guide, but the subject does not *always* come before the verb: "In unity there is *strength*." "'How odd!' said *the rabbit*." In the classroom, the best way to start toward a sense of what a subject is is to begin with archetypal sentences in which the subject is the doer, the agent—and then work from there toward the most common variations and reversals of this primordial "agent—action" pattern:

The mailman knocked.
The surface glistened.
The car was washed.

In the long run, as linguists became increasingly preoccupied with the relationship between grammar and meaning, teachers profited from the structuralist cautions by making *both* their account of outward form and their description of typical meanings more reliable and instructive. Verbs are verbs because of typical changes in form—which reflect typical differences in meaning: Verbs are the only English words with a built-in reference to time. In the typical classroom situation, technical (structural) and semantic (meaning-based) information work together. Technically, "John shot a man" and "John became a man" are different because only the first can be turned into a passive sentence: "A man *was shot by* John" (but not "A man *was become by* John"). Semantically, the two patterns are different because the two nouns linked by *became* point to the same referent. We can use such semantic correlations to describe the first pattern as "subject—action verb—target" and the second as "subject—linking verb—description of subject."

To make grammar "meaningful" to our students, we have to refer to typical and recurrent meanings of grammatical devices. While doing so, we have to remember two important points: First, our grammatical categories slice experience in ways that derive from the prehistoric past:

In English . . . all action must be conceived of in reference to three standard times. If, therefore, we desire to state a proposition that is as true to-morrow as it was yesterday, we have to pretend that the present moment may be elongated fore and aft so as to take in all eternity. In French we know once for all that an object is masculine or feminine, whether it be living or not; just as in many American and East Asiatic languages it must be under-stood to belong to a certain form-category (say, ring-round, ball-round, long and slender, cylindrical, sheet-like, in mass like sugar) before it can be enumerated (e.g. "two ball-class potatoes," "three sheet-class car-pets"). . . . It is almost as though at some period in the past the uncon-scious mind of the race had made a hasty inventory of experience, com-mitted itself to a premature classification that allowed of no revision.[8]

Second, in actual use "most structures—including the subject-verb-object structure—gather into themselves many different meanings."[9] The term *possessive*, for instance, applies to forms that often signal relationships other than ownership: *the girl's friends* (association); *the child's innocence* (quality), *the children's capers* (agent), *the general's dismissal* (object of action).

The linguist's basic quarrel with traditional grammar had been over its adequacy as a system of grammatical description. At various points, familiar categories and definitions were found to *stand in the way* of an accurate description of modern English. But from the linguist's point of view difficulties also resulted from the uses to which traditional grammar was conventionally put. Teachers typically taught grammar for an ul-terior purpose. They taught the sentence so that students would avoid sentence fragments and run-on sentences. They taught the inflectional scheme of personal pronouns so that students would avoid "Me and my friends like it" and "between you and I." Typically, in fact, teachers tried to get at "common errors" before students had enough understand-ing of basic features of English grammar to understand what was involved. From the linguist's point of view, "remedial" grammars promote a lop-sided or distorted view of the language because "they overemphasize those elements of English structure where usage is divided, and under-emphasize those elements where divided usage is impossible for native speakers and writers."[10]

In the more extreme version of the remedial approach, teachers were encouraged to "take up the students' problems as they come up." As a result, the student was often fed mere bits and snatches of informa-tion and never quite got to see how anything really worked. To recognize a sentence fragment, the student has to know some of the major features and variations of the English sentence. Consider the following pairs:

The bull pawed the ground. Its hooves were kicking up dust.
The bull pawed the ground. *Its hooves kicking up dust.*

They refused to surrender. For liberty was dearer than life.
They refused to surrender. *Because liberty was dearer than life.*

He asked his usual question. What money do they make?
He asked his usual question. *What money they made.*

In each pair, the second version contains a sentence fragment. To tell the difference, the writer has to know the difference between a verb and a verbal, between a coordinating and a subordinating connective, and between a direct and an indirect question. Not even a crackerjack teacher can improvise the necessary explanations "to help you with this point that came up on your theme."

Obviously, the linguist's re-examination of traditional grammar challenged long-established habits. Change was at first slow and painful but in the end all-pervading. The school grammar became *a more authentically English grammar* than it had been in the past. It showed the distinctive features of modern English as well as those it had in common with its Indo-European relatives. The grammar taught in the schools became *more concrete and teachable* than it used to be. It focused on things that could be shown, demonstrated, manipulated. The general orientation of the English teacher's work with language became less negative and *more productive.* The negative desire to stamp out "errors" was replaced by a positive desire to understand language better and put it to better use. The linguist made it possible for teachers to construct positively oriented programs designed to awaken students to the rich resources of their mother tongue.

LINGUISTICS: THE FIRST WAVE

In the forties and fifties, linguistics meant structural linguistics. Linguists borrowed their basic assumptions from the work of Leonard Bloomfield, whose *Language* had appeared in 1933. Teachers learned new ways of looking at language by studying the books of Charles C. Fries, Paul Roberts, W. Nelson Francis, and James H. Sledd. Rejecting a school tradition that had taken too much for granted, these writers shared a belief in a new "scientific" approach committed to an empirical, inductive method. They tried to clear away all preconceptions, all the things that "everybody knows." Ideally, they would have liked to study English in the manner of the linguistic anthropologist investigating a previously unrecorded language:

We make a tape recording of the sounds we hear, and upon careful study of this recording it turns out that the sounds uttered . . . have at least some similarities. Though many of the sounds may seem strange to our ears, we can learn to recognize, fairly well, the vowels and consonants which occurred in the speech of our subjects. Suppose we find that the various vowels and consonants we recognize sound approximately the same no matter which one of our subjects is talking, and that they occur on the average with about the same frequencies. . . . We analyze our tape recording further and find that the sounds often occur in similar sequences; if we listen carefully to the breaks between these sequences we might conclude that our subjects use many "words" in common. . . . We could go on in this way, making increasingly detailed analyses. We should want to study how the longer sequences of sounds are put together; we would try to discover certain constancies or invariances in the structure of our subjects' utterances.[11]

Linguists thus undertook to act on Bloomfield's statement that "the only useful generalizations about language are inductive generalizations."[12] Following in their footsteps, the student worked his way from sound resources (phonetics) to significant sound contrasts (phonemics) and smallest meaningful units (morphemics). He then proceeded to grammar in the more limited sense, that is, the forms of words (morphology) and combinations of words in a sentence (syntax). He thus moved "through the hierarchy of English structure, from the smallest elements, sounds, up to the largest elements, sentences."[13] In theory at least, the structural linguist aimed at an analysis of the *spoken* language before examining the writing system and its "secondary representation" of speech.

As a result of this general orientation, textbooks began to place a heavy emphasis on **phonology**, on the systematic study of the sound resources of language. To some extent, the modern investigator could here draw on earlier work in phonetics: **Comparative** or **contrastive phonetics** had charted phonetic differences between major European languages, and between their major dialects. Studying positions of lips and tongue, for instance, a phonetician like the Frenchman Passy could pin down the differences between the English *t* in *try,* the German *t* in *tragen,* and the French *t* in *trois.* Students no longer had to imitate the sounds of a foreign language by substituting the closest similar sound from their own language. The phonetician could demonstrate the exact position or movement of lips, tongue, and teeth needed to produce the "real thing." He could teach American students how to bring the tongue forward, crowding against the upper teeth, when speaking French. He could teach a Cockney flower girl how to talk like a fair lady and say "Walk: Not bloody likely" with all the phonetic characteristics of the prestige dialect.

The modern linguist, trying to work his way inductively from the flow of speech sounds to underlying principles, could profit from considerable spadework done in historical and comparative phonetics. However, insofar as he was interested in structure, in system, he was hindered by the great variety of speech sounds that phonetics had been charting. Not only is articulation different in English *try* and French *trois*, but there is a different *t* in English *team* and *steam*. A sound like English *l* is different in *lip* and in *thrill*. Many other English consonants vary considerably depending on their position in a word, and on the sounds that precede and follow them.

To systematize the tremendous range of actual speech sounds, the linguist sorted them out into **phonemes**. A phoneme is not just a sound like the *p* in *pin*. The phoneme also includes such variations of *p* as would not make a difference in meaning. We would still hear *pin*, and get the meaning of "pin," if a speaker used a slightly different *p*-sound as found, say, in *spin*, or *tip*. But we have crossed over to a different phoneme if we hear *bin*, and get the meaning of "bin." The *p* in *pin* and the *b* in *bin* are different phonemes. The *p*-sounds in *pin, spin,* and *tip* are variants (allophones) of the same phoneme.

Our writing system reflects the basic phonemes of English only fitfully, and in misleading ways. Letters like *b, p, d, t,* and *v* correlate well with the consonant phonemes they stand for. But the combination *th*, for instance, is used for two different phonemes—the ones that make the difference between *thy* and *thigh*. The letter *g* is used for three different phonemes in *good, gin,* and *rouge*. In our writing system, we list *a, e, i, o,* and *u* as vowels. The actual vowel phonemes of English are represented in a list like *hit, head, hat, palm, hot, hut, hood*. In addition, we have the double vowels (diphthongs) in *heat, hate, hide, hoist* and in *how, home, hoot*. These are glides that start low with one of the simple vowels and then glide up, with the tongue going forward in *hate, hide,* and *hoist*, backward in *how, home,* and *hoot*. Variations from this system of vowels help set major American (and British) dialects off from each other.

In charting the phonemes, or meaningful sound contrasts, of English, linguists traced sound features that are superimposed on utterances otherwise consisting of the same phonemes. Since such features are superimposed on stretches of sound cutting across the shortest possible segments, they were called "suprasegmental phonemes," or **suprasegmentals,** for short. There is a difference in meaning between the members of each of the following pairs:

John!
John?

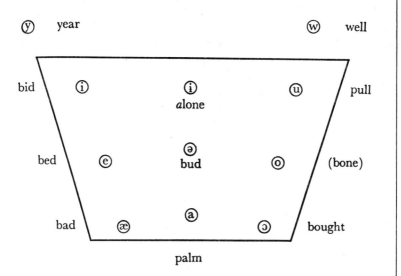

A SIMPLIFIED CHART: Nine Simple Vowels

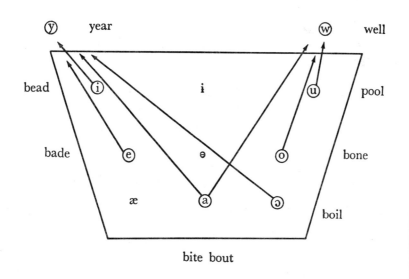

A SIMPLIFIED CHART: Seven Glides (Diphthongs)

Prodúce!
Próduce!

Donald Duck
Donald, duck!

The differences in sound here illustrated are differences in **intonation**.[14]

Of the features of English intonation here shown, the most familiar is **stress,** which makes sounds stand out in loudness and length. Stress makes the difference in pairs like *prógress* and *progréss, white hoúse* and *White House, a dáncing teacher* and *a dancing téacher.* Stress makes the difference in sets like the following:

Louise had bought us pizza. (unlike some other people)
Louise *had* bought us pizza. (so we should remember this fact)
Louise had *bought* us pizza. (and not baked it herself)
Louise had bought us *pizza!* (big deal!)

Poets regularize the varied stress patterns of natural speech in order to make language move to a metrical beat:

Did this woman set in motion the Greek expedition to Troy?
Was thís the fáce that láunched a thóusand shíps?

What matters for metrical analysis is relative stress, that is, whether a syllable has stronger stress than the ones that surround it. Linguists, on the other hand, distinguish intermediate degrees of stress between the most and the least prominent. They may identify four different degrees of stress in a sentence like "Paul's in the bedroom." Proceeding from loudest to softest these may be labeled primary ('), secondary (^), tertiary (`), and weak (˘):

Pâul's ìn thĕ bédròom.

The second feature of intonation is **pitch**, which makes the difference between shrill, high-frequency sounds and their low-frequency, slow-vibration counterparts. Significant variations in pitch are seen most clearly in the rising pitch that distinguishes "John" and "John?" or "He is ill." and "He is ill?" These questions normally have the simple rising pitch of questions to be answered yes or no. The concluding portion of such questions rises from the second, or normal, to the third level of pitch and stays there:

²He is ³ill³?
²Are you coming ³back³?

A more complicated rising-falling pitch normally marks the concluding portion of statements, and of questions requiring reply other than yes or no. The concluding segment of such an utterance rises to the third level but then drops off to the first, or lowest, level of pitch:

²The dog chased the ³cat¹?
²Where are you ³going¹?
²When should I ³call him¹?

Beyond such basic pitch patterns, other characteristic pitch contours are our major devices for signaling alarm, incredulity, insistence:

²Am I planning to marry ⁴George²!

A third feature of intonation is often labeled **juncture**. There are different kinds of noticeable breaks in the flow of speech. These breaks are not simply pauses of varying lengths; they may involve retarding of tempo in the pronunciation of adjoining sounds as well as changes in their sound quality. They are correlated with typical patterns of stress and pitch. Shifting in the least noticeable of these breaks ("open transition") makes the difference between "a name" and "an aim"; between "I scream" and "ice cream."

A more noticeable break ("level juncture") corresponds to commas that do not signal a rise in pitch in sentences like, "Mr. Smith, the janitor, turned off the lights." Marked by a sharp terminal rise in pitch, the third type of juncture ("rising juncture") is often heard before the commas in sentences like "Mr. Smith, who has served us many years, has decided to retire." Marked by a sharp drop in pitch and volume, the fourth type of juncture ("falling juncture") terminates most utterances. Level, rising, and falling junctures are often grouped together as terminals distinguished by sustained (→), rising (↗), and falling (↘) pitch.

Intonation can help establish grammatical distinctions not otherwise clear. It thus provides a bridge from phonemics to syntax. For instance, *in* functions differently in the following two sentences:

We sat ìn a car. (tertiary stress on *in*)
We took íñ a show. (secondary stress on *in*)

The first *in* is a preposition, with weak stress. But the second *in* is something else, something more prominent, more heavily stressed. In combinations like "took *in* a show" and "sent *in* a request," *in* carries the stress, carried in the contrasting sentences by the simple verbs ("*sat* in a car"). Open transition separates *took in* and *a show,* but *sat* and *in a car.*

The *in* in *took in* is part of a compound verb rather than an ordinary preposition.

Many teachers ready to be initiated into linguistics found themselves bogged down in courses or books that were essentially introductions to English phonology. Ideally, however, phonology was to be a stepping-stone to the study of larger units. The student would go on to **morphology**, studying combinations of phonemes into morphemes. A phoneme could be defined as the smallest language unit that *makes a difference* in meaning. If we change a single phoneme in a word like *him*, we change the meaning: we get *Tim*, or *ham*, or *hit*. A morpheme could be defined as the smallest language unit that *by itself* carries meaning. The *t*-sound changes *him* to *hit*, but by itself it means nothing. *Him, hit, hip, hiss*, etc., carry meaning by themselves. They cannot be split any further into *meaningful* subunits.

Much of morphology is concerned with recurrent combinations of *several* morphemes. Words like *Greeks* and *trees* combine a "base" morpheme with an inflectional ending carrying the meaning of "more than one." In a word like *seeker*, the base morpheme combines with a derivational ending that carries the meaning "one who . . ." The plural affix in *oxen* would be considered a variant, or **allomorph**, of the plural morpheme in *Greeks*. Generally, simple root words as well as familiar prefixes and suffixes would have the status of morphemes. *Pinned, redder, slowly, growth, modesty, prepare, postpone*, etc., would all be split into their base morphemes, or roots, and other "bound" morphemes, meaningful only when thus affixed to a base.

With a sound grounding in phonology and morphology, the student would at last be ready for the study of **syntax**—the study of relationships within a sentence. He could turn his attention to similar strings, or sequences, of morphemes and analyze their similarities. Suppose we collect a sampling like the following:

> the mountain climber
> the young mountain climber
> a very young mountain climber with warts
> the youngest mountain climber of all
> this very pretty freshman girl in my class
> the two prettiest freshman girls of Toledo

Such clusters occur in varying length, with a word like *climber* or *girl* still present as a kind of "hard core" even in the shortest versions. We call *climber* or *girl* the **headword** of the cluster. We see at work the two most basic grammatical devices of English, its two basic tools: (1) *Word order* rigidly determines the actual sequence of words. A computer that had gone haywire might print out a sequence like "a with very warts climber young mountain." But normally the mechanisms at work in the language center of our brains insert each little word in its proper slot. (2) *Inflections* express the relationship between "two . . . girl*s*" and between "young*est* . . . of all." Without the inflectional endings *-s* and *-est,* these words would not fit; the strings would be "broken English."

A third major grammatical device of English is represented by words like *the, a,* and *of.* The function of these words is to help tie the major units of meaning together, to help cement them in a meaningful whole. This is the kind of work done in a sentence by determiners, prepositions, connectives, and the like. We call such words **function words** (or, sometimes, structure words). We have to remember that many of these have not just their grammatical function but also a dictionary meaning, and that it is sometimes hard to distinguish sharply between the two.[15] In some uses of function words, the dictionary meaning is weak:

> Consider *to* in *I want to go.* The elements *I, want,* and *go* are referable, through the intermediary of English content structure, to aspects of human experience. But it is impossible to find a specific factor in the situation which can be considered as the "meaning" of *to.* Nevertheless, *to* does have a function, since without it *I want to go,* means nothing. [16]

In other uses of function words, the dictionary meaning is strong:

> The *to* of *what nature hasn't done to us will be done by our fellow man,* for example, is semantically of major importance to its sentence, so that if *for* is substituted there is a very considerable change in meaning.[17]

Having noted the role of the major grammatical devices, we can proceed to sort out the words in each string into major **word classes.** The nouns are words like *climber, girl, wart, class.* Like most of the words traditionally included in this class, they have inflected forms for the plural: *girls, warts.* They appear after noun-markers like *the, a, this,* and *my.* Many nouns show typical **derivational** suffixes—noun-forming suffixes like the *-er* in *climber.* These help us derive nouns from other words. In a larger sample, we would see other noun-forming suffixes at work, such as *-hood, -ness, -acy,* and *-dom: womanhood, bigness, delicacy, kingdom.* The adjectives in our sample differ from the nouns in both form and position. They have inflected forms for comparison: *younger—youngest; prettier—prettiest.* They fit in after intensifiers like *very* or *rather.* (Notice that *mountain* and *freshman,* though here used as modifiers, do not. They are nouns used as modifiers, or **modifying nouns.**) In a larger sample, we would find typical derivational suffixes used in making adjectives: *-y,*

-ish, -ous, -able, -ful, and so on. We would find these in words like *classy, girlish, mountainous, marriageable,* and *wonderful.*

Leaving the noun clusters behind, we move on to strings in which the headwords are verbs:

> was hitting
> has been hitting
> only rarely hits the target
> invariably hits the nail on the head
> would have been hit by a train
> could have hit him the first time

We are struck by the great number of forms and combinations possible for the English verb. In the sample, we encounter only three basic forms: *hit, hits, hitting.* Normally, regular English verbs are four-part verbs: *ask, asks, asked, asking.* Irregular English verbs are five-part verbs: *break, breaks, broke, broken, breaking.* Auxiliaries combine with the main verb to make possible the full range of complete verbs: *was* hitting, *has been* hitting, *would have been* hit, *could have* hit. In a larger sample, we would encounter verb-forming suffixes like *-ize, -fy,* and *-en: organize, glorify, redden.* The single-word modifiers clustering around the verb are adverbs. Many of them show the derivational suffix *-ly: rarely, invariably.* Unlike other sentence parts, adverbs shift position in the sentence with relative ease:

> *rarely* hits the target
> hits the target *rarely*
>
> *invariably* hits the nail on the head
> hits the nail *invariably* on the head
> hits the nail on the head *invariably*

Leaving aside some other elements in the verb clusters (or verb phrases), we can now look at samples of a noun cluster and a verb cluster put together. The noun cluster becomes the subject; the verb cluster becomes the predicate. We have arrived at the goal of our inductive labors—the complete English sentence:

> The very young mountain climber with warts invariably hits the nail on the head.

From a sampling of relatively simple sentences, we can form some idea of the most common **sentence patterns.** Subject, verb, and other basic sentence elements combine to set up a sentence skeleton consisting of two, three, or four basic parts. We can sort out the resulting basic patterns by asking what, if any, complements, or "completers," follow the verb. The following basic sentence patterns differ in the kind of sentence elements needed to complete the predicate:

S—V   Birds sing.
(The subject is followed by an intransitive verb that "does not go anywhere.")

S—V—O   The dog chased the cat.
(A transitive verb carries the action across to an object—the target or receiver.)

S—LV—N   Her father is a mailman.
(A linking verb pins a label on the subject.)

S—LV—Adj   The sky looked blue.
(The label pinned on the subject by the linking verb is an adjective instead of a noun.)

S—V—IO—O   Fred lent John his bicycle.
(The subject—verb—object sentence takes a detour through an indirect object that indicates destination, with the direct object indicating missive or object sent.)

S—V—O—OC   Fred made John his friend.
(The verb pins a label—the object complement—on the object.)

S—V—O—Adj   The fire kept us warm.
(The label pinned on the object is an adjective instead of a noun.)

To get from our set of simple recurrent patterns to more complicated sentences, we need above all an inventory of different kinds of **connectives**. Connectives link one subject-predicate group to another:

My brother liked Elvira, *who* ignored him.
My brother liked Elvira, *though* she ignored him.
My brother liked Elvira, *but* she ignored him.
My brother liked Elvira; *however,* she ignored him.

In setting up the necessary subclasses here, we can rely on structural criteria: *And* and *but,* for instance, are different from *therefore* and *however,* because they behave differently in a sentence. If a student asks, "Why is *but* a coordinating connective and *however* an adverbial connective?" the answer is, "*But* is stationary, whereas *however* shares with adverbs a relative freedom of movement." We do not say, "The location is good, the pay *but* is terrible." But we do say,

The location is good; *however,* the pay is terrible.
The location is good; the pay, *however,* is terrible.
The location is good; the pay is terrible, *however.*

In addition to investigating ways of joining subject-predicate groups, we will be concerned with the possible substitutions within them. For instance, pronouns, verbals, or noun clauses may take the place of nouns:

The salesman missed the train.
He missed the train.

The statement made me furious.
To hear him say that made me furious.

The reason is unknown.
What made him leave us is unknown.

Expansion, connecting, and substitution would enable us to get from the basic sentence patterns to highly complex sentences.

Since the first generation of modern linguists led English teachers to rethink their attitude toward language along these lines, linguistics as a scholarly discipline has moved on rapidly. An ambitious second generation, represented by the transformational grammarians among others, has questioned many assumptions of earlier linguists. By and large, linguists have abandoned as too confining the early commitment to rigorously inductive procedures. They have abandoned the requirement for a comprehensive phonology *prior* to work in syntax. They have moved beyond the early preoccupation with observable language behavior to sophisticated theory about the mental phenomena behind language.

Nevertheless, the impact of the first wave of applied English linguistics on English teaching in the schools was profound and lasting. Teachers learned to approach language with the attitude of "Let's look at what is there." Instead of relying on opaque verbal formulas, they learned to apply concrete structural and formal tests. Instead of cataloguing disconnected items, they learned to display typical relationships.

Above all, teacher and student learned to look at language as a living thing, functioning in accordance with basic rules and yet sprouting unsuspected complications. Wrestling with such complications, teacher and student learned what it means to represent data that do not fit one's ready-made notions. They found out what it takes to set up categories that are reasonably "leakproof," what it takes to set up usable classifications without sweeping complications under the rug. Adjectives, for instance, are in basic ways different from nouns. They follow a quite different inflectional scheme, such as *poor—poorer—poorest*. But at times they unexpectedly "cross over" and appear with articles and as subjects of verbs:

> *The poor* will always be with us.
> *The poorest* suffered most.

By encouraging students to investigate such paradoxical facts, linguists helped the English teacher to make his teaching more honest and more instructive. They restored intellectual excitement to a subject that had become cut-and-dried, illiberal, and merely conventional. Much of what English teachers learned in the process will survive changing fashions in teaching and changing emphases in research.

TRANSFORMATIONAL GRAMMAR: THEORY AND APPLICATION

Noam Chomsky's *Syntactic Structures*, published in 1957, helped inaugurate a new transformational linguistics that was rapidly popularized in articles and textbooks by R. B. Lees, Owen Thomas, Paul Roberts, and others. In the eyes of the transformational grammarians, the very emphasis on observable fact that had been the linguist's strength had become an obstacle to fruitful inquiry. Linguists were forever taking inventory of "surface" phenomena, cutting up ("segmenting") existing sentences and classifying their parts. For the new linguist, by contrast, the agenda was "to come to an understanding of the often deeply buried mechanisms that make language viable." [18] Looking for these mechanisms, transformationalists came to look at grammar, not as a system for *classifying* the elements in sentences already produced, but as a system for *generating* sentences in the first place.

A transformational grammar starts by describing the **source sentences** (or "**kernel sentences**") that provide the elementary building blocks for sentence construction. They are "the stuff from which all else is made." **Transformations** are the *operations we perform* on these "barebones" sentences to make them more complicated. "Transforms" are the resulting more complex structures. In the words of Noam Chomsky,

> We can greatly simplify the description of English and gain new and important insight into its formal structure if we limit the direction description in terms of phrase structure to a kernel of basic sentences (simple, declarative, active, with no complex verb or noun phrases), deriving all other sentences from these . . . by transformation, possibly repeated. [19]

In transformational grammar, the "rules" are formulas for building sentences. They are **desi**gned to provide a theoretical model of how native speakers "construct quickly during conversation a never-ending succession of novel sentences each of which conforms perfectly to the requirements of well-formedness of his language." [20]

Source sentences would be simple statement patterns like

> Logs burn.
> A bird sang its song.
> The train has left.
> The milkman will call.

An example of a basic transformation, bringing about a more complicated structure, would be a common question-producing mechanism we employ in English: We *split* the first auxiliary off from the rest of the verb. We then lift it out of its original slot and move it to a new position *in front of* the subject.

Statement: The train *has left.*
  Question: *Has* the train *left?*

Statement: The milkman *will call.*
  Question: *Will* the milkman *call?*

Like other basic transformational rules, the "split-the-verb" rule for questions applies more widely than we might at first suspect. If there is no auxiliary to split off, we make one up—we insert a form of the "dummy" auxiliary *do:*

>   *Source:* Logs burn.
>   *First step:* Logs *do burn.*
> *Second step:* *Do* logs *burn?*

>   *Source:* A bird sang its song.
>   *First step:* A bird *did sing* its song.
> *Second step:* *Did* a bird *sing* its song?

Basic transformations typically involve additions, deletions, and reshufflings of this sort. "Single-base" transformations are transformations applied to a single source sentence.

Source sentences to some extent coincide with the familiar basic sentence patterns we encountered earlier. The most elementary of these can be reduced to a general formula like the following:

ENGLISH GRAMMAR

A Summary

Inflections	His friend*s* stopp*ed* work*ing*.
Word order	*The man* attacked *the dog*.
Function words	*The* firemen asked *for a* raise.

SENTENCE PATTERNS

S-V	Speed kills.
S-V-O	Lincoln freed the slaves.
S-LV-N	Benedict Arnold was a traitor.
S-LV-Adj	Advice is cheap.
S-V-IO-O	Congress awarded him a medal.
S-V-O-OC	Tom called Juan his friend.
S-V-O-Adj	Macbeth considered Banquo dangerous.

SIMPLE TRANSFORMATIONS

Request	Drop the gun.
Passive	The slaves were freed by Lincoln.
Question	Where have the flowers gone?
Negation	Crime does not pay.
There-is	There is hope.

MODIFIERS

Adjectives	a *treacherous* friend
Modifying noun	a *brick* house
Number adjective	*several* bystanders
Adverb	acted *carelessly*
Prepositional phrase	the girl *in white*
Appositive	Fred Gonzales, *a senior*

CONNECTIVES

Coordinating	She called, *but* I kept walking.
Adverbial	I think; *therefore*, I am.
Subordinating	Catch me *if* you can.
Relative pronoun	He looked for people *who* cared.
Special	Tell me *that* you love me.

VERBALS

Present participle	*Barking* dogs don't bite.
Past participle	He raked up the *fallen* leaves.
Gerund	*Seeing* is *believing*.
Infinitive	*To err* is human.

First noun phrase + (possible auxiliary) + verb + (possible second noun phrase)

The rule for forming the passive from a sentence like "John ate the apple" could then be spelled out somewhat as follows:

Passive = Second noun phrase + (possible auxiliary) + appropriate form of *be* + past participle of verb + (by + first noun phrase)

Obviously, the transcription of such rules can be greatly simplified by an appropriate system of notation, such as perhaps

$$\text{Passive} = NP_2 + (\text{aux}) + be + V\text{-en} + (by + NP_1)$$

These and similar rules for single-base transformations would allow us to construct from the source sentence

John ate the apple

such transforms as

did John eat the apple?
John didn't eat the apple.
the apple was eaten by John.
who ate the apple?
what did John eat?
when did John eat the apple?
eat the apple!
etc.

"Double-base" transformations are operations combining material from *two* source sentences in a larger, combined sentence. For instance, we would employ a double-base transformation in putting together a sentence containing a relative clause:

First Source: She married *the man.*
Second Source: *The man* loved her.
Result: She married the man *who* loved her.

First Source: Rogelio returned *the book.*
Second Source: He had borrowed *the book.*
Result: Rogelio returned the book *that* he had borrowed.

First Source: Many Americans have *names*.
Second Source: *Names* show their Spanish ancestry.
     Result: Many Americans have names *which* show their Spanish ancestry.

In each case, we start with two sentences that overlap: They use the same noun. The *repeated* noun is deleted in the second source sentence, and the appropriate relative pronoun takes its place. Where necessary, the relative pronoun is *moved* to the beginning of the new relative clause. The finished relative clause is inserted ("embedded") in the first source sentence (the "matrix" sentence).

Stripped of the technical abracadabra of scholarly transformational work, such sentence-generating formulas presented a great potential contribution to constructive classroom work with language. Asked, "What is grammar good for?" the teacher could say, "Grammar pays off in sentence building." Teaching participial phrases, for instance, he no longer had to treat them simply as an existing part of mature sentences. He could show where participial phrases "came from." He could put the students through their paces by having them *lift* such phrases out of an added source sentence and use them in a more sophisticated combined version:

First Source: The fans went wild.
Second Source: They were *watching the race*.
     Result: The fans *watching the race* went wild.

First Source: The tremors subsided.
Second Source: The tremors were *shaking the building*.
     Result: The tremors *shaking the building* subsided.

First Source: George went up into the gallery.
Second Source: He was *whistling under his breath*.
     Result: George went up into the gallery, *whistling under his breath*.

A transformational approach thus provides us with a model of how information feeds into a "minimum" sentence. It provides a model of how a starved, underprivileged sentence can be packed with meaning. Starting with a sentence like "The car stopped," we can fill up the blackboard with further information like the following:
What kind of car is it?

The car is a Buick.
The car was built in 1962.
The car is red.

The car is a sedan.
A man is driving the car.
The man is wearing sunglasses.
The man is wearing a sport shirt.
The sport shirt is yellow.

How and where did the car stop?

The brakes squealed.
The car skidded.
The car stopped in front of a drugstore.
The drugstore was at the corner.
The corner was the corner of Elm and Vine.

Why did the car stop?

A woman stepped into the street.
The woman was old.
The woman was carrying a shopping bag.

We then go through the various necessary transformational steps, "cancelling out the numerous overlapping parts . . . re-forming the remaining elements; rearranging them; supplying missing connectives"; etc.[21] The resulting final product makes full use of the resources of the English sentence:

The red 1962 Buick sedan driven by a man wearing sunglasses and a yellow sport shirt skidded with squealing brakes and stopped in front of a drugstore at the corner of Elm and Vine as an old woman carrying a shopping bag stepped into the street.

Adapting the same approach, we can "reconstruct" the way actual sentences were put together by writers who are recognized masters of English prose:

    Statement: His big yellow eyes looked straight ahead.
Added Source: They were *narrowed with hate.*
      Result: His big yellow eyes, *narrowed with hate,* looked straight ahead.

(Ernest Hemingway)

    Statement: The thin sun appeared.
Added Source: It was *rapidly burning away mist and cloud.*
Added Source: It was *warming the air and the earth.*

Result: By midmorning the thin sun appeared, *rapidly burning away mist and cloud, warming the air and the earth.*

(William Faulkner)

In order to put transformational grammar to work in the classroom, teachers and textbook authors had to decide *how* to use it, *how much* to use it, and *how soon.* Transformational theory had developed, not as a rationale for constructive "sentence practice," but as an answer to unsolved problems in grammatical analysis. A transformational approach could get at grammatical relationships that "surface" analysis did not reach. Take for instance a sentence like

John was persuaded to leave.

As far as surface analysis goes, *John* here is the subject of *persuaded.* As far as meaning goes, however, John is going to *leave,* but *someone else* had to persuade him. As soon as we go beyond the surface, we realize that "*John* is understood to be the subject of *leave* and the object of *persuade.*"[22] This "underlying" relationship can be graphically shown— it can be made "explicit"—when we trace the finished sentence back to its source sentences:

Somebody persuaded *John.*
John left.

By showing these "deeper" structural relations, we can get at differences between structures that are *superficially* alike. For instance, there seems to be no formal or structural difference between "the growling of lions" and "the raising of flowers." But we recognize the different *logical* relationship between verbal and noun in each case. The distinction *is* expressed, not in the phrases themselves, but in the sources from which they are derived. In other words, their transformational history is different. The first is a transform of "the lions growl." The second is a transform of a sentence like "John raises flowers."

If a purely structural grammar has no way of formulating the felt grammatical difference between the two versions of "gerund + *of* + noun," then a transformational grammar is more "powerful" to the extent that it does. Transformational grammar in effect adds another level of analysis to our previous levels of investigation. It adds a "third dimension" that not only helps us demonstrate important differences but makes them *predictable.* Thus, Noam Chomsky, in *Syntactic Structures,* treated the *sleeping* in "the sleeping child" as an adjective, since it derives from a sentence parallel to the source sentences of "the tall boy" and "the little girl":

> The boy is tall.
> The girl is little.
> The child is sleeping.

At the same time, "The boy is tall" is a kernel sentence. But "The child is sleeping" is a transform of "The child sleeps." *Sleeping* is restricted from entering such adjective positions as "the very sleeping child" because there are no sentences like "The child very sleeps." This kind of analysis does justice to the peculiar hybrid status (between verb and adjective) of verbals like the present and past participle.[23]

Many teachers were intrigued by the power of transformational grammar to illuminate important relationships and to reveal an underlying system of regularities that helps make grammar work. They soon, however, discovered the other side of the coin: A straight transformational grammar requires complete and systematic derivation of hundreds of structures that are simply accepted as given by other grammarians. Many of these involve teacher and student in chains of derivation of formidable complexity.

Even at a very elementary level, a generative grammar raises the question of what to accept as basic and what to generate by transformational steps. We have to decide, for instance, whether to make such elements as indirect objects and object complements part of the most basic patterns—or whether to introduce them from an added source sentence:

> *First Source:*   Fred sent a message.
> *Second Source:*   The message is *for John.*
> *Result:*   Fred sent *John* a message.
>
> *First Source:*   John considered Sam.
> *Second Source:*   Sam was *a fool.*
> *Result:*   John considered Sam *a fool.*

Traveling in this general direction, we soon find ourselves taking elaborate detours through complex derivations for simple things. To put the adjective *wise* into "The *wise* man is honest," we would start with two source sentences:

> The man is honest.
> The man is wise.

We would then convert the second source into a relative clause:

The man *who is wise* is honest.

We would then delete *who is* and reverse *man* and *wise:*

The wise man is honest.[24]

In the technical jargon of the MIT linguist, we would say that to get the adjective into a phrase like *the new shoes,* we would proceed through the "relative clause transformation," the "relative *be* deletion," and the "adjective transformation":

	the shoes *the shoes are new*
Relative Clause Transformation:	the shoes *which are new*
Relative Be Deletion:	the shoes *new*
Adjective Transformation:	the *new* shoes[25]

This is a formidable way of getting the modifier *new* next to its "headword" *shoes*—where it was all along, and where it was even when the child first learned combinations like *big truck* and *good baby.* To get the adverb *extremely* in front of the adjective *tall,* we may be asked to consider a sequence of rewrites like the following:

George is *to some degree* tall.
George is *to a degree which is extreme* tall.
George is *to an extreme degree* tall.
George is *extremely* tall.[26]

Ultimately, the transformational grammarian aims at representing a major part of the program that the brain can consult in order to speak and understand grammatical English. A grammar would embody the system that we would have to code into a speech machine if it were to produce true English sentences. In such a system, grammatical rules would soon have to be bolstered with lexical information—data concerning meaning. For instance, it would not be enough to describe *frighten* as a transitive verb—a verb that appears between subject and object, that can be used in the passive, etc. Almost *anything* can frighten us (and thus become the subject of *frighten*). But who or what can *be* frightened (and thus become the object of *frighten*) is more restricted: The object of *frighten* has to be a living thing, something that can experience feelings. We frighten people or animals. The subject of *elapse,* by contrast, *cannot* be a living thing. Human beings, or animals, do not "elapse." Before we use a noun in relation to *frighten* or *elapse,* we have to know whether the noun stands for something "animate" or "inanimate."[27] When we use *who* or *which* to point back to a noun, we have to know whether that noun stands for something "human" or "nonhuman." A comprehensive transformational grammar thus has to find a way of coding such grammatically relevant information. It may use clusters of **features** that place words inside (or outside) a given category: [28]

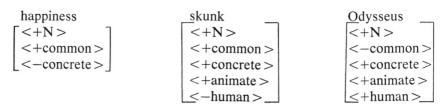

Much of this information the classroom teacher would normally leave to the already acquired, operational knowledge of language that students possess. The classroom teacher tries to promote the student's understanding of basic processes and to set up a framework for fruitful practice. The transformational linguist pursues an ideal of "true descriptive adequacy" that requires formidable explicitness for the sake of a reliable overall system.

The basic difference between the linguist and the teacher is that research is subject-centered, while teaching is student-centered. The modern linguist is a system-builder; he asks, "How does this item fit into my overall system?" Much of the technical abracadabra of modern linguistics serves the need for devices that help fit recalcitrant facts into larger general patterns. Thus, many truncated "elliptical" constructions are traced back to fuller and more regular ones. *"That's* over," for instance, is explained as derived from *"That thing* is over." It thus conforms to a general rule that the first "noun phrase" in a sentence consists of "determiner noun." Finding no *the* or *that* in "Spring is over," we would say that the determiner has been omitted, or that there is a "null" -determiner or "zero" -determiner.[29]

A "zero-determiner" is not a "fact of language." It is a bookkeeping device that makes for efficient manipulation of linguistic data. Before we introduce such concepts to our students, we ask: "Assuming that this term serves the convenience of a given descriptive system, how does it serve *my* purposes? Will it help me to make basic processes more graphic and understandable? Will it help me to build up the confidence and competence of my students?" As with the earlier structural grammar, failure to ask these questions will keep transformational grammar from making its great potential contribution to productive classroom work.

PSYCHOLINGUISTICS, TAGMEMICS, AND AFTER

While teachers have tried to put modern grammar to work in the classroom, research has moved on rapidly, increasingly becoming concerned with basic problems of language theory. Transformational grammarians from the beginning had ambitious theoretical goals: The "generative" model of how sentences were produced was to lead to an understanding of "the system of linguistic competence that underlies behavior." This understanding would in turn lead to insight into how language is *acquired* as well as used, and it would ultimately involve an understanding of how "language mirrors human mental processes." Grammar thus turns into **psycholinguistics.** The study of grammar heads toward "a study of the nature of human intellectual capacities" as manifested through language.[30] Increasingly, the search for the "hidden organizing principles" behind language turns into an examination of our built-in language aptitude, of the "internal resources" we put to work in learning and using language.

In keeping with this long-range drift, recent transformational work has moved farther away from "surface structure" toward ever more abstract "basic" relationships. In earlier transformational materials, for instance, *be* appeared as part of the basic structure in elementary sentence types like

> S—*be*—Adv   John is here.
> S—*be*—N   John is a miser.
> S—*be*—Adj   John is tall.

More recent materials have stressed the similarity between verb and adjective as the most basic "constituent" of the predicate. Both verb and adjective act as the basic "predicators" in stripped-down sentence models like the following:

> *Verb:*   John *cries.*
>   John *runs.*
>
> *Adjective:* John *honest.*
>   John *tall.*

The *be* that would serve as the linking verb in the actual finished sentence seems secondary: We can stipulate a "*be* transformation" that "introduces the correct form of *be* into the deep structure" when an adjective rather than a verb appears after the subject:

> John *is* honest.
> John *was* tall.[31]

By this kind of analysis, we in effect go *back* a further step beyond the simple "kernel sentences" of earlier work. Kernel sentences were an already finished—though *simple*—grammatical product. Current analysis goes back beyond such kernel sentences to more abstract underlying statement patterns, or "propositions." Deep structure is thus getting "deeper"; the account of basic grammatical elements and relations is getting more abstract. To describe the "network of grammatical relations" in a sentence, we would start with elements much more highly generalized than the specific grammatical signals that *convey* these relations in the finished sentence. Thus, our account of the deep structure of a question-sentence might merely include an abstract "question-marker" Q. This marker then activates specific question transformations as we derive the actual finished sentence. The deep structure of a passive sentence would have a similar marker to activate the necessary passive transformation, etc. The underlying "deep structure" would thus already include such essential meaning elements as "question," "negation," "imperative," "passive," and the like. The "surface structure" would show the specific grammatical signals that convey these meanings in the actual sentence. The "transformational component" of the grammar would trace, step by step, the transformations necessary to take us from the deep-structure relations to actual surface-structure sentences.

To reach truly basic relations, we would formulate "language-independent" definitions for central concepts, such as "subject-of," "object-of," etc. We would formulate "deep down" basic categories independent of surface grammar. Thus, in the deep structure of a passive sentence, not its final "grammatical subject," but its original "logical subject," would reappear as subject as far as "semantic interpretation" is concerned.[32] In relation to the verb *pay*, some of the following elements might appear at the most basic level:

> "Agent" (answers: "done by whom?")
> —may appear as Subject:　　*John* paid.
> 　　　　　　　　　or after *by*:　The money was paid *by John.*
>
> "Object" (answers: "affecting what?")
> —may appear as Direct Object:　John paid *money.*
> 　　　　　　　　　　or after *of*:　　Payment *of money* . . .

"Dative" (answers: "to or for whom?")
—may appear as Indirect Object: John paid *Jim* the money.
                  or after *to:*   John paid the money *to Jim.*

"Instrumental" (answers: "by what means?")
—may appear after *with:*   He paid *with a check.*

Such archetypal grammatical relationships constitute, on a deeper and quasi-semantic level, a return to the **cases** of traditional grammar. But unlike the traditional cases, these new categories are in the underlying deep structure. They remain unchanged even when a proposition is run through its many different possible surface manifestations:

1. Jones paid Smith the money with a check.
2. Jones paid the money to Smith with a check.
3. The money was paid Smith by Jones with a check.
4. The money was paid to Smith by Jones with a check.
5. The money was paid by Jones to Smith with a check.
6. Smith was paid the money by Jones with a check.
7. A check is what Jones paid Smith the money with.[33]

As we thus move from the overt grammatical signals to the under-lying meaning relationships they express, we can hope to go beyond the historical accidents and physical peculiarities of one specific language. We may hope to discover relationships that underlie all languages. Hence the concern with **language universals** that has replaced the earlier struc-turalist view that each language is "unique" and must be studied on its own terms.

While grammarians have thus worked their way closer to basic questions about the nature of language, they have shifted attention away from the problem of how to improve language competence. By and large, transformational theory has been spinning away from the teacher looking for application of linguistic know-how to classroom work. Trying to keep their feet on the ground, teachers will increasingly look for approaches that stay closer to actual performance. Hence their interest in a possible slot-and-filler grammar on the **tagmemic** model, as developed by Kenneth L. Pike and others.

In its basic view of language as a system for "encoding meaning," tagmemics is close to the current transformational perspective. Again we would assume basic meaning categories like *agent, act, goal, instrument,* "*beneficiary,*" *time, place, cause, manner,* and the like. Again, a "proposition" put together from these basic elements could be given different grammatical forms:

In order for a proposition to take form as one or more sentences, the various categories in the proposition must be assigned grammatical roles in the sentence. That is, a category such as Agent is assigned a particular grammatical role—subject, or predicate, or adjunct, and so on.

> Agent as subject: *The police* arrested my roommate.
> Agent as predicate: The streets were well *policed.*
> Agent as adjunct: My roommate was arrested *by the police.*

Because the different categories of a proposition can take various grammatical roles, and propositions can be combined in different ways, we can have a variety of sentences that have nearly the same meaning.[34]

While grammarians have thus worked their way closer to basic questions about the nature of language, they have shifted attention away from the problem of how to improve language competence.

Tagmemic description would focus on the way the actual sentence has combined "meaning" and "grammar." Each sentence provides slots to be filled by elements that *combine* a basic "propositional" meaning and a grammatical function, such as subject or object:

> A tagmeme is a composite (1) of a functional slot in a grammatical pattern (e.g., object slot), (2) with accompanying generalized plot element (a propositional category, such as Affected), (3) plus a class of appropriate fillers (such as noun phrase), (4) manifested by one chosen member of the class (such as *my roommate*):
>
> $$\text{subject} + \text{predicate} + \begin{bmatrix} \text{object:} & \text{noun phrase} \\ \text{Affected:} & \textit{my roommate} \end{bmatrix}$$
>
> as in *The police arrested my roommate.*[35]

Such basic sentence types would be changed and expanded by various familiar processes, such as substitution and embedding:

> Choice occurs at slots in a *pattern*—which we define as a conventional sequence of slots with a set of possible alternatives, or choices, that can fill the slots. Patterns, like tagmemes, are grammatical units, with slots filled by particular lexical items.
>
> Other lexical items of a category may be substituted; for example, *they* or *the cops* may be substituted for *the police*; *him* or *my friend* for *my roommate.* . . .

A sentence can also be expanded by embedding. Two clauses that share a common category can often be embedded one within the other. Thus,

My brother opened the window. The maid had closed it.

becomes

My brother opened the window the maid had closed.[36]

Emphasis on the slot-and-filler scheme of a tagmemic grammar makes it possible for the English teacher to "return to the surface." Examining typical modifier slots in front of the noun, for instance, he can strengthen the student's sense of pattern, of "what goes where," without constructing elaborate hypothetical derivations:

Predeter-miner (Predet)	Deter-miner (Det)	Number Adj (Num)	Adjective (Adj)	Modifying Noun (MN)	Noun (N)
	a		mean		temper
		three	blind		mice
		four	husky	football	players
	this		beautiful	flower	arrangement
		second			prize
both	his		wooden		houses
	my	two	tiny	song	birds
many	a		dusty	dirt	road
half	the				battle
	the	only	available	horse	cart
all	the	chief		tourist	attractions
	our	every			wish
	these	three	valuable	silver	coins[37]

This kind of scheme makes possible the effective demonstration of differences: The words in the "adjective" column are our true adjectives. Only these can be preceded by an intensifier like *very*: "These three *very valuable* silver coins" but not "these *very three* valuable silver coins" or "these three valuable *very silver* coins." The words that come between the true adjective and the headword are "modifying nouns." They are like adjectives in *one* respect: they are used as a modifier in front of a noun. But they do not share other adjective features:

> *a football* player   BUT NOT   The player is *football.*
> OR   The player is *very football.*

At the same time, this scheme sets up a framework for further *exploration*. We can turn to the student and ask: Can you change the order of the adjectives in the following examples? Can you explain what kind of adjectives follow one another in what order?

a	small	oval		plastic	button
a	big		old	wooden	bucket
the	tiny	round		golden	frame
a	huge	tall	bronzed		athlete
a		square	yellow		patch

Finally, this kind of slot-and-filler scheme sets up the context for "limbering-up" exercises that put the student through his paces:

a car
a shiny new sports car
a second huge decrepit old touring car
all these tinny inexpensive imported family cars
etc.

This kind of work with the student's linguistic repertory can be carried on without an elaborate system of symbolic notation. It can help keep alive his delight in living language, freely and imaginatively used.

LINGUISTICS AND THE STUDENT

Years ago, teaching grammar meant wading, for the umpteenth time, through the opaque definitions of the noun and the verb, the gerund and the participle. The student's job was to memorize the terms and to copy out the examples in dull textbook sentences. Today, honest work in language is not likely to be predictable and dull. In the last few decades, modern linguistics has produced an impressive revival of interest in the technical workings of language. Today there is God's plenty for teachers looking for fresh, substantial, challenging materials that can help the student better understand and use his own language.

To use such materials productively, teachers must be prepared to answer the questions that a bright student would legitimately ask:

(1) "What are we after?" What we are after is not to commit ourselves to one pet theory, or to memorize a new system of diagraming, or a new set of terms. What we are after is to *develop a fuller appreciation, and a fuller command, of the resources of the English language.* We want to extend our acquaintance with the English sentence, which, as Winston Churchill said, is "a noble thing." We want our students to acquire, gradually and over the years, a sense of what is magnificent about sentences like the following:

It was the thunder of a great bald eagle
who beat his way off the rocks and straight up over them
his claws hanging down,

his hot red eyes sparkling for one second
in the light of the sky.

(Walter Van Tilburg Clark)

One day when I went out to my woodpile,
or rather my pile of stumps,
     I observed *two large* ants,
          the one red,
          the other much larger,
          nearly half an inch long,
          and black,
          fiercely contending with one another.

(Henry Thoreau)

He saw himself
     saving people from sinking ships,
     cutting away masts in a hurricane,
     swimming through a surf with a line;
or as a lonely castaway,
     barefooted and half-naked,
     walking on uncovered reefs in search of shellfish to stave
          off starvation.

(Joseph Conrad)

(2) "What is it good for?" When we study the workings of language, we build on what we have already learned indirectly, through imitation and use. We extend it directly and systematically through study and practice. We study adjectives, for instance, because first-rate speakers and writers put the adjective to *good use:*

He was only a *little* boy, ten years *old,* with hair like *dusty yellow* grass and with *shy polite gray* eyes, and with a mouth that worked when he thought.

(John Steinbeck)

We study verbals, because verbals are a prominent feature of a mature style, in sentences written by people who know how:

The groom at the head looked back, *jerking the leading rope.*

(D. H. Lawrence)

They turned to each other, *laughing excitedly, talking, not listening.*

(William Golding)

Gazing up into the darkness, I saw myself as a creature *driven and derided by vanity.*

(James Joyce)

Seizing the sailor's arm with her right hand, and *mounting the little girl on her left,* she went out of the tent *sobbing bitterly.*

(Thomas Hardy)

(3) "How do I study it profitably?" Grammar starts from the fact that language is more than words. Words combine into sentences. To understand grammar, we focus attention on *how* this combining works, on how it is done. We begin to understand the workings of grammar when we ask: What does it take to turn a mere disjointed list of dictionary words into a coherent statement? What do we do to make words fit into a sentence? What is the difference between the broken English and the grammatical English in each of the following pairs?

Words: Afar—hunter—moose—hear—roar
Sentence: The hunter heard the roar of the moose from afar.

Words: Welcome—we—spacemen—tiny—Martian—beady—eye
Sentence: We welcomed the tiny Martian spacemen with the beady eyes.

Here we see the most basic sentence-building mechanisms at work: the shuffling of words to make them fill the right slot in the sentence, the changes in words to make them fit into their slot, the filling in of the missing links that help tie the parts of the sentence together. Soon we ask: How do simple sentences get more complicated? How do sentences "grow"? For instance, we focus on how modifiers build up a bare, uninformative sentence skeleton, adding details, spelling out qualifications:

Bare: Men tell tales.
Modified: *Dead* men tell *no* tales.

Bare: Men must obey the laws.
Modified: *Good* men must *not* obey the laws *too well.*

(Emerson)

Bare: Madness is sense.
Modified: *Much* madness is *divinest* sense
              To a discerning eye.

(Emily Dickinson)

The study of grammar becomes "productive" if the basic question remains: How do I get from here to there? How does a child first get from isolated words to "These are the cookies I don't like" and "Are the rooms really this way when it's not Halloween"? How does the beginning writer get from inhibited primer sentences to mature sentences that carry meaning?

(4) "What is there for me to do?" If the aim of instruction is to develop the students' linguistic **repertory,** there should be much practice material *putting them through their paces.* Again and again the teacher should say: "Your turn. You put it to work." For example, in a substitution exercise like the following, the student puts his study of verbals to work in improvising variations from a basic pattern:

Pattern: *Something* is a pleasure.
Variations: *Skating* is a pleasure.
              Popping corn is a pleasure.
              To walk slowly down a busy street is a pleasure.
              Swimming in a cool lake on a hot summer day is a pleasure.
              *To see someone try to worm his way to the head of a long line
                  in front of a movie theater, and fail,* is a pleasure.

Imitation exercises ask the student to fill in, with his own "content," the grammatical structure of a model sentence. Here are model sentences from Irwin Shaw's short story, "The Eighty-Yard Run," with student-written imitations:

Model 1: Darling tucked the ball in, spurted at him,
              driving hard,
              hurling himself along,
              all two hundred pounds bunched into controlled attack.

Imitations: Carol took her diary back, sneered at her,
              walking fast,
              forcing herself along,
              all her secrets uncovered by the uninvited intruder.
          James reeled the fish in, beamed at it,
              feeling exuberant,
              dragging the five-pounder up,
              all fears of defeat dispelled in an instant.

Model 2: He smiled a little to himself as he ran,
              holding the ball lightly in front of him with his two hands,
              his knees pumping high,
              *his hips twisting in the almost girlish run of a back in a broken
              field.*

Imitations: Bob cussed a lot to himself as he drove,
              holding the wheel tightly in front of him with his two hands,
              his feet braking often,
              his lips curling in an almost devilish pout of a driver in a
              traffic jam.
          She laughed a bit to herself while she swam,

kicking the float gently in back of her with her two feet,
her toes turning inward,
her legs splashing in the high waves of the surf in the ocean.

When we thus involve our students in the workings of language, we do justice to a basic fact: The human message of language comes to us through a *medium*. Many teachers, in many fields, deal in one way or another with the meanings and purposes of human experience. The English teacher, if anybody, is qualified to deal with the verbal medium through which these meanings and purposes are communicated.

If an English teacher is an expert in anything, he is an expert in how meaning is communicated through words. Meaning emerges from words in context—which means, in part, in their grammatical relations. Competence in the technical foundations of our subject keeps us honest. Who will trust our insights into ecology, or war, or prison reform, if we are at a loss when confronted with basic features of the English sound system or the English sentence? Though we may sympathize with everything, we are expected to *know something*. Above all, we are expected to know something about what language is, how it works, and how it can be made to work better for our students.

FOOTNOTES

[1]Excerpts and exercises here and later from Hans P. Guth and Edgar H. Schuster, *American English Today, 7–12* (St. Louis: McGraw-Hill Book Company, 1970).

[2]Otto Jespersen, *Growth and Structure of the English Language,* 9th ed. (New York: Doubleday & Company, Inc., 1956), pp. 73–74.

[3]Noam Chomsky, *Language and Mind* (New York: Harcourt, Brace & World, Inc., 1968), pp. 20, 34–36.

[4]Otto Jespersen, *Language: Its Nature, Development, and Origin* (New York: Holt, Rinehart & Winston, Inc., 1922), pp. 22–23.

[5]Walter G. Friedrich, ed., "A Modern-Grammar Chrestomathy" (Valparaiso, Indiana; mimeo., 1961), p. 12.

[6]Jespersen, *Language,* p. 23.

[7]Charles Fries, "Meaning and Linguistic Analysis," *Language* 30 (January–March, 1954), 57–68.

[8]Edward Sapir, *Language: An Introduction to the Study of Speech* (New York: Harcourt, Brace & World, Inc., 1949), pp. 99–100.

[9]Dona Worrall Brown, "Does Language Structure Influence Thought?" *ETC.: A Review of General Semantics,* 17 (Spring 1960), 341.

[10]James H. Sledd, "Grammar or Gramarye," *The English Journal,* 49 (May, 1960), 300.

[11]John B. Carroll, *The Study of Language* (Cambridge, Mass.: Harvard University Press, 1959), p. 7.

[12]Leonard Bloomfield, *Language* (New York: Holt, Rinehart & Winston, Inc., 1933), p. 20.

[13]Archibald A. Hill, *Introduction to Linguistic Structures: From Sound to Sentence in English* (New York: Harcourt, Brace & World, Inc., 1958), p. iii.

[14]Structural treatments of intonation, and phonology generally, were heavily indebted to George L. Trager and Henry Lee Smith, Jr., *An Outline of English Structure* (Washington: American Council of Learned Societies, 1957).

[15]Edgar H. Sturtevant, *An Introduction to Linguistic Science* (New Haven: Yale University Press, 1960), p. 61.

[16]H. A. Gleason, Jr., *An Introduction to Descriptive Linguistics,* rev. ed. (New York: Holt, Rinehart & Winston, Inc., 1961), p. 55.

[17]Ralph B. Long, *The Sentence and Its Parts: A Grammar of Contemporary English* (Chicago: The University of Chicago Press, 1961), p. 5.

[18]Paul Roberts, *English Syntax: Alternate Edition* (New York: Harcourt, Brace & World, 1964), p. 411.

[19]Noam Chomsky, *Syntactic Structures* (The Hague: Mouton & Co., 1957), pp. 106-107.

[20]Robert B. Lees, "The Promise of Transformational Grammar," *The English Journal,* 52 (May 1963), 327.

[21]Arthur A. Stern, "Spatial and Temporal Grammar," *The English Journal,* 57 (September 1968), 882-883.

[22]Chomsky, *Language and Mind,* pp. 30-31.

[23]Chomsky, *Syntactic Structures,* pp. 72-75.

[24]Chomsky, *Language and Mind,* p. 26.

[25]Roderick A. Jacobs and Peter S. Rosenbaum, *Grammar 1* (Boston: Ginn and Company, 1967), p. 37.

[26]Owen Thomas, *Transformational Grammar and the Teacher of English* (New York: Holt, Rinehart & Winston, 1965), pp. 170-171.

[27]Noam Chomsky, "Topics in the Theory of Generative Grammar," in Thomas A. Sebeok, ed., *Current Trends in Linguistics* III (The Hague: Mouton & Co., 1966), p. 45.

[28]Jacobs and Rosenbaum, *Grammar 1,* pp. 42-43.

[29]R. B. Lees, "On Departures from Respected Traditions," *College Composition and Communication,* 18 (October 1967), 152-163.

[30]Chomsky, *Language and Mind,* pp. 1-4, 24.

[31]Jacobs and Rosenbaum, "Teacher's Guide" to *Grammar 1 & 2,* p. 39.

[32]Chomsky, "Topics," pp. 34-42.

[33]W. Ross Winterowd, "The Grammar of Coherence," *College English,* 31 (May 1970), p. 829.

[34]Richard E. Young, Alton L. Becker, and Kenneth L. Pike, *Rhetoric: Discovery and Change* (New York: Harcourt, Brace & World, 1970), p. 293.

[35]Young et al., *Rhetoric,* p. 295.

[36]Young et al., *Rhetoric,* pp. 295, 349.

[37]Guth and Schuster, *American English Today, 12,* pp. 134-135.

FOR FURTHER STUDY

A.   Study the following discussions of *sentence structure* by two prominent modern linguists. What terms, concepts, and procedures would be
familiar to someone who has studied traditional school grammar? What
would be unfamiliar or new? How familiar, or how different, is the overall
perspective implied in these quotations?

Language study, by which I now mean attempts to do what linguists do, can
proceed without prior information gathering. The data are readily available.
For example, suppose that a class had been working along and had reached the
conclusion that sentences were grossly binary in structure (i.e. contained subjects and predicates). It's a good generalization, one that children intuitively
decide on in their gross parsing of sentences. Suddenly somebody realizes
that sentences like

> Tell me a story.
> Give him a penny, etc.

are not binarily structured in the same way. Do we give up the generalization?
Well not quite, for many members of the group sense that there is a subject for
sentences of this kind. In fact they know that it's "you." In other words we might
save the generalization by modifying it somewhat to say that sentences in their
abstract structure have subjects and predicates, but that in some of these (in
particular for commands) the subject is later deleted (the "you understood" of
traditional school grammar).

Is there any evidence beyond the intuitive that justified there being a
"you" in the abstract structures of commands? Well, says somebody else, you
can say

> Tell yourself a story.

but not

> Tell himself a story, tell ourselves a story, etc.

and we know that a "–self" of this kind is added to a form when the subject
and that form refer to the same thing. That is, we can have

> John bought himself a treat.
> I helped myself to another piece of pie, etc.

but not

> John bought ourselves a treat.
> I helped themselves to another piece of pie, etc.

These facts would suggest that a "you" subject must be present in the abstract
structure of commands so as to allow sentences like (x) and exclude sentences
like (xi). The facts also suggest that "you"–deletion would have to follow in order
of application "self"–insertion, etc. . . .

Now, without trying to go into too much detail here, let me simply say
that in this way a class can proceed to come up with insightful generalizations,
a consistent set of them that accounts for the complex array of English sen-

tences. Grammar becomes then not a procrustean bed of *do's* and *don't's* in which every sentence must be laid, forced, crushed; but rather the grammar, the set of generalizations, becomes as complicated as is required by the data. The study of language then can in part be the writing of a grammar of a class's own language. What is learnt will of course be far more general than any set of generalizations upon English sentences, which is anyway guaranteed to prove wrong upon further examination. What is learnt is theory construction itself, how to come to grips with the problem of offering consistent explanations of complex arrays of data.

—Wayne A. O'Neil, in *The Urban Review*

Let us consider such a sentence as *John wants to know how you like him.* As it is spoken, it consists of a chain of eight words in succession. But it conveys a complex message containing at least three distinct propositions. The dominant sentence is that *John wants something.* What is that something? It is *to know something else.* There is no immediate subject of *know*—it has been deleted by a regular rule—but it is plainly John who is *to know something else.* And that something else is *the extent to which,* or *how you like him.* We can suggest the complexity of this sentence by a diagram such as the following:

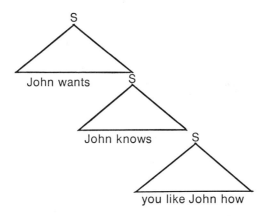

It might be possible for a language to glue these three propositions together by simple adjunction into something like *John wants John knows you like John how.* But we never hear anything like this; every school child is in control of a complex series of deletions, substitutions, and foregroundings which produce *John wants to know how you like him.* To produce this sentence he must at least

1. Attach the second sentence to the first as an infinitive with *for . . . to* as complementizer
John wants for (John) to know . . .
    2. Drop the second *John* as identical with the first
John wants for . . . to know . . .

3. Drop the first half of the complementizer *for*
John wants to know . . .
4. Bring the question word *how* in the third sentence to the front
John wants to know how you like John . . .
5. Convert this *John* into the appropriate pronoun *him.*

One cannot overemphasize how abstract and complex the organization of language rules is. By "language rules" we do not mean the small number of rules that can be taught explicitly in school but rather the very large number which the child learns for himself before he comes to school.
—William Labov, *The Study of Nonstandard English*

B.   Albert C. Baugh says in *A History of the English Language:*

we still find all too often provincialism and prejudice masquerading as scientific truth in discussions of language by men and women who would blush to betray an equal intolerance in the music or furniture or social conventions of other parts of the world than their own. Doubtless the best safeguard against prejudice is knowledge, and some knowledge of the history of English in the past is necessary to an enlightened judgment in matters affecting present use. Such knowledge warns us to beware of making arbitrary decisions on questions which only time can settle. It teaches us that reason is but a sorry guide in many matters of grammar and idiom, and that the usage of educated speakers and writers is the only standard in language for the educated. It should make us tolerant of colloquial and regional forms, since like the common people, they claim their right to exist by virtue of an ancient lineage. And finally, it should prepare us for further changes since language lives only on the lips and fingers of living people and must change as the needs of people in expressing themselves change.

(p. 403)

Select a book which places current English in its *historical context,* such as Albert C. Baugh, *A History of the English Language,* 2d ed. (New York: Appleton, 1957); Thomas Pyles, *The Origins and Development of the English Language* (New York: Harcourt, Brace, 1964); Otto Jespersen, *Essentials of English Grammar* (rptd. University of Alabama Press, 1964) or *Growth and Structure of the English Language,* 9th ed. (New York: Doubleday & Company, Inc., 1956). Study the historical information the book provides on one familiar feature of English grammar: the case forms of pronouns; the forms of "irregular" English verbs; the tense system of English verbs; the forms and uses of auxiliary verbs.

C.   Compare and contrast the treatment of a major feature of English grammar in a *language textbook* published in the forties or fifties and in a more recent book. How is the construction described? How is it explained? How is it illustrated? What is the student expected to do with it? Choose one of the following:

Passive Voice: "President Lincoln *has been shot.*"

Participial Phrase: "*Standing on his toes*, he could see the hero."

Relative Clause: "Columbus, *who was looking for India*, discovered America."

D.   The following articles examine major issues affecting the *application of linguistics* to the teaching of language in the classroom. Select *one* of these, or a similar article of a later date. Identify the author's general perspective; discuss his handling of specific topics or specific issues.

Ralph B. Long, "The English Verb: A Traditional View," *College Composition and Communication,* 17 (May 1966), 100–106;

R. B. Lees, "On Departures from Respected Traditions," *College Composition and Communication,* 18 (October 1967), 152–163;

Michael Grady, "The Uses of Linguistics in the Schools," *English Journal,* 57 (September 1968), 870–879;

Keith Schap, "The Feature System in the Classroom," *English Journal,* 56 (January 1967), 74–80, 99;

Philip H. Cook, "Putting Grammar to Work," *English Journal,* 57 (November 1968), 1168–1175;

Andrew MacLeish, "Some Structures for Written English," *English Journal,* 58 (September 1969), 877–885, 891;

Ralph B. Long, "English Grammar in the 1970's," *College English,* 31 (May 1970), 763–773.

E.   The following exercises will make you explore and put to work some of the *resources of English grammar*:

1.   Assume that you have built a *speech machine* that can speak a simplified form of American English. You have found that English is too complicated a language for even a very intelligent machine to speak. Here is how you have made it simpler:

—We usually have different words for a quality (*good*) and its opposite (*bad*), and even for a higher degree of the quality (*excellent*). The machine uses only the one basic word and then applies the following code:

good	Opposite: *un*good	High degree: *plus*good
hot	*un*hot	*plus*hot

—We have many different ways of changing a word from present to past: break-*broke*; sneeze-*sneezed*; sing-*sang*; and so on. The machine uses only the basic word and then applies the following code:

sing	Past: sing-*past*	Future: sing-*fut*
sneeze	sneeze-*past*	sneeze-*fut*

—We have various ways of changing a word from one to several: boy-*boys*; child-*children*. The machine simply uses the following code:

One: boy-*one*   Several: boy-*more*

—The machine cannot remember, for instance, all the names we apply to different brass instruments: *trumpet*, *trombone*, *tuba*. It uses an all-purpose word like *horn*. Instead of *car*, *truck*, *convertible*, *sports car*, and so on, it uses a word like *auto*.

When you apply all four of these rules, you get the following kind of translation:

PEOPLE-ENGLISH: The trumpeter parked his little sports car.
MACHINE-ENGLISH: The hornblower-*one* park-*past* his *un*big auto-*one*.

Do the following to show that you understand how the machine works:

a.   Translate the following sentences into machine-English:

His truck looked huge next to the sports car.
Her uncle played an excellent solo on the tuba.
Cold days will soon drive the tourists away.

b.   Write a brief joke or anecdote in machine-English. See whether your classmates can translate it back into people-English.

c.   Assume that you have to build a cut-rate model of the speech machine. To cut the price, you have to *simplify further* the machine language that the machine is designed to produce. Can you help to make machine-English simpler than ordinary English? Write *one* rule that would eliminate one or more additional complications of people-English.

2.   Most English sentences fall into the subject-predicate category. However, various combinations that do *not* have a subject and a predicate are treated as complete, self-contained units in both speech and writing. Can such *nonsentences* too, like sentences, be sorted out into a few predictable patterns? BE YOUR OWN GRAMMARIAN—how many types would you say are illustrated in the following list? How would you describe the different types?

1.   Good work!
2.   And so to bed.
3.   A likely story!
4.   Like father, like son.
5.   Nothing ventured, nothing gained.
6.   What a liar!
7.   Good riddance.
8.   Now for the important part.
9.   How true!
10.   Penny wise, pound foolish.
11.   The more, the merrier.
12.   What a lovely view!
13.   How strange!
14.   So much for Alfred.
15.   No wonder!

3.   In questions, we normally put the first auxiliary in front of the subject: "*Have* the guests left?" "Where *can* we park the car?" If there is no auxiliary, we put a form of *do* in front of the subject: "*Do* your friends like books?" "How *does* this machine work?"

Do these rules apply to sentences that start with *who*, *whom*, or *what*?

Study the following sample sentences carefully. State any special rules that they seem to follow. A hint on strategy: First check off any sentences that seem to follow the familiar rules. Then try to find out what is different in the rest.

1. What did the man say?
2. What changed your mind?
3. What has Jim bought?
4. Who took my paper?
5. Whom did your sister invite?
6. What can I give her?
7. What had the speaker forgotten?
8. What had upset his plans?
9. What does an ornithologist study?
10. Who washed the windows?
11. Who wrote *Moby Dick*?
12. Who could the stranger have been?
13. Who could have warned these people?
14. Whom did the part nominate?
15. What will his title be?

4. *Do* is used as an auxiliary in questions and in negative statements wih *not*. What other uses of the word *do* and its various forms (*does, did*) can you discover? Two major additional uses of the word are illustrated in the following sentences. *Describe these two uses as accurately as you can.* Again, check off those sentences first that use the word in familiar ways. Then sort out the remaining sentences into the two major categories.

1. Where did the host go?
2. These decorations *do* look attractive.
3. The boys did their work.
4. *Do* remind your mother.
5. This solution does not seem right.
6. The soldiers did their duty.
7. The liquid *did* leave a stain!
8. Did the caller leave a message?
9. My sister does the dishes.
10. Fred *did* neglect his assignments.
11. Do the group a favor.
12. His comments *did* seem ill-advised.
13. The reviewer did the book justice.
14. How does this gadget work?
15. Do teen-agers admire artists?

5. Typical adjectives have four major features in common: They appear as modifiers immediately preceding a noun (a *busy* day). They appear as complements following a linking verb (The line was *busy*). They fit in after *very* or *extremely* (He was very *busy*). They have forms with -*er* and -*est*, or *more* and *most*, for use in comparisons (*busier* than usual). One special subgroup of adjectives shares only *one* of these four features. Can you find these special adjectives in the following examples? Write down all the adjectives that you can use only in

one of the four different ways. Is there anything they have in common—meaning, position, form?

1. The food was *delicious*.
2. Our *chief* objection concerned the food.
3. We followed our *talkative* guide.
4. The teacher drew a *straight* line.
5. The *main* course was fish.
6. Mr. Simson was the *principal* speaker.
7. Jim had forgotten the *unfortunate* incident.
8. Fred took the *only* copy.
9. His *sole* handicap was his height.
10. Your advice has been *helpful*.

6.   Normally, nouns and adjectives are two quite distinct classes of words. Nouns serve as subjects and objects; they are often preceded by noun-markers like *the*, *a*, *this*, *my*, or *his*; they have special plural forms, often formed by adding *-s*. Adjectives serve as *modifiers* of nouns; they fit in after *very* or *extremely*; they have special forms for use in comparisons (*brighter-brightest; more beautiful-most beautiful*). To some extent, nevertheless, the two classes overlap. A word that is typically used as a noun sometimes seems to be used as an adjective and vice versa. Can you find examples of such "crossing over" in the following sentences? Does the word that crosses over share all the features of the other class? Study the examples carefully. Describe the overlapping between these two categories—nouns and adjectives—as accurately as you can.

1. Uncle Tim hated the rich.
2. The wealthiest are not always the most charitable.
3. The city government had been reorganized.
4. Art teaches us love for the beautiful.
5. Herbert had been a child prodigy.
6. The nurses were tending the sick.
7. Newspaper readers like the unusual.
8. Her beauty treatments had cost a fortune.
9. His parents bought a brick house.
10. Books are printed in Braille for the blind.
11. Steel doors barred our way.
12. His doors were open to the most humble.
13. Only the very strong survived.
14. Grandfather wore a gold watch.
15. The stronger helped the weaker.

7.   Write several sentences illustrating simple English sentence patterns. Then write *three different versions* of each sentence, each time building up the bare-bones pattern with material drawn from the full range of English modifiers. (Do not add whole clauses.)

Example: The cowboy mounted his horse.
                The handsome screen cowboy slowly mounted his horse.

Swearing irritably, the overdressed imitation cowboy clumsily mounted his wary horse.

In the cluttered backyard, the incredibly dirty little cowboy happily mounted his battered wooden toy horse.

8. The following model passages show the full resources of the English sentence as used by masters of American prose. Use each of them as a model sentence. Fill in your own words, but preserve, as far as possible, the grammatical structure of the original.

a. Darling tucked the ball in, spurted at him,
   driving hard,
   hurling himself along,
   all two hundred pounds bunched into controlled attack.

(Irwin Shaw)

(Example of a sentence modeled on 1.:
   Stephen took his coin back, looked at it,
   swallowing hard,
   pulling himself up,
   all his dreams shattered by the unexpected rebuff.)

b. A man has a right *to be employed, to be trusted, to be loved, to be revered.*

(Emerson)

c. He stood watching the approaching locomotive,
   his teeth chattering,
   his lips drawn away from them in a frightened smile.

(Willa Cather)

d. *At the head of the gulch, on one of the largest pine trees,* they found the deuce *of clubs* pinned *to the bark with a bowie knife.*

(Bret Harte)

e. I always go to sea as a sailor,
   because they make a point of paying me for my trouble,
   whereas they never pay passengers a single penny that I ever heard of.

(Herman Melville)

f. The injured captain . . . was buried in that profound dejection which comes to even the bravest and most enduring when, willy-nilly, *the firm fails,*
   the army loses,
   the ship goes down.

(Stephen Crane)

Teaching Standard English

Regional Dialects and Standard English—The Doctrine of Correctness—The Liberal View of Usage—English for the Disadvantaged

English teachers walk into their classrooms hoping to teach their students how to speak and write educated English. The more literary and academic the teachers' expectations, the more sensitive they are to how far their students' language falls short of the goal. The struggle then starts to make students "say it right":

Student: My book is—
Teacher: The book you read.
Student: Yeah. The title is called *Macbeth* by Shakespeare.
Teacher: Its title *is* . . .
Student: I ain't never read it before.
Teacher: I never read it.
Student: Me neither. In this book the author depicks—

Teacher: Depicts.
Student: Depicks how this guy he wants to——
Teacher: Who?
Student: Him.
Teacher: He.
Student: Yeah. He potrays that this here——
Teacher: He *says.*[1]

Here is the trap waiting for every teacher of English at every level: Our aim is to help the student use "good English," but our attempts at "correction" in effect shut him up. Constant interruption makes it impossible for people to attend to what they are saying. Constant unpredictable criticism makes people insecure. Constant negative criticism of their natural language patterns makes students hate English. Our means defeat our ends: We want students to appreciate the power and beauty of language, but we are trapped into teaching "how not to write, what not to say."

With linguists drastically redefining "good English," and with students rejecting the arbitrary say-so of teachers, a thorough rethinking of our responsibilities in this area has become necessary. Most of the traditional teaching of good English has dealt with *choices* available within the repertory of English vocabulary and grammar. "He blamed *me for it*" and "He blamed *it on me*" carry roughly the same message. "*Me and Jim* cut wood" and "*Jim and I* cut wood" report the same activity. Choices between roughly synonymous words, constructions, and pronunciations are matters of **usage**. The basic fact is that *usage varies.* Usage varies from one place to another: Before the days of newspapers, radio, television, and universal schooling, regional dialects could drift far apart. Today, the crucial variations in usage are no longer regional but *social.* Standard English is the prestige dialect of white-collar occupations. It is office English, school English, media English. Nonstandard English is blue-collar English, neighborhood English. The reason for mastering standard English is that it has national currency as a prestige medium of communication.

Over the years, a massive shift has taken place in our attitude toward standard English. Many old-style prohibitions on "uneducated" usages have come to be recognized as petty, arbitrary, and uninformed. Many of them have quietly faded away from stylebooks and guides to "effective English." Furthermore, much that used to be condemned as careless or substandard has come to be recognized as perfectly appropriate to the more *informal* uses of standard English. Finally, the nonstandard English that many of our students bring to school has come to be regarded as not inferior but merely *different*—viable on its own terms, and serving millions of people for self-expression and communication in their daily lives.

The general shift toward a more liberal view offers English teachers a second chance for productive, positively oriented work in the area of usage. To make such work fruitful, we have to establish three basic points:

(1) To deal with language differences effectively, we have to *distinguish between grammar on the one hand and usage on the other*. Grammar and usage are closely related but different in their goals. Grammar answers the question, "What is our language *like*?" It examines the way words work in sentences. It studies the principles of arrangement and mutual adjustment that make our language work. Usage is concerned with the question "Given roughly synonymous forms or constructions, which is *the right choice*?" Questions of usage arise when our language offers us several possible ways of saying roughly the same thing. Pronunciation, vocabulary, and grammar all vary slightly from region to region, from group to group, and from occasion to occasion. The student of usage explores differences like those that set apart the following excerpts from Walter Van Tilburg Clark's *The Ox-Bow Incident*:

Rural Dialect:
Half an hour since *I seen* how *they was lally-laggin'* around. . . . Tommy, you *git for home*. . . . I s'pose if they had ten hours' start you'd jest *set to home* and wait for 'em. . . . I *ain't* excited; I'm *jest plumb* disgusted.

Informal Standard:
He was just sitting there with a sullen *dead-pan* and *raking in the pots* slow and *contemptuous*, *like* he expected it. The only variation *he'd* make would be to signal Canby to fill his glass again when he'd *made a good haul*. Then he'd *toss the drink off* in one gulp without looking at anybody or saying a "mud," and set the glass down and flick it halfway to the middle of the table with his finger.

Formal Platform Speech:
You *cannot flinch* from what you believe to be your duty, of course, but certainly you *would not wish to* act *in the very spirit* which *begot the deed* you would punish. . . . If such an awful thing has actually *occurred*, it is *the more reason* that we should *retain our self-possession*.[2]

(2) To deal with language differences effectively, we have to *abandon our moralistic attitude* toward "bad English." It is morally obtuse to call a child careless or sloppy for speaking the variety of English that he has learned at his mother's knee. The linguist starts from the simple fact that "different sorts of English do exist." From the linguist's point

of view, such different varieties are equally interesting and equally complex. As teachers, we realize that the kind of English the student speaks greatly affects his chances for academic success and social mobility. Our most basic task is to help students move *beyond* a variety of English that has a limited currency. We try to equip our students with the language resources that will work for them in a given situation. In the words of Dudley Bailey, "The question of standards, of 'good English,' is not a question of moral right and wrong but rather a question of suitability to the occasion. The mark of an educated person is his ability to shift linguistic gears."[3]

(3) To deal with language differences effectively, we have to *recognize the force of linguistic habits*. The student uses forms and structure unconsciously. They are firmly entrenched as part of his language; through years of exposure and reinforcement they have gotten into his bones. In the words of Robert Lado,

> The student's use of his native dialects and styles is anchored on firmly established systems of habits, and as in foreign language learning, we can assume that in spite of himself he will transfer those habits to the new dialect and styles he is trying to learn. . . . In order for the student to have at his command the new resources of the language, he will have to acquire new sets of habits.[4]

If we want to extend the student's linguistic repertory, mere analysis, mere half-understood "explanation," is not enough. We have to develop *habit-building* programs that give "new ways of saying it" a chance to sink in, to become second nature.

In teaching usage, we face a twofold task. First, it is our job to teach a realistic understanding of differences in language use and a positive appreciation of the color and humanity that linguistic variety adds to our lives. Thus, our students will not be hobbled by artificial dos and don'ts; they will be free to attend to what gives language honesty, strength, and beauty. Second, it is our job to *make sure that a nonstandard dialect* (not of their own choosing) *does not hold our students back*. Nonstandard English, or too limited a repertory in standard English, stands in the way of the student who wants to move on. By helping the student toward an effective command of standard English, we help him extend his range of choice.

REGIONAL DIALECTS AND STANDARD ENGLISH

Historically, the major source of variety in usage has been the development of **regional dialects**. As members of a speech community spread out over a larger area, the language of the different groups drifted apart. The separate strands first became dialects and finally separate languages. The Low German of the Netherlands became Dutch; the colonial Latin of the Roman provinces in Gaul became French. When modern nation-states developed, the regional dialect of the court, or of the capital, or of the major trading center, gradually became a passport to public employment, economic advancement, and, finally, appearance in print. It became the language of traders, scribes, and, generally, city people. The peasants continued to speak their local dialect, which soon began to sound rustic to educated ears. The **prestige dialect** of the capital gradually became the "standard" national language. In England, London English became the national standard and thus school English, office English, book English.

When near-universal public education became a reality, teachers of "school English" often found their charges speaking a local variety of English of the kind that seldom finds its way into print. Here are some attempts to reproduce such regional dialects in writing:

Rural New England:
(Peter) Whar in tarnation d'ye s'pose he went, Sim?
(Simeon) Dunno. He druv off in the buggy, all spick an'span, with the mare all breshed an' shiny, druv off clackin' his tongue an' wavin' his whip. I remember it right well. . . . I yells "whar ye goin', Paw?" an' he hauls up by the stone wall a jiffy. His old snake's eyes was glitterin' in the sun.

—Eugene O'Neill, *Desire under the Elms*

Industrial British Midlands:
Do you think if I won the football pools I'd gi' yo' a penny on it? Or gi' anybody else owt? Not likely. I'd keep it all mysen, except for seeing my family right. I'd buy 'em a house and set 'em up for life, but anybody else could whistle for it. I've 'eard that blokes as win football pools get thousands o' beggin' letters, but yer know what I'd do if I got 'em? I'll tell yer what I'd do: I'd mek a bonfire on 'em.

—Alan Sillitoe, *Saturday Night and Sunday Morning*

Irish English:
Is it dhreamin' I am? Is somethin' happenin' to me, or is it happenin' to you? O, man, it's mixin' mirth with madness you are at thinkin' St. Pathrick ever looped his neck in an orange sash, or tapped out a tune on a Protestant dhrum! Let us only keep silent for a minute or two, an' we'll hear him sayin' that th' hymn St. Pathrick sung an' he on th' way to meet King Laeghaire, an' quench th' fire o' Tara, was Lilly Bullero Bullen a Law!

—Sean O'Casey, *Red Roses for Me*

In linguistic terms, all dialects have equal merit. They serve the needs of their users with equal efficiency and flexibility. The French trouba- dours, using a Southern French dialect, wrote love poetry as articulate, sensitive, and poetic as any written in the Northern, Parisian French that was destined to become the national standard. William Langland's powerful *Piers Plowman* was written in a mixed fourteenth-century dialect with strong midland and west-of-England features. What handi- caps the user of a regional dialect is its *limited currency*. Dialectal splint- ering becomes a barrier to communication for anyone trying to go beyond a relatively small, unified speech community. As Chaucer said in concluding his *Troilus and Cressida*:

> And for there is so gret diversite
> In Englissh and in writyng of oure tonge,
> So prey I God that non myswrite the,
> Ne the mysmetre for defaute of tonge.

Historically, only the emerging dominance of prestige dialects has pro- vided the answer to Chaucer's cry: "That thow be understonde, God I besech!"

The spread of a prestige dialect as the standard medium of education and literature means a loss in color and variety. Since it is often ac- quired through schooling rather than absorbed from early childhood, its adoption means a loss in naturalness and ease. At the same time, it means a tremendous gain in effectiveness and range. It becomes our major means of participating in a culture that goes beyond narrow boundaries in space and time.

In his dealings with language, *the teacher must reconcile a receptive attitude toward dialectal variety with loyalty to the common medium.* In Thomas Hardy's *The Mayor of Casterbridge*, Michael Henchard objects to Elizabeth-Jane's use of dialect words—"those terrible marks of the beast to the truly genteel":

> "Bide where you be," he echoed sharply. "Good God, are you only fit to carry wash to a pig-trough, that ye use words such as those?" (Ch. 20)

Readers of this passage would probably agree on a number of points: first, Elizabeth-Jane's use of dialect words is pleasing and natural, and social intercourse would be the poorer for their loss. Second, Michael's reaction reveals the insecurity of a man who has only recently risen from the lower social ranks and who sees in telltale dialect features a challenge to hard-won social status. At the same time, however, the reader is grateful that Hardy himself writes in a prestige dialect without obvious geographical, social, or temporal limitations.

In the United States, regional dialects reached only a limited development and have now practically disappeared as a barrier to communication. Current research into regional varieties of American English is being recorded in the *Linguistic Atlas of the United States and Canada*. According to one study of linguistic-atlas findings,

> Typical intonation patterns, customary subject-verb-object word order, the inflectional -*s* which signals plural number or third person singular of the present tense, and the vast majority of vocabulary items belong without distinction to all dialects of American English. Consequently no functional block in communication normally obtrudes between native users of English.[5]

In the United States, the normalized standard thus comes much closer to being a genuine common denominator than the national standard superimposed on the often sharply divergent regional dialects of other countries. One obvious reason is the intermingling of people from different dialect areas, through early migrations and later through mobility unknown in more static societies. Other factors are the establishment of political unity at an early stage in the nation's history, the fact that many immigrants' children learned English not at home but at school, and the unprecedented development of standardized mass media of entertainment and communication. The linguist is in fact hampered in his effort "to collect a body of valid and reliable information on American dialects" because

> The wide spread of education, the virtual extinction of illiteracy, the extreme mobility of the population—both geographically and from one social class to another—and the tremendous development of a number of media of mass communication have all contributed to the recession of local speech forms.[6]

Such dialect differences as did exist in this country became the subject of **dialect geography**. The dialectologist spends his time "eliciting from socially classifiable speakers of American English the linguistic forms which they habitually use" and "classifying such forms according to regional and social patterns of distribution."[7] The question is not what an informant thinks or prefers but simply what he does in fact use. Typically it is a question of whether he pronounces the *s* in *grease* like the *s* in *cease* or the *s* in *please*; of whether he calls an object a *pail* or a *bucket*, a *spider* or a *skillet*. Thus, when linguists establish in the Eastern United States such major dialect areas as "North" (including

New England), "Midland" (including most of Pennsylvania, Ohio, West Virginia), and "South," the boundaries rest mainly upon vocabulary evidence:

> Characteristic Northern expressions . . . include *pail, swill, whiffletree* or *whippletree, comforter* or *comfortable* for a thick quilt, *brook, co-boss* or *come-boss* as a cow call, *johnnycake, salt pork*, and *darning needle* for a dragonfly. In the Midland area we find *blinds* for roller shades, *skillet, spouting* or *spouts* for eaves, a *piece* for food taken between meals, *snake feeder* for a dragonfly . . . The South has *lightwood* as the term for kindling, a *turn* of wood for an armful; string beans are generally *snap beans*; *hasslet* is the term for the edible inner organs of a pig, *chittlins* for the small intestine; and in this area cows are said to *low* at feeding time.[8]

Awareness of dialectal differences helps the teacher understand or anticipate the usage problems of students from a given regional background:

> The American Negro, especially one recently arrived from the South or reared in a black ghetto, may not use in his speech the conventional inflectional suffixes on nouns or verbs, so that he may omit them in writing where they belong or write them in the wrong places . . .
>
> . . . an educated Southerner may use such combinations of auxiliaries as *might could, used to could*, or *ought to could*, reflecting the familiar cultivated usage of his own region. . . . The Northerner, on the other hand, may say *sick to the stomach* or *hadn't ought*. . . . The Eastern Kentuckian may convert *used to* into an adverb, as previous generations converted *maybe*, and transfer it to the beginning of the sentence, as in *"Used to*, everybody around here would bake their own bread."

The teacher who is responsive to expressions with a regional flavor will agree with the dialectologist that

> For such students the remedy is not to decry their native dialect or to attempt to alienate them from their habitual linguistic behavior, but to recognize that in their situations the problem of fit between speech and writing, never a simple matter for any speaker of English, has special complications.[9]

He will further agree that similar complications lie in wait for such students as they move from "neighborhood speech" to the kind of oral English that will serve them well in school and on the job.

For a long time, dialect study meant primarily the study of *rural* dialect; it focused on the speech of culturally and socially peripheral nonurban areas. Only in recent years have dialectologists come to grips with the dialect problems of people in "the heavily urbanized areas in which most Americans now live." Here a major factor determining a child's language patterns is not regional origin but social status. Dialect study thus becomes **sociolinguistics**. It becomes intimately involved in contemporary social problems and acquires strong political overtones.

Whether we deal with regional or with social dialects, the central question is whether and how we can make standard English available to all our students. Can we help our students master the kind of standard American English that has true national currency and that in fact serves as an effective means of communication far beyond national borders? If the answer is to be yes, English teachers will need a realistic understanding of the nature of standard English and its relation to other major varieties of English usage. They will need a realistic estimate of both the obstacles and the opportunities in their path.

THE DOCTRINE OF CORRECTNESS

A major job of public education is to help establish and preserve the common bond of a national culture. In a nation of immigrants, a major job of English teachers has been to teach the national language as a common medium. To do so effectively, they naturally looked for a clearly defined common standard. They looked for a definition of "good English" that was the same in Maine and California, the same for the merchant's and the sharecropper's child, and the same for yesterday's classic and today's newspaper. Their basic attitude toward language was **normative**, aiming at the highest common denominator in a country that was assimilating people from many diverse cultural strands.

In looking for a rationale for a strong and stable common medium, English teachers embraced the eighteenth-century **doctrine of correctness**. Here they found a tradition committed to "polishing" and "refining" the language and giving it greater stability and permanence. This normalizing tendency had early found its expression in attempts to "ascertain," that is, to fix, the language in a form closer than current usage to hypothetical standards of clarity, efficiency, and consistency. Adopting this general perspective, teachers concentrated on hunting down deviations from a correct norm in the student's speech and writing. Teachers and textbook authors made it their business to stamp out "common errors."

The great unanswered question about the error-centered approach to English has always been: "How do we *know* an error is an error? Who *says* we must not put a preposition at the end of a sentence? Who *says* 'it's me' should really be 'it is I'?" When neoclassical writers like Dryden and Swift first started to "correct" their prose, they were apparently trying to bring English closer to the beauty, clarity, and vigor of classical Latin. They looked at their native language as a wild growth that had to be carefully pruned to serve for literary purposes. One way to prune was to condemn features that were at odds with the rules of Latin. Latin word order did not allow a preposition at the end of a sentence. Latin did not use the object form of a pronoun after a linking verb. It had two clearly separate forms for *who* and *whom*, and it did not tend to merge the two.

Obviously, there was no way to remodel the great bulk of English along the lines of Latin and Greek, and such influence as the classical models had was bound to be spotty, indirect, and largely unacknowledged. In practice, there simply was no clear standard of what made one usage "correct" and another erroneous, "illiterate," or "vulgar." Thus, Samuel Johnson shared the eighteenth-century preference for "the durable materials of a language" as against the "tyranny of time and fashion," "the corruptions of ignorance," and "caprices of innovation." However, when, in his *Dictionary of the English Language* (1765), he set out to regulate the confusion of English usage, he found that

> choice was to be made out of boundless variety, without any established principle of selection; adulterations were to be detected, without a settled test of purity; and modes of expression to be rejected or received, without the suffrages of any writers of classical reputation or acknowledged authority.

Like other early lexicographers and grammarians, Dr. Johnson then improvised his own "tests of purity": the practice of the great writers of the past (but admitting "no testimony of living authors"); conformity to "the genius of our tongue"; authentic derivation from the original languages; freedom from latter-day French influence in "structure and phraseology"; absence of the merely temporary, local, and technical.[10]

Other writers were less respectful of the practice of the best authors and the "genius of the language." Thus, Bishop Lowth, in *A Short Introduction to English Grammar* (1764) denounced as a "very great corruption" the use of the identical form for the past and the past participle in *have spoke, has wrote,* and *was took.* He insisted on the distinct past participle, in spite of his recognition that "the general bent and turn of the language is towards the other form" and that this other form "is too much authorised by the example of some of our best writers." According to his own citations, these writers included Milton, Pope, and Swift.[11]

When the rules of correctness were codified by the authors of nineteenth-century textbooks, the arguments offered in support were typically *ad hoc* arguments. Apparently logical arguments were improvised to discredit a specific debatable usage, but the same kind of argument was seldom applied across the board to other items of the same kind. Thus, respect for etymological derivation was said to require that *between* not be applied to more than *two* of a kind—since the word was related to both *two* and *twain*. "Arguments *between* my three brothers" thus had to be corrected to "arguments *among* my three brothers." But no attempt was made to "call back" to their original meanings thousands of other words that had similarly moved away from their etymological derivation—such as *December*, originally the "tenth," not the "twelfth," month.

Up to modern times, English instruction in the schools has been haunted by the ghosts of eighteenth-century British grammarians, whose aim had been to purify the language and arrest its "natural tendency to degeneration." In the meantime, however, language scholarship had gone through a massive shift away from a prescriptive toward a more **descriptive** approach. Scholars no longer looked upon change as deplorable and instead accepted it as a basic feature of language considered as a living, growing thing. Historical linguists were tracing the changes that led from the earliest-known Indo-European documents to contemporary speech. They saw a continuous development from the Latin of imperial Rome through Old French to the dialects of Modern French. They showed how earlier Germanic dialects became Old English, Middle English, and finally English in its modern form. As heir to this tradition of historical scholarship, the modern linguist has insisted that "language doesn't stay the same":

> There are the forces of internal organic change, in phonemic, morphological, and syntactic matters; of internal borrowing (analogy); and of external borrowing, from related dialects, related languages, and non-related languages. All these kinds of change are going on all the time. Their work is like that of geological forces, in erosion and building up: at one place, the structure of the language may be wearing away through phonemic and morphological reduction, while at another place it may be building up through phonemic splitting, analogical new-formation, change of meaning, and borrowing. And, like the work of geological forces, linguistic change is, in the present state of human technology, irresistible. We may try to dam it up at one point, but it's sure to burst forth at another, and where we are least expecting it.[12]

The linguist's emphasis on linguistic change and his interest in dialectal variants helped promote an openminded interest in language in all its copious variety. Students began to study language, not as a wild growth to be pruned, but as a rich, various, and dynamic thing to be appreciated in all its marvelous complexity.

When English teachers tried to defend the traditional rules, they were defending conventions that had lost their historical and intellectual foundations. Familiar arguments used to make the corrector's instinct intellectually respectable proved hard to maintain in serious debate. First, the appeal to efficient communication too often proved futile. As Harold Whitehall said in discussing the *it is me—it is I* quandary, "Clarity of statement has nothing to do with these matters; one form is as clear as the other."[13] The most damaging feature of traditional language instruction is the teacher's pretending not to understand, or to misunderstand, usages that are perfectly clear to him and to the student. There is no doubt in either the teacher's or the student's mind that "*Can* I leave the room?" is a request for permission. There is no point in pretending to the student that "tie it *tightly*" means "tie it as if you were drunk."

Objections to the supposed redundancy of debatable usages proved similarly hollow. *The reason is because* was said to be redundant because both *reason* and *because* contained the idea of cause. But the phrase is no more redundant than the double genitive signal in "a friend *of* my brother's." We must distinguish between the built-in redundancy of the linguistic system and the stylistic redundancy that results from padding and ineffectual repetition. As Paul Roberts said:

> One of the important characteristics of any working language is a very high degree of redundancy. The meanings of a message will be signaled not once but many times in the course of an utterance. Consider such a sentence as "There were several children in the room," and notice how often the plural meaning is signaled. We get it in the *were*, in the vowel of *child-*, in the *r* of *children*, and the *en* of *children*, and in the word *several*. We need hear only one of these signals to know that more than one child is meant.
>
> Redundancy is what makes language work as well as it does. If there were no redundancy, then communication could not go on in the presence of any kind of noise, since it would be necessary to hear every particle of the message.[14]

Other traditional arguments were similarly at odds with the way language works. Students were told that *like* was a preposition and could not be used as a connective: "like my father" was possible but not "like my father *said*." But many other words do double duty as prepositions and connectives. *After, before, until* are all double-duty words: We say "We left *after dinner*" but also "We left *after we finished dinner*." Countless English words serve as more than one part of speech. Nouns turn into verbs: We *ape* a teacher, *knight* a merchant, and *lock* a door. We *lord* it over somebody, or try to *bell* the cat. What law would bar *like* from crossing over from one major grammatical category to the next?

The author of the traditional textbook did not say, or did not know.

When an expression "sounds right" to the speaker, and clearly conveys the intended meaning, objections on the basis of logic easily become futile quibbling. There is no point in claiming that in a double negative like "I *don't* want *none*" the two negatives cancel each other out. If the speaker had indeed wanted something, he would have said so. The English double negative is no more illogical than the French *personne* and *rien*—which once meant "a person" and "a thing" but now mean "no person" and "nothing." Historically, the *me* replaced the *I* in "It is *I*" because "It's *me*" sounds right—the slot after the verb is now usually "object-territory," and the object-form *me* seems natural. For similar reasons, the Old English "*Me* was given the book" (originally an indirect object) changed to "*I* was given the book," since the slot *before* the verb seems natural for the subject form. The resulting forms are no more illogical than the French *c'est moi*, or the archaic "*me*thinks" and "*me*thought." If these are mistakes, then it is true that "seen from the perspective of history, language consists almost exclusively of errors."[15]

Living language does not fit into neat logical schemes. The Latin word for farmer, *agricola*, is feminine in form. The German word for girls, *Mädchen*, is used with the neuter article. The relationship between language and logic is often perplexing and intriguing. Otto Jespersen said,

> In most cases where, so to speak, the logic of facts or of the exterior world is at war with the logic of grammar, English is free from the narrow-minded pedantry which in most languages sacrifices the former to the latter or makes people shy of saying or writing things which are not "strictly grammatical." This is particularly clear with regard to number. *Family* and *clergy* are, grammatically speaking, of the singular number; but in reality they indicate a plurality. . . . In English one is free to add a verb in the singular if the idea of unity is essential, and then to refer to this unit as *it*, or else to put the verb in the plural and use the pronoun *they*, if the idea of plurality is predominant. . . . Inversely, there is in English a freedom paralleled nowhere else of expressing grammatically a unity consisting of several parts, of saying, for instance, "I do not think I ever spent a more delightful three weeks" (Darwin) . . . "Three years is but short" (Shakespeare) . . . "ten minutes is heaps of time" (E. F. Benson).[16]

Whatever the theoretical arguments in support of "correct" English, its rulings were often contradicted by the daily spoken practice of educated people. Notoriously, English teachers themselves used in their own unguarded, natural speech many of the usages that they condemned in the speech and writing of their students. In reading the great literature of the present and the past, students found that the rules were contradicted also by the practice of the "best writers." The best writers could be shown to employ usages like the following, all in violation of traditional rules:

> He was a preacher that made it his care to give everyone *their* meat in due season. (*Cotton Mather*)

> The impertinence of *these kind* of scrutinies, moreover, was generally concluded with a compliment. (*Jane Austen*)

> The practical *reason why* . . . a majority are permitted . . . to rule is not *because* they are most likely to be in the right . . . but *because* they are physically the strongest. (*Henry David Thoreau*)

> They felt that they would sooner have had *less* figures and more food. (*George Orwell*)

> The Utopians do not believe that any civilized man *can* omit any of the subjects that are included in the course of study. (*Robert M. Hutchins*)

Modern statistical studies bore out such observations. A traditional rule, for instance, had allowed the use of the *-s* genitive for animate nouns (the *boy's* bicycle, the *soldier's* lament) but had ruled it out for inanimate nouns. Writers like John Donne had used it freely in *either* case:

> This is my *play's* last scene, here heavens appoint
> My *pilgrimage's* last mile . . .
> My *span's* last inch, my *minute's* latest point . . .

One investigator found that in a national magazine uses of the *-s* genitive were "about equally divided between living beings and inanimate objects." Another investigator said in concluding a survey of the widespread use of locutions like "the play's structure" in violation of traditional rules:

> A large portion of my data is from writers who cannot exactly be classed as "skimmed milk." Such novelists as Faulkner, Hemingway, Evelyn Eaton, and Sherwood Anderson, such literary figures as Louis Untermeyer and Archibald MacLeish, such scholars and critics as David Daiches, Howard M. Jones, O. J. Campbell, John Mason Brown, and the *New York Times*— to mention a few sources for my materials—presumably know something about style.[17]

Extending their inquiries into the past, modern investigators commanded the vast resources of the *New English Dictionary on Historical Principles*, reissued in 1933 as the *Oxford English Dictionary*. There they found extensive quotations showing, for instance, that, contrary to the traditional rule, *myself* had from Middle English down been commonly preferred to *me* in combinations like "my friend and *myself*."[18] They found other debated usages supported by quotations from authors ranging from Bacon and Shakespeare through Addison and Goldsmith to George Meredith and William Morris. In sum, modern re-examination of traditional standards of correctness led many teachers to agree with H. L. Mencken: "Some of the rules laid down with most assurance by pedants have no support in either history or logic, and are constantly violated by writers of unquestionable authority."[19]

Whatever its intellectual and scholarly weaknesses, English teachers have not found the tradition of correctness easy to shake off. The belief in correct English has been a major cultural phenomenon, with exact parallels in countries like Germany and France. Even today, the person questioning it may trigger strong emotional reactions. In fact, the permanent legacy of the doctrine of correctness has been our continuing linguistic timidity. When the reader mumbles "*as*, damn it" every time we use *like*, communication is effectively cut off. The public speaker, and the practicing writer, are better off if they know how to sidestep such irrelevant reactions. It is for this reason that in working with ambitious, academically oriented students we take time "to point out the current shibboleths . . . and to advise how much they are observed and by which people."[20] We thus tell our students that careful writers avoid *like I said* because many people have been taught that this use of *like* is ungrammatical. We tell them that an important point might be lost while a conservative reader worries about the supposed redundancy of *reason is because*.

THE LIBERAL VIEW OF USAGE

In the forties and fifties, those championing a positively oriented "permissive" attitude toward usage started to do battle in earnest with the conservative attitudes demonstrated in countless handbooks, stylebooks, and dictionaries. Porter G. Perrin's pioneering *Writer's Guide and Index to English* (1942) patiently examined the pros and cons of hundreds of debatable usages. Hundreds of investigations, like those collected in Margaret M. Bryant's *Current American Usage* (1962), patiently recorded the actual usages of educated speakers and writers. In 1961, the G. and C. Merriam Company, whose citation files have been called the "national archives" of our language, joined forces with the linguists in *Webster's Third New International Dictionary*, the unabridged volume from which books like *Webster's Seventh New Collegiate Dictionary* are derived. Many expressions formerly labeled "incorrect" or "careless" were here recognized as widely used by educated people.

For the traditional distinction between simple "right" and "wrong,"

MODERN AUTHORITIES ON USAGE (I)

Can, may

Webster's New International Dictionary, 2nd ed.
>   can . . . Loosely, to have permission, to be allowed; equiva-
>   lent to *may*; as, can he go to the picnic?

Webster's Third New International Dictionary
>   can . . . have permission to—used interchangeably with *may*
>   (you *can* go now if you like)

Perrin, *Writer's Guide and Index to English*
>   1. *In General English.* In General usage *may* occurs rather
>   rarely except in the sense of possibility:
>>   It may be all right for her, but not for me.
>
>   *Can* is generally used for both permission and ability:
>>   Can I go now? You can if you want to.
>>   I can do 80 miles an hour with mine.
>
>   This is in such widespread usage that it should be regarded
>   as Standard English in speaking and in writing.
>   *Can't* almost always takes the place of *mayn't* in the United
>   States:
>>   Can't I go now?
>>   We can't have lights after twelve o'clock.
>
>   2. *In Formal English.* In Formal English a distinction is
>   sometimes made between the auxiliary *can*, with the mean-
>   ing of ability ("being able to") and *may*, with the meaning of
>   permission.
>>   You may go now. He can walk with crutches.
>>   You may if you can.
>
>   The distinction makes possible the classic dialog at many
>   tables:
>>   "Can I have some more meat and potato?"
>>   "You *may* [with a withering accent] have some more
>>   meat and potato."   (p. 446)

Bryant, *Current American Usage*
>   *Can* is almost universally employed in negative expressions
>   instead of the unused *mayn't.* "Why *can't* I go to the beach?"
>   will be used rather than "Why *mayn't* I go to the beach?"
>   and the negative answer is likely to be "You *can't*." Even if
>   the question is "*May* I go?" a negative answer may well be
>   "You *can't* go today, for I want you to meet your father at the
>   airport." *Can* is, therefore, standard usage in the negative.
>   Children also generally employ the negative *can't* in asking
>   permission: "*Can't* I go to the movies tonight?"   (p. 49)

MODERN AUTHORITIES ON USAGE (II)

The reason is because

Webster III

> (*one of the reasons why* it has seemed to me to be desirable to speak on this subject *is because* it may contribute . . . —E. N. Griswold) . . . in reputable use though disapproved by some.

Perrin, *Writer's Guide and Index to English*

> In Formal English the construction beginning "The reason is . . ." is completed by a noun or a noun clause, to balance the noun *reason*:
>
> > The reason for my poor work in French was [noun:] my intense dislike of the subject.
> >
> > The reason for my poor work in French was [noun clause:] that I disliked the subject intensely.
>
> Since in speech not many noun clauses are introduced by *that*, and *because* is the connective that most obviously stresses the notion of reason, in spoken English we usually find:
>
> > The reason for my poor work in French was because I didn't like the subject.
>
> "The reason is because . . ." is also frequently found in writing:
>
> > In general it may be said that the reason why scholasticism was held to be an obstacle to truth was because it seemed to discourage further enquiry along the experimental lines.—Basil Willey, *The Seventeenth Century Background*, p. 7
>
> Marckwardt and Walcott [1938] call this construction "Acceptable colloquially" (pp. 31, 112). In such use the *because* clause, in spite of its form, is a noun clause, not adverbial. Because of widespread prejudice against the construction, students should usually follow Formal usage. (pp. 668–69)

Evans and Evans, *Dictionary of Contemporary American Usage*

> As a rule, the example given of the misuse of *because* is a sentence containing *the reason* or *the reason why*, as in *the reason why he failed was because he tried to do too much.* It is claimed that only the word *that* can be used here. If the claim is based on theory, there is no reason why *because* should not refer back to a noun, such as *reason*, as well as to a pronoun, such as *it, this, that.* And if it can refer to a noun, there is no reason why the clause cannot function as a noun. If the claim is based on practice, the facts are that this construction is relatively new, that it offends some people, but is used freely by the best modern writers. (p. 56)

the new liberal view substituted a more realistic and more flexible attitude. The basic contribution of the liberal movement was its recognition of different legitimate *varieties of usage*. For practical purposes, teachers began to make two major kinds of distinctions. First, they recognized a major difference in usage related to social background and amount of formal schooling. Standard English was basically "educated" English—school English, office English, book English. It was the language of education, administration, business, journalism, the mass media. Nonstandard English was basically "working man's" English. It served him on the job, in his neighborhood, in his home. Second, teachers recognized two major **functional varieties** of standard English. One, the more formal variety, was the language of platform speech, of "edited" English, of serious discussion in both speech and writing. The other, the more informal variety, was the language of casual conversation.

The second major contribution of the liberal movement was to substitute *appropriateness* for correctness as the criterion of "good English." To use good English meant to use language right for the occasion, fit for the job at hand. A solemn formal tone would be appropriate for an important document; a stylized formal tone might be appropriate for an important invitation. A still formal but not starchy kind of English would be appropriate for vigorous discussion. An informal, chatty kind of English would be natural among friends. Usage becomes a problem when it does not fit the setting, when it does not suit the occasion. The worker who asks his foreman, "To *whom* did you assign this punch press?" is likely to find himself considered a stuffed shirt. The motorist who says "Come off it, Mac" to a policeman is likely to get a ticket.

The liberal approach to usage made it possible for students to explore the true range of their native language in all its plentiful variety. They could become interested in true popular speech without constantly running into off-limits signs saying "illiterate" or "vulgar." They could study some of the characteristic features of **nonstandard speech**, discovering there traces of older forms (such as the double negative) as well as newer forms carrying forward familiar processes of analogical extension (*knowed, growed*):

> *Verb Forms:* he *don't*, you *was*, I *says*: *knowed, growed*; have *wrote*, had *went*; I *seen* him
> *Pronoun Forms: hisself, theirself*; *this here* book, *that there* animal; *them* potatoes
> *Connectives: without* you pay the rent; *on account of* he was sick; *being as* she couldn't come
> *Double Negatives:* we *don't* have *no* time; a little rain *never* hurt *no one*

These and similar forms turned out not to be "mistakes" but simply language features illustrating familiar linguistic principles at work. When in nonstandard English *know-knew-known* switched over to *know-knowed-knowed*, it merely followed dozens of other formerly "irregular" English verbs that at one time or another adopted the prevailing *-ed* ending for the past. Thus, the earlier *help-halp-holpen* in Modern English became *help-helped-helped*. When a speaker uses a nonstandard form, he is not blundering about, making up his own "errors." He is merely following the established conventions of the kind of English that is natural and familiar to him. If he uses *hisn*, for instance, he uses it the way that in his kind of English it is *supposed* to be used. His particular variety of English "observes its own laws." Thus, as Albert Marckwardt points out in *American English*, the form *hisn*, if it appears in a speaker's repertory, "is the absolute, not the secondary or adjectival form." *His* appears before a noun; *hisn* stands alone. People say, "The book is *hisn*"; they never say, "This is *hisn* book."[21]

Nonstandard speech is part of our human landscape. We can turn to it as a source of human variety and local color when our standardized official world becomes too glib, too plastic, too impersonal. We can turn to it as a source of authentic, idiomatic folk speech when academic English becomes too pedantic and jargon-ridden. Ideally, we make our students appreciate the efficiency and range of standard English without cutting them off from nonstandard as a medium rich in humor, imagination, and humanity:

> We stood there, it was cold, listening to the fellow in the radio talking, only I couldn't make no heads nor tails out of it. Then the fellow said that would be all for a while, and me and Pete walked back up the road to home, and Pete told me what it was. Because he was nigh twenty and he knowed a heap: about them Japanese dropping bombs on Pearl Harbor and that Pearl Harbor was across the water.
>
> "Across what water?" I said. "Across that Government reservoy up at Oxford?"
>
> "Naw," Pete said. "Across the big water. The Pacific Ocean."
>
> We went home. Maw and pap was already asleep and me and Pete laid in bed, and I still couldn't understand where it was, and Pete told me again—the Pacific Ocean.
>
> "What's the matter with you?" Pete said. "You're going on nine years old. You been in school now ever since September. Ain't you learned nothing yet?"
>
> "I reckon we ain't got as fer as the Pacific Ocean yet," I said.
>
> —William Faulkner, "Two Soldiers"

A liberal attitude toward nonstandard English made it possible for people to become educated without feeling ashamed of the language of their parents, their relatives, their friends. Similarly, a liberal attitude toward informal standard English made possible a general rehabilitation of **colloquial** English—the casual, conversational variety of the prestige dialect. The term *colloquial* has nothing to do with "localisms" or with "speech forms of the lower classes." Colloquial English is the language white-collar people naturally use when off duty, when not speaking or writing "for the record." It is chatty English, "talky" English. If it is good enough for the teachers' lounge and the company president's barbecue, it is also good enough for the informal speech of our students.

Here are some typical features of informal standard English:

Contractions:	*don't, doesn't, isn't, won't, can't; I'm, you've, they're*
Conversational Tags:	*Well,* . . . ; *why,* . . . ; *now,* . . .
Pronoun Forms:	it's *me,* that's *him;* who *did you invite*
Pronoun Reference:	everybody took *theirs;* somebody left *their* gloves
Intensifiers:	*so* glad; *such* a surprise; *real* miserable; *awful* fast
Connectives:	*because you say so* doesn't make it right; a rebate *is when* . . .
Abbreviations:	*ad, gym, phone, exam, bike*
Idioms:	*chip in; check up on; come up with; blame* (something) *on* (somebody)

The vocabulary of informal English is the small change of everyday talk: *act up, fake, flunk, folks, gang up on, goof, gripe, josh, mean, mess, mope, pal, skinny, sloppy, stump, swap, wangle.* A familiar part of the informal repertory are the many clichés of shirt-sleeve talk:

> let's not kid ourselves
> something's got to give
> throw in the sponge
> pull out all the stops
> hassle over something
> here's the pitch
> have a crack at it
> hold your horses
> let's get down to brass tacks
> use some elbow grease
> if you want to know the truth
> you can say that again

While informal English is basically spoken English, it does have familiar legitimate uses in writing. It is appropriate for a very personal kind of writing, in which the writer talks about things close to himself, without necessarily treating them as a "big deal":

When the interrogation began the questions came *hot and heavy.* "Fat man" was on his feet pacing the creaky floor in his massive wing tip shoes that *just happened to be* well polished and out of place in contrast with the rest of his *grubby* half dressed appearance. Why did you do it? Who *put you up to* it? How long have you been involved with this type of behavior? You know what's going to happen to you don't you? *This kind of jazz* went on for over ten minutes. All I could say was yes, sir; no, sir; I don't know, sir; I think so, sir; shut up, sir; you make me sick, sir! I was *so scared I could die and melt away, and if he had breathed on me I would have.*

(Student theme)

On the other hand, informal English makes possible the humorous effect a writer achieves when he treats things that are *usually* treated solemnly in a much more casual fashion:

Dr. George Gallup recently demonstrated that while knowledge is exploding *all over the place* it is hitting remarkably few targets. Dr. Gallup found that only 11 per cent of the population is behaving knowledgeably. A *whopping* 76 per cent of the population is still *carrying on* in *pretty much* the *same damn fool way* their ancestors did. Thirteen per cent is unde-cided.

(*Patrick Butler*)

When colloquial English becomes extremely informal, it shades over into **slang.** Slang has been described as "language that is being slung about instead of being handled with stately consideration." It has a free-wheeling, disrespectful quality that makes it inadvisable for use with teacher, preacher, policeman, and judge. American slang especially tends toward the drastically graphic metaphor that makes no attempt to be polite: *rubberneck, sawbones, eyewash, hayseed, bonehead, windbag, rotgut, loan shark, stool pigeon, fall guy.* As H. L. Mencken said in *The American Language,* "Such a term as *rubberneck* is almost a complete treatise on American psychology," showing along with "boldness and contempt for ordered forms" a delight in pungent epithets and grotesque humor.[22]

What limits the usefulness of slang is its deliberate defiance of con-vention, authority, respectability. "Head" becomes *bean;* "jail" becomes *jug* or *clink.* Slang metaphors are deliberately extravagant, exaggerated out of all proportion: "that kills me," "hit the ceiling," "fly off the handle," "go whole hog." On the other hand, slang shows in action some of the forces that keep language colorful, vigorous, alive. Slang keeps alive the power of invention, our naïve delight in word-making, our naïve pleasure in having a rich set of synonyms from which to choose:

Nonsense:	claptrap, bosh, flapdoodle, twaddle, baloney, bunk
Money:	folding green, dough, bread, moolah, mazooma
Dullard:	chump, hayseed, rube, jerk, drip, sap, clod, dope, square
Face:	kisser, mug
Miser:	tightwad, cheapskate, skinflint
Top Person:	big shot, bigwig, big wheel, big cheese, VIP

But slang is not merely entertaining; it is also often functional. Much slang has a pointed, no-nonsense quality that keeps language from going soft and sticky. In printer's slang, an exclamation mark becomes simply a "bang." Many typical slang words are short and to the point: *blab, click, fizzle, jell, jibe, scram, wow.* Much of our language is slang that has made the grade: *bogus, boom, carpetbagger, crook, graft, handout, hike, hobo, honky-tonk, racketeer.* Though much slang comes and goes, some slang terms were first used centuries ago:

grub (food) — 1659; *hick* (rustic) — 1690; *sap* (fool) — 1815

Having defined nonstandard and colloquial English in realistic, positively oriented terms, teachers adopting a liberal perspective could give their students a businesslike account of **formal standard English** as the basic medium of serious writing. What we write down is generally more important than what we merely mention. It is typically intended for a larger audience. Formal language indicates that we are taking our subject and our audience seriously. Language that is too breezy may make our audience feel that what we have to say does not merit serious attention. Though formal English is first of all written English, "edited" English, it is also the language of much public speech, of much serious discussion.

Trying to show our students what kind of English is fit for serious writing, we have to establish a basic point: *Effective formal English is vigorous and natural.* It avoids excessive formality as well as breezy informality. We don't produce serious written English by always preferring the big word to the simple word, the dictionary word to the everyday word. If we always avoid the simple everyday expression, we make our writing stilted, pompous, and unnatural. Often the most natural word is in between:

Very Formal	In-between	Slang
retire	go to bed	hit the sack
fatigued	exhausted	bushed
vanquish	trounce	clobber
wedded	married	hitched
spouse	husband	old man

Students must not come to feel that English teachers are happy only with the most stilted and unidiomatic kind of language. When teachers always criticize every informal touch in the student's writing, he all too often begins to write a tortured, pseudo-formal style, desperately trying to avoid anything that sounds natural or familiar.

A formal style does not use "big words" to impress the reader. The best writing uses much of the *common stock* of the language:

> Many critics through the years have pointed out that almost all anti-war novels and motion pictures are, in fact, pro-war. Blood and mud and terror and rape and an all-pervading anxiety are precisely what is attractive about war—in the safety of fiction—to those who, in our overprotected lives, are suffering from tedium vitae and human self-alienation.   (Kenneth Rexroth)

Rexroth makes use of an "educated" vocabulary that goes beyond every-day talk: *all-pervading, anxiety, overprotected, self-alienation* (not to mention the "learned" *tedium vitae*). But the terms that give the passage its force are blunt common-stock words (*blood, mud, rape*). Much of the working vocabulary of the passage is businesslike, workaday English (*point out* instead of *demonstrate* or *call attention to the fact*; *suffer from* instead of *be affected by*). The key terms that bring the passage into focus are not pretentious and polysyllabic but clear and direct: *antiwar, prowar*.

The following passage illustrates the same in-between quality of much effective modern prose. It is formal enough to fit serious discussion, but it has the informal touches that keep it from getting too far away from the natural rhythms of speech:

> It happens to be a fact that all classic works without exception deal directly or indirectly with problems of conduct. That is their great virtue for school use. Not that they teach a plain goody-goody morality, but that they show and discuss and solve dilemmas that a shipping clerk or an athlete can be made to understand. For this understanding, the discussion of any classic *must be superficial.* If you dive below the surface with your pupil you drown him. Certain teachers are always terrified of superficiality; they seem to think other teachers will scoff or that the dead author will scold. Let them remind themselves that their colleagues' profundity would strike the great author as either surface scratching or pedantry; and let them remember that for every reader there is a time when a given book is being read for the first time.   (Jacques Barzun)

Again, the author does not *limit* himself to the familiar, the simple His vocabulary ranges beyond the conversational: "terrified of superficiality," *scoff*, "colleagues' profundity," *pedantry*. His sentences are deliberate and effective. They repeatedly become insistent ("show and discuss and solve"). There is the kind of parallelism that helps give well-structured prose direction and impact ("let them remind themselves . . ."; "let them remember . . ."). But again the author stays close enough to common speech for his style to remain personal, natural, alive. He uses conversational phrases ("it happens to be a fact that . . ."), an occasional colloquialism ("goody-goody morality"), the informal *you*. His metaphors have a homely, familiar quality: "if you dive . . . you drown him"; "surface scratching."

The net effect of the modern liberal approach to usage was to restore the native speaker's confidence in his command of his own language. The liberal approach rehabilitated many authentic features of American English that had been arbitrarily proscribed. It made it possible for teachers to base advice about speech and writing, not on the fear of error, but on a positive appreciation of what was appropriate and effective. Many traditional taboos, in fact, had dealt, not with substantial questions of effective communication, but with niggling points of external form. For daily classroom work, an important side effect of the liberal movement was to help loosen the pedantic rigidity that used to mark the teaching of **mechanics**. Many rules about commas and semicolons had once been taught with deadly seriousness as essential to good English and sound thinking. These turned out to be what they always were—*conventions*, rules of thumb, customary ways of doing things (which in the traditional handbooks had by no means been accurately or reliably described). Slowly, handbooks and style manuals started to describe these conventions more realistically and to *recognize the range of acceptable variation from familiar rules*. Thus, any attentive reader of the "best authors" could verify established practices that violated traditional taboos:

Sentence Fragment in Response to a Question:

Where do I start? *With personal relationships.* (E. M. Forster)

What does Morocco mean to a Frenchman? *An orange grove or a job in Government service.* (George Orwell)

Descriptive Fragment:

Pale, dry, baked earth, that blows into dust of fine sand. Low hills of baked pale earth, sinking heavily, and speckled sparsely with dark dots of cedar bushes. A river of the plain of drought, just a cleft of dark, reddish-brown water, almost a flood. And overall, the blue, uneasy, alkaline sky. (D. H. Lawrence)

Sentence Fragment That Elaborates on Previous Statement:

> But the look he gave me was not in the least the kind of look you might ex-
> pect. *Not hostile, not contemptuous, not sullen, not even inquisitive.* (George
> Orwell)

**Comma Splice for Closely Related Ideas (Even When There Is No Direct
Grammatical Parallelism):**

> Thousands of them perish in obscurity, a few are great names. (E. M.
> Forster)

> The hours passed, it grew hotter and hotter. (Aldous Huxley)

> Owning a car was still a major excitement, roads were still wonderful and
> bad. (E. B. White)[23]

These familiar practices are not the result of "carelessness" or
"sloppy thinking." They are convenient and perfectly intelligible ways of
handling the lowly punctuation marks that help regulate the flow of verbal
traffic on the written page. If English teachers want to reach today's students, let alone have an effect on society at large, they will have to learn
to see sentence fragments and comma splices in perspective. English
teachers have too long taken their cue from people with little minds,
people who saved their moral indignation for alleged misuses of the semi-
colon and the period. They have listened too long to people who were
prepared to mount their last stand on the issue that "regardless of what
any edition of Webster may say, the word is still *salame,* not *salami.*"
For years, liberally oriented teachers wasted their energies doing battle
against traditionalist misconceptions about language. The time has come
for English teachers to concentrate their energies on the real language
needs of their students.

ENGLISH FOR THE DISADVANTAGED

Among the charges leveled against English teachers in recent years, one
largely justified indictment stands out: Our obsession with "good English" has masked our failure to solve the language problems of those of
our students who are most in need of help. While English teachers have
spent their time on trivia, they have neglected the basic communication
needs of the disadvantaged. Euphemisms aside, a disadvantaged student

> is isolated from the mainstream of culture in a given society by the acci-
> dent of birth or upbringing. A child who grows up in a family and a com-
> munity which are economically deprived or socially stigmatized, or both,

SPEECH SAMPLES OF DISADVANTAGED CHILDREN

Puerto Rican girl, age 13 (in Chicago 1 year)

I say their names. The first is Ginovar Aguilar. She *tiene* (has) let's see . . . she *tiene* (has) five children. The other one is Coranácion Serra. She *tiene* (has) two children. I don't see another one of his. I see any more but two. Let's see. Ginovar Aguilar is in New York. She speaks English. Yes . . . yes. I don't see . . . let's see . . . I don't see any more but one children of her. Any more. But the other I see the two childrens. Yes . . . no . . . let's see. One have . . . let's see . . . one have ten years . . . ten years old. Her name is Lupita or Guadalupe. The other is Esto Flores . . . Esto. He has . . . he had a thirt- . . . no, fourteen . . . Aunts . . . He work in the factory. My mother work . . . my mother is the wife house . . . the wife house . . . house wife.

Kentucky boy, age 10 (in Chicago 1 year)

They ain't got no ponies; they got big horses. . . . I rode one, real big uns. Scare me. . . . I had a pony. I could ride hit real good —a little pony. . . . Ouno (I don't know) . . . Yeh we had one . . . See his really named Frankie. When you call him Peanut, he'll buck ye. . . . He will. Ya say, get up Peanut, den he'll say, yonk, shuum! . . . I ont know. . . . A red one. . . . And it had a slick back, it goes mmn, like kat. . . . He got down 'n wallered wif me. See he started to lay down an when he started wallerin I got off. Wif dis new saddle, he tore dis new saddle off. My father got mad. He wentnt down 'n got wallered wif this new saddle. Me on him too. But I got off. . . . I know. He did dat to my cousin too, and she hopped off like everything. She wouldn't get on him no more.

Negro girl, age 14 (Memphis)

English. Our teacher when we firs got in here "I haven't got a pe." Girl sittin nex to me. She a teacher's daughter. Teachers always like the teacher's daughter over the other children, expecially if the teacher go—is a teacher at that school. Her mama was a teacher dere las year. This year she teach at another school. She si righ nex to me. So she so stingy. I have some candy uh sumpin, she'll as me for some and I don't be wantin to give it to her, but I'll go on and give it to her and so nen one day she as me how de spell a lil ole simple word. Wha was that word? It star with a 'S'. It was scot, I think. SCOT. She didn't know how to spell it, and I tol her. It was on a cross word puzzle. An nen I axed her for sompin. Naw, the girl sittin on the other side of me named Delores. She ax her le 'er use her ink pen. She say, "After today you not gon use my ink pen anymore, you better bring your own." An so Delores gave her the ink pen bac. And nen teacher came ta'in 'bout uh "I don't have any pets in here." Eribody cin come in the room and si down. Here go Teresa, "May I go over to so and so and so and so's room?" "May I go over to so and so and so's—?" She have 'bout ten places to go when she git in that room, and teacher let her go ery place. And one day I had my brother's lunch money and I wanted to give it to him. And I tol her the reason I wanted to go and she wouldn't even le me go but —and, and she say she say couldn't nobody go and nen Teresa jes walked up there and had ten places to go and she went to all ubum, but I couldn go take my brother his lunch money.

(Tape-recorded and transcribed by N. Louanna Furbee, Emily Pettigrew Morris, and Dagna Simpson, in A. L. Davis, ed., *American Dialects for English Teachers*, USOE, 1969) has a disadvantaged start in life. The school, which is supposed to bring him back to the mainstream of culture, has generally failed to achieve this goal because the teacher is not equipped to handle him and his problems.

The disadvantaged child, whether poor black or poor white, speaks a variety of English

considered unacceptable by the teacher and the members of the prestigious group who use standard English. The disadvantaged child, therefore, has an additional task to cope with, the task of learning standard English in school, whereas the middle-class child has already learned it at home. He also has greater difficulty in learning to read, because, among other things, his reading materials are written in standard English.

The child from a linguistic minority,

such as the Indian child from the reservation or the Spanish-speaking child from Mexico or Puerto Rico, presents another kind of language problem, that of learning a language entirely different from his native tongue. This task of learning English, not an easy task in itself, is often complicated by the child's learning from another disadvantaged child of his age the non-standard dialect, which, instead of winning him the encouragement of the teacher, only brings him the teacher's disapproval and a subsequent sense of confusion and futility.[24]

The traditional solution to the problem of the disadvantaged child has been to reject his first dialect, or his first language, completely. The teacher, armed with workbook and test, set out to eradicate all deviations from standard English. For most minority children, this all-or-nothing approach did not work. It amounted to the teacher's condemning the child's language without providing a workable alternative, without truly making a "new" dialect available. Holding on to the purity of standard English, many teachers were in effect "throwing the baby away and keeping the bath." For many disadvantaged children, standard English became part of the barrier that shut them off from what the school and the larger society presumably had to offer. As the child is "constantly corrected and harassed" for using the language of his own family and community, hostility or withdrawal is a natural result:

A black child runs up to a teacher and says, "Is you da new physical education teacher?" The teacher steps back, looks at the child disdainfully and says, "ARE you THE new physical education teacher?" With this, the child lowers his head and looks away. This type of encounter occurs daily in black schools throughout America.

When a child enters school, he brings a language system which is intimately woven with the culture of his community and it is through this system that he perceives his reality. For middle-class white children, the development and refinement of this language system is continued and enhanced at school, but for most black children there is no continuation or enhancement of his system. Instead, his language is not accepted and the school becomes a battleground where the child and the authority figures engage in open warfare over his right to humanity (his language). He is told that the language it has taken five years to master is incorrect, sloppy, lazy, vulgar, and crude.[25]

The most basic need here is for a fundamental change of attitude on the part of teachers: *They must learn to respect the child's language,* for one cannot reject the child's language and claim to accept the child. They must see that the child's language is for him "an essential means to maintaining communication and rapport with his family and peers. To attack this dialect, whether directly or by implication, is to attack his loyalty to his group, his identity, his worth."[26]

The teacher must learn to let his students be **bidialectal.** They must be allowed to use their dialect without ridicule during their early years of schooling, and without constant interruption and criticism in the more informal classroom situations in later years. While the ignorant denounce minority speech as ignorant, a new generation of idealistic young teachers is experimenting with ways to have minority students "write in their own language and out of their own experience and emotions," thus releasing some of the rich expressiveness too often dried up by rigidly enforced premature standardization.

For the teacher, exposure to the students' own language and their world helps clear away the negative preconceptions that often defeat attempts to give minority students a positive self-image and positive motivation in their school work. Writers like William Labov have vigorously attacked the concept of "verbal deprivation," the notion that "Negro children from the ghetto area receive little verbal stimulation" and "hear very little well-formed language, and as a result are impoverished in their means of verbal expression." Such children may engage in "defensive, monosyllabic behavior" with interviewers, teachers, and other authority figures. But in natural surroundings they demonstrate the spontaneous fluency and exuberance of their own "highly verbal culture."[27] The black folk culture is rich in traditions of oral improvisation and oral art, with its games of verbal abuse, such as the "Dozens"; with the rich verbal mimicry of black folk humor; with the eloquence of spiritual and blues. H. Rap Brown says about his own ghetto childhood, "we learned what the white folks call verbal skills . . . By the time I was nine, I could talk Shine and the Titanic, Signifying Monkey, three different ways." Signifying could be used to "make a cat feel good or bad," but it could also be used to express personal feelings:

> Man, I can't win for losing.
> If it wasn't for bad luck, I wouldn't
>   have no luck at all.
> I been having buzzard luck
> Can't kill nothing and won't nothing die
> I'm living on the welfare and things is
>   stormy
> They borrowing their shit from the Salvation
>   Army
> But things bound to get better 'cause they can't
>   get no worse
> I'm just like the blind man, standing by a
>   broken window
> I don't feel no pain.
> But it's your world
> You the man I pay rent to
> If I had your hands I'd give 'way both my arms.
> Cause I could do without them
> I'm the man but you the main man
> I read the books you write
> You set the pace in the race I run
> Why, you always in good form
> You got more foam than Alka Seltzer . . .[28]

The highly verbal character of the black subculture is indeed obvious to anyone except people with tin ears. As V. S. Pritchett said, for instance,

> The word is everything in Harlem. The long word or the book word beautifully uttered by the man driving his cab or talking in his shop; the rambling or the inciting word of the street meeting; the Biblical or inflaming word of the unctuous ranting preacher. These people have the gift of tongues which is scarcer among American whites; indeed conversation is commoner there than in white New York.[29]

All constructive work with minority students must start from a positive appreciation of their own culture, so that they can become educated, not by rejecting their heritage, but by building on what they are and what they have. Similarly, all attempts to extend the range of the student's language repertory must start from a positive understanding and appreciation of the language resources he brings to school. Linguists are actively exploring the nature and origin of the language patterns of the disadvantaged child: How uniform is the **black dialect** spoken by many urban Negro children as the result of mass migrations of rural Southern Negroes to the cities? How much *local* urban dialect is there in New York City, Detroit, Washington, D.C.? How close is, or was, the "black dialect" to nonstandard Southern American in pronunciation, syntax, vocabulary? What influence, if any, is there of early pidgin (or "creole") versions of English adopted by African slaves in order to communicate both with their white masters and with fellow slaves from different tribal groups? How much influence of assimilated "Anglo" terms and idioms is there in the "street" Spanish spoken by Chicano children in California, by Puerto Rican children in New York?

While these and other questions are being debated, teachers can adopt a few preliminary rules of thumb:

(1) *Stay close to actual specimens of the real thing.* The best remedy against prejudice, as always, is to adopt a "What have we got here?" approach. It is educational for teacher and student simply to get examples of minority speech and look at them together. Increasingly, more or less authentic approximations of minority dialect appear in print in books, newspapers, magazines:

> "See i's like ma mov' tell me da put some limon, hot limon 'n some tea and go da bed an' git up un'er de cover. An' I be hot, I be so hot unti' I jus' cain' do. I jus' gotta take de cover off me. So I be takin' off my bajama shirt. I be takin' off everythin'. An' so, din, din I wake up nix mornin', ma col' be worse, seem like."
>
> An' teach say I'ma, teach' say I'ma tell dis to de princiba, too, dat chu go 'roun' stealin' school prope'ty. My muvver pay for dis whin she paid for de tax. She say, you muvah ain' pay for dis. Dis b'long to de school. An' she start talkin' all lat ov' ol' junk an' waste half de peri'd. Din we start talkin' 'bout light, how, speed o' light an' na speed o' soun' an' all 'a' kinna stuff."[30]

(2) *Treat dialect features not as two-headed monsters but as English.* Many features of a black dialect that dialectologists have identified draw on elements and procedures well within the familiar repertory of English grammar. Speakers of a black dialect use these elements according to somewhat different *rules*—and often in ways that have direct parallels in other varieties of English. Thus, Negro nonstandard uses the uninflected third person singular: "He *say*"; "She *live* down the block"; "School *start* early." Similar uninflected third-person singular forms appear in standard English as exceptions: "He *dare* not deny it"; "She *need* not come back." They are quite regular for the modal auxiliaries:

"he *can*"; "she *may*"; "it *will.*" Again, black nonstandard speech uses uninflected forms of the noun for the possessive: "That lady *John* mother" (for "*John's* mother"). Standard English does the same with uninflected forms of the noun for various irregular plurals: *deer, sheep,* and the like.

Here are some other features of black nonstandard speech that have parallels in other kinds of English:

Reversal of subject and verb (or first auxiliary)—used in standard English for questions; used in nonstandard also for statement patterns:

Standard:	*Isn't* anybody here?
	Didn't anybody hear you?
General Nonstandard:	*Ain't* nobody gonna boss me around.
	Ain't nobody here but us chickens.
Black Nonstandard:	*Didn't* nobody hear him.
	Don't nobody know the answer.

Reversal of subject and verb (or first auxiliary)—extended in nonstandard to *indirect* as well as direct questions:

Standard:	*Can* he come?
	Ask him *if he can* come.
	I don't know *if Robert can* play.
Black Nonstandard:	Ask him *can he* come.
	I don't know *can Robert* play.
Informal British:	Go and see *is he* hurt. (Samuel Beckett)

Duplicated subject:

Standard:	*My mother* doesn't like it.
Black Nonstandard:	*My mother she* don't like it.
	My sister she work at the bank.
Early Modern English:	*Our father he* hath writ, so hath our sister. (Shakespeare)

Double negative—in nonstandard, related parts of a sentence each in turn reflects negative meaning:

Standard:	I *don't* play with him anymore.
General and Black	
Nonstandard:	You *ain't* going to *no* heaven.
	I *don'(t)* want *none.*
Middle English:	He *nevere* yit *no* vilainye *ne* said. (Chaucer)

Use of dummy "it" as a sentence opener (before a postponed subject)—in black nonstandard possible in positions filled in standard by *there*:

Standard:	*There's* a difference.
	It's the doorbell.
General Nonstandard:	*They's* a difference.
	They's no one there.
Black Nonstandard:	*It's* a difference.
	It's no one there.

Attrition of final consonants (and consonant clusters):

Standard:	*There's* more bread.
	Ask your mother.
General Nonstandard:	*They's* more bread.
Black Nonstandard:	*As' you* mother.
	This *they* big chance.

(3) *In teaching standard English, focus clearly on what really matters.* Much traditional grammar book and workbook material is useless because it condemns much that is current in informal educated speech. It thus leaves the student with no model except a hyperformal book English that exists only in English classes. As Virginia Allen has said,

> If the class has not yet learned to use high-priority features of standard English, it will be pointless to spend valuable time on grammar-book rules ... which condemn usages like "different than" and "neither are." It will be futile and foolish to dwell upon rules governing *between* and *among* and *who* and *whom*. It is sad to think how much precious energy is being squandered on such esoteric distinctions in courses for students who need all the help they can get in mastering the basic hallmarks of standard speech.[31]

Instruction in standard English has a chance of taking only if the variety of English taught appears to the student as the actual working medium of communication in our culture, reinforced not only by his contacts with teachers, but by the language of sportscasters and disc jockeys; of Batman and Superman and Mighty Mouse; of Eldridge Cleaver, LeRoi Jones, and other leaders of minority communities.

(4) *Experiment with teaching methods that stress habit-building rather than analysis and correction.* The student has to take in, and repeat, key usage patterns until they begin to sink in, until they become a part of his language repertory. **Pattern practice**, modeled on modern

methods of teaching foreign languages, provides the extensive exposure and repetition needed before the new usage pattern becomes a habit. The more resourceful the teacher, the more successfully will the practice patterns simulate real situations for language use:

Teacher: Now let's all mention things we saw on our way to school this morning. I saw a fire engine. What about you, Paul?

Paul: I saw a garbage truck on my way to school.

Teacher: Good! Laura, tell us what Paul saw, and then tell us something you saw.

Laura: Paul saw a garbage truck on his way to school. I saw a . . . a . . . I saw a black kitten in front of the supermarket.

Teacher: Fine! Anthony, what did Laura see?

Anthony: She seen . . .

Teacher: She saw. *Please say, "She saw . . ."*

Anthony: She saw a kitten.

Teacher: Yes. And what did you see?

Anthony: I seen . . . I saw a . . . a motorcycle.

Teacher: Good. Class, what did Anthony say he saw? Use saw *in your answer.*

Class: He saw a motorcycle.

Teacher: Right! Now, then, let's play the game in a different way. Did anyone see a taxi or a jeep on the way to school today? Gregory, did you see a taxi or a jeep?

Gregory: I didn't see a jeep, but I saw a taxi.

Teacher: Good. Daphne, did you see any dogs or horses on your way to school?

Daphne: I seen—saw some dogs, but I didn't see no horse.

Teacher: I didn't see any horses. That's the standard English way to say it. Say: "I didn't see any horses."

Daphne: I didn't see any horses.

Teacher: Fine! George, what did Daphne see, and what didn't she see?

George: She . . . she . . . (silence)

Teacher: Daphne, tell George what you saw and what you didn't see.

Daphne: I saw some dogs, but I didn't see no . . . I didn't see any horses.[32]

(5) *Reinforce pattern practice with a variety of role-playing activities.* In a mock trial, judge, court reporter, lawyers, and expert witnesses can serve as models of standard English. In mock interviews, officials and

celebrities can speak the prestige dialect. Students can improvise such activities; they can also write scripts for them, rehearse and tape their parts. As Charles G. Hurst, Jr. has said,

> Role-play as a valuable technique for achieving accelerated development of language skills represents one of the few means which gives a student the opportunity to engage in the kind of practice that he needs. In few other situations does he get the chance to engage in positive practice with standard English. The rapidity with which many youths develop the ability to play various roles accompanied by appropriate language styles including standard English is amazing.[33]

Radical critics of American education have shown little enthusiasm for new initiatives and new methods aimed at teaching standard English to the disadvantaged. Once we lose faith in the capacity of our society for regenerating itself, dialect engineering may seem a mere palliative, raising false hopes. Members of America's black and brown minorities may increasingly opt for separatism, cultural and linguistic as well as political and economic. Obviously, teaching standard English to the disadvantaged is mere window dressing unless it is part of a much larger effort to break down old patterns of exclusion and discrimination. But at least English teachers can take comfort in the thought that they are trying to increase the disadvantaged student's options, while other people are trying to nail him into a box.

Contrary to what radicals imply, mastery of a prestige dialect as a condition of success in school and society is not just another sinister feature of our particular political and economic system. Socialist teachers in East Germany are teaching the official High German to children from Low German dialect areas; Maoists are promoting the spread of Mandarin Chinese. In our society, as in others, "a full and contributing citizenship . . . requires fluency in the standard forms of the national language." Throughout the student's schooling, lack of confidence and fluency in school English handicaps the student in reading, writing, and all other basic school subjects. Whatever else English teachers are responsible for, one of their most basic tasks is to provide students with the "language tools which are basic to educational as well as to economic success."[34] The question is not whether people can effectively switch dialects or become to a degree bidialectal. Millions of people have done so—city-bound rural children in Europe and in this country, upward-mobile poor city children, many members of the "black bourgeoisie." The question is what English teachers can do to help with the job.

FOOTNOTES

¹Bel Kaufman, *Up the Down Staircase* (Englewood Cliffs, N.J.: Prentice-Hall, Inc., 1964), p. 191.

²Walter Van Tilburg Clark, *The Ox-Bow Incident* (New York: Random House, Inc., 1940).

³Dudley Bailey, ed., *Introductory Language Essays* (New York: W. W. Norton & Company, Inc., 1965), pp. x–xi.

⁴Robert Lado, "Sentence Structure," *College Composition and Communication,* 8 (February 1957), 14–15.

⁵Jean Malmstrom, "Linguistic Atlas Findings versus Textbook Pronouncements on Current American Usage," *The English Journal,* 48 (April 1959), 197.

⁶Albert H. Marckwardt, *American English* (New York: Oxford University Press, 1958), p. 133.

⁷Raven I. McDavid, Jr., "Dialectology and the Classroom Teacher," *College English,* 24 (November 1962), 111.

⁸Marckwardt, *American English,* p. 138.

⁹McDavid, "Dialectology," pp. 113–115.

¹⁰Samuel Johnson, *Dictionary of the English Language,* in *English as Language: Backgrounds, Development, Usage,* eds. Charlton Laird and Robert M. Gorrell (New York: Harcourt, Brace & World, Inc., 1961), pp. 136–142.

¹¹In Laird and Gorrell, *English as Language,* pp. 205–206.

¹²Robert A. Hall, Jr., *Linguistics and Your Language* (New York: Doubleday & Company, Inc., 1960), p. 189.

¹³Harold Whitehall, *Structural Essentials of English* (New York: Harcourt, Barce & World, Inc., 1956), p. 91.

¹⁴Paul Roberts, Teacher's Guide to *Patterns of English* (New York: Harcourt, Brace & World, Inc., 1956), p. 19.

E. Standop, *"Was ist Grammatik?,"* *Praxis des Neusprachlichen Unterrichts,* 9 (1962), 131.

¹⁶Otto Jespersen, *Growth and Structure of the English Language,* 9th ed. (New York: Doubleday & Company, Inc., 1956), pp. 14–15.

¹⁷Russell Thomas, "Notes on the Inflected Genitive in Modern American Prose," *College English,* 14 (January 1953); in *Introductory Readings on Language,* eds. Wallace L. Anderson and Norman C. Stageberg (New York: Holt, Rinehart & Winston, Inc., 1962), p. 311.

¹⁸Albert H. Marckwardt and Fred G. Walcott, *Facts About Current Usage* (New York: Appleton-Century-Crofts, Inc., 1938), p. 38.

¹⁹H. L. Mencken, "The American Language," *Yale Review,* 25 (March 1936), 538–552.

²⁰Sumner Ives, "Linguistics in the Classroom," *College English,* 17 (December 1955), 165–172.

²¹Marckwardt, *American English,* p. 148.

²²H. L. Mencken, *The American Language,* 4th ed. (New York: Alfred A. Knopf, Inc., 1937), p. 92.

[23]James L. Green, "Acrobats, Plowmen, and the Healthy Sentence," *English Journal*, 58 (September 1969), 894–898.

[24]San-su C. Lin, "Disadvantaged Student? or Disadvantaged Teacher?," *English Journal*, 56 (May 1967), 751–756.

[25]Toni Searles et al., "Speech Therapy for Human Dignity," *Changing Education*, 3 (Winter 1969), 42.

[26]Lin, "Disadvantaged Student? or Disadvantaged Teacher?," p. 753.

[27]William Labov, "The Logic of Nonstandard English," *The Florida FL Reporter*, (Spring/Summer 1969), 60.

[28]H. Rap Brown, *Die Nigger Die!* (New York: The Dial Press, Inc., 1969), pp. 29–30.

[29]V. S. Pritchett, "Striverstown," *New Statesman,* Aug. 16, 1963.

[30]Peggy Thomson, "Negro Education—Bilingual Problem?," *Los Angeles Times*, June 11, 1967, Section F, p. 3.

[31]Virginia F. Allen, "Teaching Standard English as a Second Dialect," *Teachers College Record*, 68 (February 1967), 362.

[32]Allen, "Teaching Standard English," 363.

[33]Charles G. Hurst, Jr., "Standard and Non-Standard Dialects: An Educational Dilemma," *California English Journal*, 5 (April 1969), 11–22.

[34]Hurst, "Standard and Non-Standard Dialects," 11–22.

FOR FURTHER STUDY

A.   How familiar or how new are the *attitudes toward usage* expressed in the following passages? Which of them would you strongly support, and how? Which of them would you take issue with, and why?

1.   A professor of English just turned fifty said recently that in his boyhood in Michigan he had an English teacher who assiduously trained him and his classmates to say *somebody's else* and never *somebody else's*. That was somewhere around 1925. *Somebody's else*, you may recall, is the idiom of Dickens, Thackeray, George Eliot, and Mark Twain. On July 31, 1881, the New York *Times* headlined a story about public school teachers being told that *somebody else's* is correct. Approval of this idiom was immediately disputed by a purist of the time, Alfred Ayres in his *Verbalist* (1881). Forty-five years later at least one English teacher agrees with Ayres and is still hammering away an insistence upon using *somebody's else*.

Before leaving Ayres we might observe other examples of his prescriptiveness. He objects to the verb *donate* as an abomination, to the noun *dress* for an outer garment worn by women instead of the proper term *gown*, to the noun *lunch*, an inelegant abbreviation for *luncheon*. He even points out in passing that the question "Have you had luncheon?" is preferable to "Have you had your luncheon?" because "we may in most cases presuppose that the person addressed would hardly take anybody's else luncheon." The adjective *underhanded* "though found in dictionaries, is a vulgarism" for *underhand*.

Some of these may sound unbelievable . . . But they are no sillier than some of today's pronouncements about *like, who, more unique, different than, due to, do not think, cannot help but, back of, blame it on*. One of the surprising things about these shibboleths is their small number: you can easily classify them in a list of well under a hundred.

—Philip B. Gove, "A Perspective on Usage,"
Language, Linguistics, and School Programs

2.   When a child is said to speak 'ungrammatically' the fact is always that he is obeying a vast number of grammatical rules, a very small fraction of which happen to be different grammar rules from the ones that the critic subscribes to. The critic does not notice . . . that the child is obeying any rules at all. For that vast majority in which there is identity between the child's grammar and the critic's grammar, the critic notices no rules because there is no conflict; in that small minority of all the rules for which there is conflict instead of identity, the critic notices only the conflict and does not recognize that the child's pattern has its own logic and is part of a different grammar just as rigid as the critic's own. Hence the critic says that the child has no grammar at all, when in fact he has just as much grammar as anybody, very little of it non-standard.

Normal fluent speech obeys about five or six grammar rules per second; a critic can seldom detect, in a child's speech, more than one conflict with standard grammar per ten seconds on the average. And the one time that he was 'incorrect' feels no different, to the child speaker, than the fifty times when he was 'correct.' This means that the child must feel every critical intervention to be an unjustified interruption of his fluent speech, and must regard the form of every correction as completely arbitrary, not conceivably motivated otherwise than by some mysterious urge to interfere with normal human behavior and to distort it into a kind of marionette-dance.

—Martin Joos, "Language and the School Child,"
Harvard Educational Review

3.   I can best illustrate what I mean by a positive approach by giving an account of the school experience of one of my own children. Recently she wrote a review of the book entitled *The Silent World*. In it she had written the sentence, "You can expect the unordinary under water." This sentence was criticized for faulty diction on the ground that unordinary was not a word because, so the teacher said, it did not occur in the dictionary. Being a child of mine, she straight-away consulted the *Oxford English Dictionary* and discovered not only that the word was recorded there, but that it had been used in English as early as 1547 and as late as 1909. At this point, the teacher somewhat grudgingly withdrew her criticism. Unfortunately by making this a question of whether or not the expression was permitted by authority, the teacher simply challenged the child to pit one authority aginst the other. Consequently little or nothing of any value came out of this episode. Had the student been invited to develop for herself a synonymy of such formations as *unordinary*, *out of the ordinary*, *extraordinary*, and *unusual*, the result could have been positive rather than negative.

—Albert H. Marckwardt, "Implications of Language Processes
for the Teacher," *Language, Linguistics, and School Programs*

4.   There is no language today to rival English for its expressiveness through the range of the sciences and the arts, nor any literature to rival in richness that written in English in all parts of the world. It is a fact, and it would be dishonest to pretend otherwise, that one can not take part in our complicated society without mastering its language at a fairly high level. Yet, as the ills and inequities of our society are revealed, young people lose confidence in the political, economic, educational, and social system which produces a plethora of consumer goods at the expense of our natural environment and distributes these goods with an inequity that leaves starvation in the midst of plenty and rotting slums alongside palatial skyscrapers. Language and the use of language is what knits our marvelous technocracy together. At the same time, language and the use of language marks indelibly those who are outside the pale, who can not participate fully, but must forever look on.

     In the past, the effort has been to invite all who were able inside the pale. And the school—in particular, the English class—was the avenue of access. This procedure was tolerated during the flux of the 19th and earlier 20th century, when the immigrant and agrarian population all were starting about equal and the "educated middle class" was open for the taking. But, as the society has matured, the inadequacy of the educational avenue—and particularly the English class—has become manifest. A child born into the proper family has acquired, by the age of three, the standard dialect and has achieved, by the time he goes to school, an intuitive awareness of the symbolic process of literature which permits him to pass through formal education at a rate impossible for those who first have to acquire the rudimentary tools. This is not a matter of either intelligence or aptitude. It is rather like throwing an English-speaking child into a Spanish-speaking first grade. As more and more children are born into proper middle-class families, the diversity in the public schools becomes so difficult to cope with that one may despair over the future of a common education. While this diversity shows itself in many ways, the chief emblem remains language—call it vulgarity, reading level, comprehension, or what you will. And those who teach the stylistics of Strunk and White or the complexities of Shakespeare and Hemingway simply drive the poles further asunder, for this is a level of language usage which is beyond the farthest ken of the disadvantaged."

—John C. Fischer, "Language as Emblem," *School and Society*

5. Teachers must simply abandon the theory that usages differ in quality, as between good and bad, correct and incorrect, and instead build their methods and reconstruct their emotional reactions on the plain facts that are already known in part to their pupils. Teacher and pupil must come to terms with each other—and of course all the burden of coming to terms must rest upon the one who is supposed to be wiser and better informed—on the basis that usages can be learned without condemning those which they replace, that the learner has an indefeasible right to speak as he likes without school penalties, while the teacher has no rights in this respect but only the duty to demonstrate what usages are profitable in the adult world. . . .

. . . you must not circle or cross out what he wrote—you owe at least this much to common decency.

Your aim should be to make the child's own resources available to him. He comes to you able, apparently, only to write simple sentences eight to twelve words long. Why? He is afraid to write the long compound sentences which he can and does use lavishly in conversation, because he has been regularly condemned for 'comma-faults'; he is afraid of complex sentences because his teachers have foolishly insisted that he was making the wrong clause subordinate; he has not been encouraged to experiment with devices like saying 'without noticing' and 'heedlessly' instead of adding two more clauses to the sentence, but has instead been slapped down for beginning a sentence with 'The trouble being. . . .' He confines himself to the eight-to-twelve-word simple sentence for one reason only: self-defense. In other words, he is inhibited.

—Martin Joos, "Language and the School Child,"
Harvard Educational Review

6. With respect to language study there is a clear goal for elementary education to reach in informal ways: students (urban, suburban, rural) should have understanding of the naturalness of language differences. Instead of "enriching" the lives of urban children by plugging them into a "second" dialect (if that enterprise is so "enriching": why don't we let everyone in for the fun and games; "enrich" the suburban kid with an urban dialect), we should be working to eradicate the language prejudice, the language mythology, that people grew into holding and believing. For there is clear evidence that the privileged use their false beliefs about language to the disadvantage of the deprived. One way to stop this is to change nonstandard dialect speakers into standard dialect speakers at least for some of the time, i.e. when the nonstandards are in the presence of the standards, currying favor of them, jobs of them, etc. This seems to me intolerable if not impossible. Another response to language differences would be to educate (especially the people in power) for tolerance of differences, for an understanding of differences. This could be naturally done, easily done in ele

mentary schools, but only by teachers who are themselves free of language prejudice. In many ways this is the more important kind of language study that needs
to be accomplished in the schools.

—Wayne A. O'Neil, "Paul Roberts' Rules of Order,"
The Urban Review

B.   In the forties and fifties, the battle over *"correct" versus "permissive"* usage consumed much of the time and energy of English teachers.
Study the echoes of this controversy in one of the following articles or in a
more recent article dealing with the same general topic. Describe the kind
of synthesis or compromise that seems to determine the author's perspective
on usage. Choose one:

Robert C. Pooley, "Teaching Usage Today and Tomorrow," *English
Journal*, 56 (May 1967), 742–746;

William Morris, "The Making of a Dictionary," *College Composition
and Communication,* 20 (October 1969), 198–203;

Paul Faris, "Two Views of English Usage," *College English*, 31 (May
1970), 836–44.

C.   In recent years, *standard English for the disadvantaged* has become
a hotly debated issue. The following articles reflect current arguments
over relevant linguistic knowledge, the effectiveness of new methods, and
underlying social and political assumptions. Your instructor may ask you
to present and defend one key position in the controversy as part of a panel
discussion staged by your class. Choose one, or a more recent contribution:

Raven I. McDavid, Jr., and Virginia Glenn McDavid, "The Relationship
of the Speech of American Negroes to the Speech of Whites," *American
Speech*, 26 (February 1951), 3–17;

Virginia F. Allen, "Teaching Standard English as a Second Dialect,"
Teachers College Record, 68 (February 1967), 355–370;

San-su C. Lin, "Disadvantaged Student? or Disadvantaged Teacher?,"
English Journal, 56 (May 1967) 751–756;

William R. Slager, "Effecting Dialect Change Through Oral Drill,"
English Journal, 56 (November 1967), 1166–1176;

Luis F. Hernandez, "Teaching English to the Culturally Disadvantaged
Mexican-American Student," *English Journal*, 57 (January 1968), 87–92, 121;

John C. Fisher, "Generating Standard Sentence Patterns—And Beyond," *College Composition and Communication*, 21 (December 1970),
364–368;

James Sledd, "Bi-Dialectalism: The Linguistics of White Supremacy,"
English Journal, 58 (December 1969), 1307–1315, 1329;

Wayne O'Neil, "The Politics of Bidialectalism," *College English*, 33
(January 1972), 433–438.

D. How do *current dictionaries* treat informal English and slang? Study the treatment of some of the following items in dictionaries, including *Webster's Seventh Collegiate, Webster's New World, Random House Dictionary, Standard College Dictionary,* and *American Heritage Dictionary.* Which of the items do *you* consider informal or slangy? How can you tell? *How* informal or slangy are they?

1. second-rate, so-so, blah
2. monkeyshines, monkey business, monkey around, grease monkey, monkey on my back
3. straphanger, road hog, hot rod, jalopy, meter maid
4. sit tight, lie low, sit pretty, hang loose, hold steady
5. wishy-washy, hoity-toity, topsy-turvy, slap-happy, punch drunk

E. In 1960, Robert C. Pooley listed the following items, once widely condemned by English teachers, as now "tolerated at least, and in some instances . . . in very general use":

1. *will* instead of *shall*
2. split infinitive ("to *sincerely* approve")
3. *like* as a conjunction ("like I said")
4. *different than*
5. "he is one of those boys who *is* . . ."
6. *myself* as a polite substitute for *I* or *me* ("I understand you will meet Mrs. Jones and *myself* at the station")
7. *the reason is because*
8. plain form (instead of possessive) before a verbal noun ("imagine *John*—instead of *John's*—winning a scholarship")

Study the current treatment of several of these items in *three current language texts* or handbooks of English intended for school or college.

F. The following assignments will give you a chance to explore areas of usage that are of concern to English teachers.

1. The following scene is from Lorraine Hansberry's *A Raisin in the Sun*, a play about a Negro family in Chicago. Study the scene carefully and then answer the following questions:
　　(1) What familiar features of nonstandard English appear here?
　　(2) Does this selection show anything about the use of different kinds of language on different occasions?
　　(3) What kind of people are these—how are they presented by the author? How does this selection confirm your ideas about speakers of nonstandard English? How does it change them?
　　Walter I want so many things that they are driving me kind of crazy . . . Mama—look at me.

Mama   I'm looking at you. You a good-looking boy. You got a job, a nice wife, a fine boy and—

Walter   A job. (*Looks at her*) Mama, a job? I open and close car doors all day long. I drive a man around in his limousine and I say, "Yes, sir; no, sir; very good, sir; shall I take the Drive, sir?" Mama, that ain't no kind of job . . . that ain't nothing at all. (*Very quietly*) Mama, I don't know if I can make you understand.

Mama   Understand what, baby?

Walter (*Quietly*)   Sometimes it's like I can see the future stretched out in front of me—just plain as day. The future, Mama. Hanging over there at the edge of my days. Just waiting for me—a big, looming blank space—full of *nothing*. Just waiting for *me* (Pause) Mama—sometimes when I'm downtown and I pass them cool, quiet-looking restaurants where them white boys are sitting back and talking 'bout things . . . sitting there turning deals worth millions of dollars . . . sometimes I see guys don't look much older than me—

Mama   Son—how come you talk so much 'bout money?

Walter (*With immense passion*)   Because it is life, Mama.

Mama (*Quietly*)   Oh—(*Very quietly*) So now it's life. Money is life. Once upon a time freedom used to be life—now it's money. I guess the world really do change . . .

Walter   No—it was always money, Mama. We just didn't know about it.

Mama   No . . . something has changed. (*She looks at him*) You something new, boy. In my time we was worried about not being lynched and getting to the North if we could and how to stay alive and still have a pinch of dignity too . . . Now here come you and Beneatha—talking 'bout things we ain't never even thought about hardly, me and your daddy. You ain't satisfied or proud of nothing we done. I mean that you had a home; that we kept you out of trouble till you was grown, that you don' have to ride to work on the back of nobody's streetcar—You my children—but how different we done become.

2.   Nonstandard English is spoken in many different parts of the United States. The following sentences have been taken from novels by John Steinbeck, Claude Brown, and Marjorie Kinnan Rawlings. The sentences illustrate nonstandard English used in a California farm community; in Harlem, New York City; and in a rural community in northeastern Florida. Point out all features of nonstandard English here illustrated. How authentic are they? How widespread are they? How would you normally react to them? Why?

   A.   *California farm community*
 1.   I've knew him for a long time.
 2.   That dog is so old he can't hardly walk.
 3.   They was so little.
 4.   I been mean, ain't I?
 5.   If them other guys gets in jails, they can rot.
 6.   You taking his pay away from him?
 7.   Answer when you're spoke to.
 8.   Know what he done Christmas?
 9.   Brang a gallon of whiskey right in here.
10.   Suppose he don't want to talk?

   B.   *Harlem, New York City*

1. Boy, why you so bad?
2. I'll tell you what they is.
3. Who teached you how to work roots?
4. I didn't get no gooder.
5. You only been back in New York three months and four days.
6. Mama want you.
7. I seen him do that.
8. He got too much devil in him to be tricked by them root workers.
9. In a couple of weeks, all you children going home.
10. I even got badder than I was.

C. *Rural community in northeastern Florida*

1. How's Jody to learn to hunt if his daddy don't carry him along and learn him?
2. I had to look after the rest of them till they was old enough to shuffle around for theirselves.
3. You climb up this here live oak.
4. I takened a shot at him.
5. The minute I shot, I knowed I was high.
6. Leave me have it, Pa.
7. That school teacher didn't scarcely know.
8. You said no man couldn't live on Baxter's Island without the Forresters was his friends.
9. If a fellow can't get out and shoot it for hisself, venison has a mighty fancy taste to him.
10. He's lucky he didn't get his fine nose broke.

3. The following paper is a student's attempt to imitate a certain variety of American folk speech. How successful is he? What features, idioms, familiar sayings, etc., seem authentic? Why, or why not? What kind of mentality, outlook, or atmosphere goes with this kind of talk? How well did the student reproduce it?

It was a lovely creek, really it was; winding down there by the mill below Roger's Bluff. Don't ask me why they called it Roger's, but they do, and always have. Well, this creek see, was as smooth as a mirror's reflection and moved slow like the stars. Red Creek 'twas called. Don't ask me why they called it Red, but they do, and always have. Some folks say it got its name from the Civil War. They say up creek a ways the Blue and Gray met and tangled. It's said their blood made the waters turn crimson red. Anyways, that's what it was called. The thing was as darn near as quiet as sunlight, but don't let that fool ya' for it 'twas a mite bit cool to the touch. The Coloreds' used to fish down there. Even was a favorite swimming hole of us here, when we's was young. Ya' know that's over now. Trees towered over that creek. Made it nice and cool. With all them bushes, it looked like someplace out of them jungle movies: real nice. Saul, the post clerk, says they's was going to build a park along the sides of that creek. But don't pay no mind to Saul fer he don't know a turtle from a toady frog. Bet ya' think it was a little creek, don't ya'? Heck, ya' couldn't throw a rock across it if ya' was a standing in the middle. Well, almost that big . . . but it wasn't no puny trickle either. Really no need to argue about it for that's over now. Paper says

nearly a thousand cars can park around them big stores. Even got a movie house.
Yes sir, a big 'en too.

Well anyway, it was a lovely creek, really it was.

4.   Herbert Kohl printed the following paper written by a Puerto Rican boy in his *Teaching the "Unteachable"* (New York: The New York Review, 1967), pp. 45–46. You be the linguist: How well does this student manage in his use of American English? What patterns, idioms, parts of the educated vocabulary, etc., has he mastered? What are his major problems with "school English"? (Your instructor may send you out to collect and study similar examples of spoken or written English as used by bilingual Americans.)

One cold rainy day I was going to school and I had to go 1,000 miles to get there and there wasn't no cars and no buses and train so I had to walk. I got soke a wet. I still had 500 more miles to go at last I almost got there and went I got there the school was close and I thought for a minute and then I remember it was a haliday and then I droped deid.

It rains too much and my flowers vegetable and gardens they get too much water. I got to think of something fast because if it keeps on like this my plants can't grow. So one day I was walking in the street when I saw this store selling rain supplies so I went in and got some then I went back home and I had one that will just rite rain so I planted in the ground and the next day I couldn't believe my eyes all the plants were just growing up. So I live happly ever after.

I just don't like to think because every time I think I get a headache because one time I was thinking about the world fair and I build a mental picture in my mind I was enjoying myself then I stop thinking. I was going home went suddenly I felt something in my mind and I got a headache and I was criing because my mind hurt. From that day on I can't think.

It happens every time I go to bed I forget to brush your teeth. Then the second time I forget to brush your teeth. Then the second time I forgot the third time I forgot too so I had to do something, so one day I was very sleepy I was going to my bed then sudently I open my eyes then I remember and I ran back to bath tob and I brush my teeth you didn't got me this time so I went back to bed and then every single day I brush my teeth live happly ever after.

(Carlos, age 12)

5.   When do questions of usage become part of larger questions about style? How fully are you aware of the register of different styles that we draw on different occasions? Study the following example of *possible* ways of saying roughly the same thing. What sets them apart? How important are the differences? Write two or three similar sets.

Listener expressing his disagreement with the speaker:
    A. Well, bud, that is the stupidest thing I ever heard.
    B. Well, sir, I'll have to disagree with that.
    C. I couldn't agree with you more, but there are some points that I'd like to clear up.
    D. Pardon me, but I believe you are mistaken.
    E. Has it occurred to you that for once you might be wrong?
    F. Your position on this issue is not in accordance with the best thinking currently available.
    G. I've heard a lot of crap in my time, but this really takes the cake.
    H. Come on—you don't really expect me to go along with that.

Chapter 4

Composition as a Creative Process

The Rhetoric of Order—The Rhetoric of Discovery—The Rhetoric of Confrontation—The Creative Spark

When we teach composition, we are close to the center of English as a subject. Whatever else we do, we are ultimately concerned with the student's ability to use language for his own purposes. As English teachers, we start from the fact that man uses language. He uses language to record his observations, to express his feelings, to verbalize his needs. He uses language to interpret the past and to map out the future. He uses words to reach out to his fellows, to plead with them, to make them do his bidding. When we work with oral composition, we stress the spontaneity, the immediacy of live language use. When we work with written composition, we stress what makes a more lasting impact. We stress what we can go back to—to ponder it, to learn from it, to put it to future use.

The most basic task in teaching composition is to convince the student of its *rewards*. Recent decades have seen a massive shift to the teaching of both oral and written discourse as a source of positive satis-faction. As a speaker and as a writer, the student has to feel that he is learning what he can do with words. He is learning what words can do for him rather than to him. Especially when we teach writing, the student has to have a chance to become motivated by its *built-in* incentives:

(1) Most simply, writing is a way of *responding to experience*. Anyone who has done any honest writing has to that extent become more observant, more aware. Even the most elementary writing task requires the writer to take something in, to pay attention to something that he otherwise might have passed by. The first thing that a writer learns is to be *receptive*. To write anything worth reading, the student writer must experience the kind of satisfaction that the author of the fol-lowing paper felt when he relived a part of his past:

I SKATE FOR A LONG TIME

My legs are pushing, gliding, pushing, gliding as I skim along the ice in pursuit of my shadow. I skate for a long time. I leave the ring of firelight and friends and skate out into the darkness.

On and on I skate, to the end of the pond and up the small brook that is its source. Now I feel like an explorer. I'm one of Roger's Rangers, scouting this body of water for Indians. But finally I tire of my game and sit on a tree trunk to rest. Now that I've stopped, I'm aware of the dead silence of winter. This spot in summer would be alive with the sounds of insects and birds. Now there is nothing. The land is cold and silent. And the sky is huge and silent. In this silence, I imagine myself to be the only person in the universe. I sit and try to think grave thoughts, worthy of this unique position. But finally the cold begins to penetrate my clothes and I know it's time to start back.

Arriving back at the pond, I find everyone gone. Putting my boots on beside the glowing embers of the almost dead fire, I find myself hoping that my mother will have some hot cocoa waiting when I get home.

I, who was him, know that there will be cocoa there, served by a warm, loving mother. I also know that he'll take them for granted just as he's taken tonight for granted. As I watch him trudging towards home, I can't help but wish that I could speak to him and tell him how precious this time of life is. But I can't, and it'll be ten years before he realizes it himself.[1]

(2) We derive a second basic satisfaction from writing as a means of *thinking things through*. As we ponder a subject, as we explore a question, we experience the satisfaction of seeing something come into

focus. We say to ourselves, "First I was confused, but now I *see*. I begin to *understand*." As we explain an incident to ourselves, as we sort out miscellaneous data, something that was at first confusing, frustrating, alienating begins to fall into place. The student writer must come to experience the satisfaction we feel when, on a given subject, we know we have something to *say*. He must feel the satisfaction the author of the following paper felt when he explained to himself the *meaning* of something that had been a part of his life:

ENJOY

My father is a ten-gallon-hat man, big and tall. When he opened a bag of potato chips, he never ate any himself; he gave them to me: this was satisfaction, knowing I was happy. My brothers and I could never enjoy ourselves enough for him. "Enjoy life while you can. Have fun," he would say. "Don't study so hard."

Sometimes I carried my books home, wearing them between my shirt and my chest, and then hid with them and some crackers in the attic next to the grayed windows with light filtering through and down upon me. The attic smelled of stale dry air. There I could lie and read.

Then my father would roar up the stairs. "Why don't you go play baseball? Enjoy yourself!"

I stood up without answering.

"Your mother said you were playing baseball, but I said I'd find you reading!"

I studied his watch.

"I worked hard, studied long hours, and got little sleep all my life. Saturday is not a day to study. Hah?"

I couldn't say anything.

"What's the matter, cat got your tongue? Don't you feel good? You want to lay down?"

"I want to go outside and enjoy myself," I finally said. Instead of taking it up or carrying it any further, he would let it drop.

My father had worked hard all his life. He never had any time to enjoy life until he was older. For these reasons he always wanted me to enjoy life.

(3) Finally, a writer *interacts with other people*. He participates actively in a dialogue. Somewhere early in his apprenticeship the student writer must come to experience the satisfaction we feel when we cease to be a mere echo. We cease to ask anxiously: "What is expected? What do they want?" Writing is a way of establishing our identity and of having

it recognized by others. A writer must start to tell himself: "I am *not* at the mercy of other people's fixed ideas. I can use words to get out from under. I can make people listen to *my* point of view. I can make them take notice—perhaps even make them think." The following student paper reflects the writer's satisfaction in *not* repeating the clichés. It reflects his satisfaction in making us listen to words that suit *his* experience and *his* purposes rather than those of someone else:

ZAP! POW!

For years now, the "experts" have preached with hellfire-and-brimstone enthusiasm against all the violence and sordid excitement contained in the comic books. There have even been attempts by irate mothers and other concerned people to have state and even federal legislatures pass laws of censorship concerning comic books and their publishers. All of this activity has arisen from the belief that comics provoke the young mind to thoughts of violence and crime by somehow giving the underworld a romantic appeal, which destroys the developing conscience nurtured by the child's parents. This claim, however, is all an unsubstantiated alarmist's myth.

I feel that I speak with some degree of authority on this subject, having been a dedicated and impassioned young follower of Superman, Batman, Green Lantern, and the rest. Likewise, my father and my uncle before me, and all my friends have also walked through the valley of moral and spiritual death of the comic book. I am sure that you, the reader, have also read at least two or three of these subversive publications in your younger days. And, somehow, all of us, I, my father, my uncle, and perhaps you yourself, have weathered the destruction, the incurable damage perpetrated upon our once young and impressionable little brains. Indeed, thousands upon thousands and by far the vast majority of young comic book readers, like ourselves, have matured into the adult world without any latent effects whatsoever.

I consider myself to have been a somewhat typical fan of the funny books, and, in retrospect, they were actually an important benefactor of my development. The comics were an intermediate step between first-grade "Run, Spot, run, run, run!" and the later, more sophisticated enjoyment of *Black Beauty*. It is because of the comics that my interest in reading developed, for, at the age at which one masters its techniques, the plots must be simple, the action funny or exciting (and in the comics they certainly are) in order to retain the wandering attention of young readers. . . .

Perhaps the most immediate factor concerning the young is the vast amount of pleasure they find in lying on the floor on a drizzly day and donning Superman's uniform to apprehend Evil and to make things right for Metropolis. This is what is important: letting a child have the food his hungry imagination desires, food of which comic books are a source.

Instruction in writing is beginning to take when students write with some sense of satisfaction, with some sense of accomplishment. A composition program has to be flexible enough so that we can persist and improvise and change course as necessary to produce this kind of student response. Since each student, and each generation of students, is to some extent different, an authentic composition program is always to some extent improvised from day to day: We bring in a dittoed copy of an editorial or a student theme, we try out new assignments, we experiment with new ways of getting the student involved. Even so, a pattern will emerge over the year, and over the years—shaped by the teacher's past experience, his tacit assumptions, his response to larger trends.

THE RHETORIC OF ORDER

How we plan our schedule of writing assignments, what we say about the work of professional writers, what we say or don't say about "how to write"—all these reflect assumptions about what writing is or should be. In selecting papers for discussion, in reacting to what a student has said, we show what kind of writing we value. All teaching of composition implies some kind of **rhetoric**—some more or less systematic understanding of what writing is, how it is produced, and by what standards it should be judged. What we say about the topic sentence or the mixed metaphor is not really neutral—it implies larger assumptions about what gives good writing its strength, its honesty, its relevance. These assumptions in turn are related to larger questions of the student's personal identity and commitment.

Every teacher who takes writing seriously to some extent asks his students to make themselves over in his image. The question for the teacher to ask himself is, What *is* that image? What is its validity? What are its larger implications beyond the classroom? Styles of writing are related to styles of thinking and feeling. Our standards of what is responsible or effective writing are related to our standards of what is responsible and effective in other kinds of behavior. Not surprisingly, the major schools of rhetoric that help shape our composition programs are related to major ways of thinking outside the classroom. These schools of rhetoric range from a conservative, traditional rhetoric of rational order, through a liberal rhetoric of discovery and inquiry, to a radical rhetoric of challenge and confrontation. Much of what we concretely teach about writing acquires a larger meaning as we relate it to these major prevailing points of view.

For many years, texts and programs seriously dealing with written composition were dominated by a conservative rhetoric that set up explicit goals, and that set out to reach these goals by direct precept and example. The conservative rhetoric was basically a rhetoric of order. Its definition of good writing stressed clear thinking and accurate expression. Its watchwords were ORDER, STRUCTURE, ORGANIZATION, COHERENCE, UNITY, CLARITY, EXACTNESS, ACCURACY, PRECISION, SIMPLICITY. Good writing was informative, purposeful, rational—free of degressions, repetition, and woolly ambiguities. To be educated meant to be able to use one's mind— use it to lay things out lucidly and coherently and to communicate the results. Much of the conservative rhetoric dealt with *obstacles* to order and clarity: inadequate logical categories, lack of transition, illogical comparisons, gaudy figures of speech, blurred popular uses of terms, disregard of exact historical or technical meanings, confusion of words similar or related, and the like.

The strength of the conservative rhetoric was that it did deal directly with basic requirements of communication. Its teachings could be verified by someone looking at a good solid piece of prose and asking: How does this writer get his point across? Why does he "make sense" when other people beat around the bush, confuse the issue, get bogged down? How does he carry the reader along from point to point? In class, the teacher could spend his time analyzing sample paragraphs and sample passages to show: This is the writer's plan. This is how he develops it. This is how this passage is put together. Teacher and student could concentrate on the virtues of the *finished product*. Ideally, following the teacher's precepts and emulating the models, the student writer would develop his own sense of structure, of direction, of purpose.

To this day, we turn to the conservative rhetoric if we want to identify the three or four rock-bottom qualities of successful writing. First, successful writing has **focus**. A successful writer does not just chat, mentioning one thing after another. *He does justice to one thing at a time.* He brings something into focus, and he stays with it long enough for us to say, "Yes, I see what you mean." The most basic question we ask of a writer is, What are you talking about? What is the point? What are you trying to prove? And what do you offer in *support* of your point, so that I may be sure it is worth attending to? Focused writing is to the point; it keeps the reader oriented:

Main Point: *Romantic love was not a major theme either in serious American literature on its highest level or in familiar American folklore.*
Example: After the first few chapters, *Moby Dick* has no female characters except mother whales. There were not many women, either,

Example: in the *great cycles of myth* that dealt with the wilderness, the river, the cattle ranges, and the mining camps. All consisted of stories about men, working or wandering, hunting, fighting, enduring hardships, getting rich, or running away from civilization,
Example: but seldom or never passionately in love. *Huck Finn* was of course too young for love, but all the familiar heroes were boys
Example: at heart. *Old Leatherstocking* died a bachelor.

(Malcolm Cowley)

Main Point: *Latin American culture has been and is a dynamic element in the development of our own.* It has, for example, furnished more
Example: than 2000 *place names* to the United States postal directory. Its
Example: *languages* have influenced American English, as such simple examples as "rodeo" and "vamoose" indicate. Its customs are part of our "Westerns" on television. Its *housing, its music, its dances, its*
Examples: *scenery, its ruins and its romance* have been imitated and admired
Example: in the United States. *One third of the continental area of* this republic was for a long period, as modern history goes, under the governance of Spanish viceroys or of Mexico. The largest single
Example: Christian church in the United States is identical with the *dominant church* in Latin America.

(Howard Mumford Jones)

  In the traditional sense of the term, the material in such a paragraph has relevance: It is relevant to the point at issue. The **topic sentence** states the main point; the paragraph as a whole develops it, backs it up. We may not agree with the point, but we know what the point is. We also know that there is enough to it for us to give it some serious consideration.

  The second basic quality of successful writing is closely related to the first: Successful writing has **coherence**. What the writer tells us should *hang together.* His ideas should be logically connected. We want to see how he moves from A to B, and from there to C. When a writer moves ahead logically, we don't have to ask "How did this get in here?" or "How does this follow?" If a piece of writing is to take the reader along, he has to see how one thing is related to the next. He has to see the logical link between two ideas:

Rule and Specific Example:

  Experience has made it quite apparent that marriage calls for mutual sacrifice. Most of the marriages that fail, marriage counselors tell us, fail because the partners lack this quality. Dishwashing, by general agreement, is a classic *example* of domestic drudgery that requires a sacrifice of the husband who shares in it. It is an excellent test of his willingness to do his share.

Effect and Its Cause:

Just about everyone likes biography. The *reason* for this is not hard to find. It is the pleasure we get in identifying ourselves with real people who have attained eminence of some sort. By the magic of biography we are transported out of ourselves into kings and queens, generals, poets, lovers, and bankers.

Cause and Its Effect:

In those days after the Civil War, it was the good women, wives and school-mistresses, who bought the books and read the magazines; most men read only the newspapers. To be successful an author had to please a feminine audience. Women liked love stories and *hence* the magazines were full of them, while all the popular novels ended to the peal of a wedding march.

Contrast of Then and Now:

Yesterday, African history, shutting out the colored man and all his cultures, began with Livingstone, Stanley, Cecil Rhodes, . . . *Today,* beginning with the arts of prehistoric peoples, it mentions explorers and European annexations as but tiresome, trivial interruptions.

Two Parts of One Process:

Your heart is divided into two parts, right and left, by a bloodtight wall. Each part forms a separate pump. Each of these two pumps, in turn, has *two interacting chambers*: *the auricle*, which receives blood into the heart from the veins, and *the ventricle*, which forces it out again into the body through the arteries.

One Major Category and the Next:

Among the perennial heroes of American comic strips, we thus see the super detectives, the *righteous crime fighters*: Dick Tracy, Robin Malone, . . . But equally strong seems to be the staying power of the familiar *comic stereotypes*: Dennis the Menace (the lovable, innocent-looking all-American boy who drives parents and neighbors out of their minds); Dagwood (the hen-pecked American husband); Bugs Bunny (the tough-talking dead-end kid).

Focus and coherence add up to the third basic quality of successful writing: Successful writing follows an overall *plan*. It is organized. There is a purposeful forward movement that carries the reader from the beginning through the middle to the end. Early in a piece of writing, the reader begins to feel that things are under control. He does not have to keep asking: "Where are we going? Where are we headed? What are you trying to do?" A successful writer lays out the subject for our inspection; we follow him without abrupt turnabouts, awkward backtrackings, or trails that lead nowhere. Among the paraphernalia of the conservative rhetoric, the **outline** is the test of whether the author has succeeded in reducing his subject to order:

Odysseus and Achilles as Epic Heroes

I. Odysseus as epic hero
    A. Great warrior (unsurpassed in archery, etc.)
    B. Accomplished orator (successful in pleading his own cause)
    C. Shrewd counselor (carefully weighing facts and situations)
    D. Very human character (loves good food and wine)
II. Achilles as epic hero
    A. Great warrior (triumphs over Hector)
    B. No great speaker (tends to be haughty and insolent)
    C. Impulsive person (quick to yield to resentment)
    D. Half divine (indifferent to food)

The author of this outline has not merely followed the chronological order of events or the plot outline of a book. *He has performed a service for the reader.* He has identified four major epic qualities and laid them out in a plausible scheme—going from the expected (warlike prowess) to the less obvious (great talker, shrewd plotter, prodigious eater). Once he has established this overall scheme, he has then arranged the qualities of the second epic hero in **parallel order**. He is thus lining things up for the reader—so that the reader can see the connections: the similarities, and the differences. Well-organized writing makes the reader feel: The author has thought this matter through, and I understand it better as a result.

Finally, along with a clear presentation of the larger logical relationships, the conservative rhetoric demanded clarity and accuracy in the use of words. It is true that in practice much time was spent in quibbling over minor verbal problems and confusions. It is doubtful that we really promote clear thinking by correcting the Founding Fathers' desire for a "more perfect union" to a desire for a "more *nearly* perfect union."

When we read in a passage by William Faulkner that "a horse . . . *infers* only weight and speed while Lion *inferred* not only courage . . . but endurance," we merely swim against the tide by changing *infer* to *imply*. But in spite of its pedantic quibbling, the conservative rhetoric did promote a *respect for words*. If a writer wants to communicate successfully, his words must have substance; they must have clear and substantial meaning. If we throw terms like *communist* and *fascist* at people merely because we are opposed to their ideas and their ways, these words cease to inform, to clarify, to denote. They become mere ignorant abuse. If we want to talk about politics in a way that informs and clarifies, we have to be prepared to say things like "democracy . . . by which I mean majority rule through elected representatives of all the people" or "fascism . . . by which I mean a strongly nationalistic ideology that tends toward a quasi-military organization of many aspects of a nation's life." By asking, "What exactly do you mean?" the teacher teaching composition in the conservative mode helps keep alive our respect for language as a common medium, for words as common currency.

The conservative rhetoric assumes that a person "whose language is muddled cannot have a very clear understanding of anything that has to be put into words." Part of our job as teachers then is "the hard job of clarifying our students' language and the thought it constitutes."[2] Ideally, the student will come to see that communication is something people have to *work at*. He will see what it takes to make words meaningful that we often use loosely, in a spirit of easy rejection or of self-congratulation:

> What do I mean by *narrow-mindedness*? I have seen it in many different situations, all of which reveal a preoccupation with the idea of moral standards. Narrow-minded people from what I have observed have one idea of good and another completely different one of what is bad. Everything that happens from day to day will fall either into their strict category of good or the category of bad. There is no between, no median. If something is good, all possibilities of bad are immediately removed. The narrow-minded person is so affected by one small sign of something bad that he fails to remain objective in viewing a situation. He greatly exaggerates the degree of badness that exists. This tendency to misjudge characterizes a narrow mind. Inevitably there will be bad as well as good, and the narrow-minded person as a result will view life from the bad side.   (Student Theme)

For years, teachers who were serious about composition taught the topic sentence, the formal outline, the thesis sentence, the formal definition, and other paraphernalia of a clarity-and-order rhetoric. Not surprisingly, composition thus taught was a serious business. There was something grim and literal-minded about it. There was something *too* solid, too orderly, too rigid about its formulas and categories. Strong on what gives writing structure and clarity, the conservative rhetoric was weak on what gives writing life and sparkle, what makes it human. It was too intolerant of the unpredictable *personal* element in writing: the revealing aside, the apparent digression, honest bafflement, confused but honest feeling. A revealing feature was its lack of interest in **humor**— in irony and sarcasm, in whimsy, in the oddball element in language. The traditional text had nary a good word for such verbal fauna as the lowly pun (Herb Caen: "Today's Brownie is tomorrow's cookie"). Sad to say, the most entertaining, and often the most human passages in a conservative textbook were the horrible examples—the verbal accidents, the inspired malapropisms, the garbled metaphors:

> Israel and Egypt are now separated by the sewage canal.
> Socrates died of an overdose of wedlock.
> Contralto is a low form of music that only ladies sing.
> Platonic love is a relationship in which sexual relations are illuminated.

Generally, the treatment of style in a conservative rhetoric is too cautionary, too restrictive. Mixed metaphors, extravagant comparisons, and bad puns may not promote clear thinking, but they do lend a touch of color to the passing day:

> In this poem, the poet seems to be coming out of a dream world and stepping into the face of reality.
>
> In such ripe discourse as this the syllables literally crawl with maggots of meaning for the epicure with a stomach for poetic Gorgonzola.
>
> The Congressman insults his constituents' intelligence by dragging a red herring into the arena and by wrapping himself in the mantle of his war record to shield himself from honest criticism.
>
> Once we legitimate burghers meekly fall for this whopping non sequitur reasoning, we will be sitting ducks from then on for every ivory tower nut who wants us to chain the front wheels together every time we put the car in a parking lot. . . . Unless we step firmly upon this burgeoning toadstool of a trend, we will end up with laws compelling us to bar all the doors and shutter the windows before we leave the house to walk the dog.

Stepping too firmly and too routinely on the burgeoning toadstools in the students' prose, the conservative teacher by and large encouraged a gray, drab "theme" style in which ultimately neither weeds nor flowers had a chance to grow.

ON HIGH SCHOOL STUDENTS

To be a member of the "in crowd" is to be the chosen one of a small world. You're the darling of campus life with control over everything from campus politics to the major social events of the year. In the case of the boys you're either a super jock or a super stud. Girls are always either a fox or a rah-rah girl for the teams . . . Then we come to the "really into's." They are forever trying to solve all the world's ills with one simple solution—whatever it is that they are really into. The subjects for "really intoing" are endless. You can be into anything from politics to natural food fads . . . Our last group is the majority group but also the most inactive one. For these reasons we'll call them "breathers." The name is really self-explanatory. Their biggest contribution is just breathing and existing.   J.M.

My classes always possessed at least one uncompromising conservative with very forceful opinions, so that it created a right-wing atmosphere from which my ears never rested. For example, one girl was a strong-headed Republican, a dedicated Mormon, and teetering on the edge of John Birchism. She had a great reverence for the flag and her country, but hated certain peoples that existed in her great America—blacks, Mexicans, Jews, and so on. She was a staunch supporter of white supremacy, with the school whitened beyond salvation to her pleasure. E.P.

The extremist or radical are extreme in their hair and dress modes. The outwardly appearance they project is somewhat "early truckdriver," they choose clothes strictly for comfort and not appearance, they give a bit of a slobbish appearance. Dirty dungarees, and tie-dyed Tee shirts are the garb of the day. The "frizzes" are the "in-look" in hair styles, and everything is strictly "anti-establishment." They are rebelling against the so-called establishment's ideas and morality, and the simplest and most easily recognizable methods are to display their feelings through their clothes. It's not that they are lazy or unclean, it's that they are trying to show that they are individuals and are of a different generation than their parents, and like it that way. T.K.

I guess my best friend was a "plastic hippy" or a phoney hippy. He was an outspoken left-wing radical. He was always talking about protest and overthrow. His idol was Che Guevara and the revolutionary movement. He dressed in blue, holy levis, long hair, T-shirts, a fringe jacket and mocassins. He didn't care much for social life because he was a sworn individualist. I guess that I saw through his act because I was his best friend.   S.P.

There are only a handful of people sympathetic to social injustices. When it comes to social matters, I have never met a completely sincere person . . . I do feel that some of my class-mates were deeply concerned with social problems. They would volunteer their minds and souls to work in mentally retarded homes or join organizations to help raise funds for poverty-stricken people. I think these people found some meaning in life and wanted to share it with less fortunate individuals. Members of this group are deep thinkers, hard workers, strong believers in equality of the sexes, races, religions, nationalities, and most of all *real* human beings.

This excessive rigidity in matters of style was a symptom of a more basic problem: We live in an age and in a society that has become increasingly hostile to predetermined patterns. Confronted with rigid categories set up by someone else, we feel hemmed in; we feel pushed. We do not have enough breathing space. Young people, especially, today have an almost paranoid suspicion of **structure**, believing that each group, like each individual, "must stumble on its own toward a sensible structure, beginning from scratch, from raw experience."[3] The fatal flaw of the conservative rhetoric was that it did not make sufficient allowance for this process of stumbling, for the search. It did not allow for the questioning that a person must go through if he wants to find answers of his own. The traditional approach often seemed to imply that order exists, that the student can put familiar patterns to work for him the way we take tools down from a rack. The conservative rhetoric typically dealt with finished patterns. It said little about how the student would work out the patterns that would fit his own experience. It said little about how he would find the answers to his own questions.

Modern literature and modern art have long been hostile to the kind of established order that the conservative rhetoric implies. When we send our students to the theater, what they find is not a theater of order, or a theater of clarity, but a theater of the absurd. After we define the anecdote as "a story with a point," the next anecdote the student reads may be similar to this one from Ionesco's *The Bald Soprano*:

> *Mr. Smith:* I'll tell you one: "The Snake and the Fox." Once upon a time, a snake came up to a fox and said: "It seems to me that I know you!" The fox replied to him: "Me too." "Then," said the snake, "give me some money." "A fox doesn't give money," replied the tricky animal, who, in order to escape, jumped down into a deep ravine full of strawberries and chicken honey. But the snake was there waiting for him with a Mephistophelean laugh. The fox pulled out his knife, shouting: "I'm going to teach you how to live!" Then he took to flight, turning his back. But he had no luck. The snake was quicker. With a well-chosen blow of his fist, he struck the fox in the middle of his forehead, which broke into a thousand pieces, while he cried: "No! No! Four times no! I'm not your daughter."[4]

So much for coherence! The point of this anecdote is that it does not have a point. Like Ionesco's plays, much modern literature rebels against conventional patterns found to be too constraining, too superficial, or too irrelevant.

Once teachers began to sense the discrepancy between the traditional rhetoric taught on Monday and the modern literature they taught on Tuesday, they became receptive to ways of teaching writing that were more nearly in harmony with the modern temper. English teaching as a profession had long suffered from a fundamental paradox: Teachers who tended to be liberal in their political sympathies assumed an extremely conservative stance in their attitude toward language and composition. A gradual but pervading shift toward a more modern rhetoric made it possible for teachers to bring their teaching of composition more nearly into harmony with who they were as people.

THE RHETORIC OF DISCOVERY

Over the years, textbooks for composition have shifted the emphasis from the finished product to *how the finished product is produced*. Conventional instruction used to offer the student orderly outlines and tidy patterns. But when he looked in his own mind, he found confusion, half-formed ideas. The real question for the student always was how to *arrive* at something ordered and substantial. The real question now is how the student can *generate* something worth writing down.

Writing is a creative process. The art of writing is the art of making up our minds. When we start, our first impressions are contradictory, our memory faulty, our information incomplete. To make any headway, we go through a crucial preliminary stage of exploration, investigation, discovery. We allow for the inevitable woolgathering, discouragements, and false starts. Gradually, something takes shape. Something comes into focus. We are bringing together material. We are *working out* an overall pattern.

When we stress the **process** of composition instead of the product, we start further back. We spend less time trying to strengthen and revise and polish *after the fact* something that was not substantial enough from the beginning. We ask: What does it take? We begin to realize that much depends on what the writer *brings* to the job. A good writer has to be receptive. He must know how to take things in before he starts to hold forth. He must be willing to learn. His typical response to a question or a problem is: Let me think about it. Let me check this out. Let me see what I can do.

As a rhetoric of discovery replaces the rhetoric of order, a new set of catchwords replaces the old insistence on coherence, unity, and clarity. We begin to make a virtue of OPENMINDEDNESS, SCEPTICISM, TENTATIVENESS, FLEXIBILITY, DIVERSITY, DIALOGUE. We become more tolerant of COMPLEXITY, IRONY, PARADOX. We put the emphasis on authentic observation, openness to experience. We encourage honest doubt. We prize the qualities that make for productive thinking.

A modern "liberal" rhetoric thus shifts the emphasis from the writer's finished work to the actual working of the writer. It presents composition not as a "putting forth of a something that is already there" but as a "putting together." Writing becomes a "laboring *toward*" form and organization. We start with the "clashing thoughts and feelings, ideas and urgings that jangle in the personality." We take in information as "what we think with" and about. We go through a process of shaping and molding and ordering that involves the resolution of discords, the compromising with difficulties, a "coming to terms with counter-forces."[5] This kind of writing and thinking should serve us well in the diverse and changing modern world, where the truths we live by "are tentative and subject to change"; where we must be "discoverers of new truths as well as preservers and transmitters of the old."[6]

Emphasis upon the process of discovery has a far-reaching effect on what teachers do in the classroom from day to day. Basically, we spend less time describing the destination and more time discussing how to get there. In fact, teaching composition in the liberal mode, we may first find it necessary to *clear away the obstacles* to any true exploration. We may first have to break down the barriers, to remove the blinders. Before true discovery becomes possible, we have to do battle against ready-made ideas, hand-me-down ideals, secondhand abstractions. The student cannot do any honest writing as long as every assignment produces only tired familiar notions, received ideas, dutiful sentiments. Writing honestly taught cannot help tending toward a kind of intellectual awakening, a broadening of perspective. It produces a kind of urban renewal of the mind.

Thus, before the student writer can start taking an honest look at actual people, we may have to wean him from the **stereotypes** that provide a lazy set of ready-made attitudes toward a whole group: the bungling woman driver, the monocled Prussian Junker, the ivory-tower intellectual, the money-grubbing businessman, the corrupt politician. The student who is lazily repeating snide clichés about politicians should be made to confront the testimony of someone who knows them in their natural habitat:

> I like politicians. Ever since I started work as a city-hall reporter in New Mexico some thirty years ago, I have spent a lot of time in their company— *in smoke-filled rooms, jails, campaign trains, shabby courthouse offices, Senate cloakrooms, and the White House itself.* Mostly I've been reporting their doings, but on occasion I have served them *as speech writer, district leader, campaign choreboy, and civil servant.* On the whole, they have proved better company than any other professional group I've had a chance to know well . . .
> —John Fischer, "Please Don't Bite the Politicians," *Harper's*

Before the student can write honestly about any social issue, we may have to bring him face to face with the brutal prejudices of the callous and the fortunate—and then confront him with authentic testimony from the other side, from the people at the receiving end:

> The area in which the fruit workers live is typically rundown, dirty and depressing. These people don't care; it is the way they were brought up, and for most of them, this is the way they will live until they die. I knew families on welfare who worked harvesting crops during the summer and spent the time drinking during the winter. The more kids they produce, the more money flows in for cars, color T.V., and drinks. What an easy life!
>
> (Student theme)

> . . . one day in the second week of picking, when the hops were good and I stayed grimly sweating over my long gray sack hung on a child-sized frame, I knew that this was going to be the day. As the afternoon waned and I added the figures on my weight tags over and over again in my head, I could feel the excitement begin making spasms in my stomach. That night the man at the pay window handed me a silver dollar and three pennies. He must have seen that this was a day not for paper but for silver. The big coin, so neatly and brightly stamped, was coolly distant from the blurred mélange of piled vines and melting heat that had put it into my hand. Only its solid heaviness connected it in a businesslike way with the work it represented. For the first time in my life I truly comprehended the relationship between toil and media of exchange, and I saw how exacting and yet how satisfying were the terms of the world.
>
> —Lois Phillips Hudson, "Children of the Harvest"

As familiar notions clash with new ideas, the student learns something basic: Honest writing is not simply a matter of recording one's "opinions." It is often first of all a matter of clearing away preconceptions, of cutting through the fog. It is a matter of finding some foundation for an opinion *that is worth writing down.* In honest writing, the writer, as well as the reader, learns something from the experience. Honest writing leads through the kind of inquiry that, when necessary, makes the writer change his mind:

Previous Opinion: People on welfare are loafers who prefer the easy money to honest hard work.

Results of Inquiry: Of the about eight million on relief, more than two million, mostly women, are 65 or over; more than 700,000 are totally blind or disabled; almost four million are children whose parents cannot support them; about one million are their mothers; about 100,000 are their physically or mentally incapacitated fathers. Less than 100,000 are "able-bodied men."

A basic part of the liberal teacher's program is to help students "escape the narrow cabin" they "had lived in for so many years at home and at school."[7] In part he will do this by discouraging reliance on the secondhand and the ready-made. But much of the time he will do the same thing more positively and more directly. *To write honestly, the student writer must relate words honestly to his own authentic experience.* He must try to make the word fit the thing. He must learn to respect the map-making function of language; he must learn something about the way an honest map does justice to the stubborn contours of the terrain.

Honest words are anchored in the experience of the writer. The same word means different things to people with different experiences. The word *welfare,* for instance, means one thing to the journalist who watches a Hollywood actress collect unemployment compensation when she cannot find a TV part just right for her:

> In Hollywood the quaint idea that the dole line is a squalid place, steeped in the shadow of shame, is dramatically dispelled. Here it is the most light-hearted joblessness, not to say larceny, within the boundless reaches of the welfare state. Here, they receive the dole and it's like an honorary degree. . . . They tell of movie luminaries pulling up in Rolls-Royces and Bentleys. While master gets in line inside, chauffeur retires to the donut shack on the corner to have a hot dog. . . . They tell of the mink-clad wives of producers in the $50,000 bracket, who, as sometime actresses, also qualify for compensation and stride in to collect their $65 a week without blinking a lash.
> —Jordan Bonfante, "Cash on the Line," *Life*

But "welfare" meant something completely different to Dick Gregory when in his autobiography he described what it meant to his family to be on relief:

> I remember how the social worker would poke around the house, wrinkling her nose at the coal dust on the chilly linoleum floor, shaking her head at the bugs crawling over the dirty dishes in the sink. My Momma would have to stand there and make like she was too lazy to keep her own house clean. She could never let on that she spent all day cleaning another woman's house for two dollars and carfare. She would have to follow that nasty woman around those drafty three rooms, keeping her fingers crossed that the telephone hidden in the closet wouldn't ring. Welfare cases weren't supposed to have telephones . . . she couldn't explain that while she was out spoon-feeding somebody else's kids, she was worrying about her own kids, that she could rest her mind by picking up the telephone and calling us—to find out if we had bread for our baloney or baloney for our bread, to see if any of us had gotten run over by the streetcar while we played in the gutter, to make sure the house hadn't burnt down from the papers and magazines we stuffed in the stove when the coal ran out.   —Dick Gregory, *Nigger*

To get our students to use words as an honest exploration of their own experience, we have to convince them that one authentic incident, honestly told, is worth many dutiful sentiments about school spirit or student government. But at the same time, *we* must be prepared to accept the student's honest contribution. Honest writing is not necessarily always "gutsy," provocative, challenging, "different." When we ask students to be open to experience, we must convince them that we mean open to *their* experience—ordinary experience, common settings, everyday people as they are. We must manage to give them a sense for the beauty of ordinary things—when we stop to observe them, when we begin to notice. This is the spirit, for instance, of some of Hemingway's prose when it does *not* deal with climactic moments but simply with a world that is real, whose beauty is that it exists:

> Nick laid the bottle full of jumping grasshoppers against a pine trunk. Rapidly he mixed some buckwheat flour with water and stirred it smooth, one cup of flour, one cup of water. He put a handful of coffee in the pot and dipped a lump of grease out of a can and slid it sputtering across the hot skillet. On the smoking skillet he poured smoothly the buckwheat batter. It spread like lava, the grease spitting sharply. Around the edges the buckwheat cake began to firm, then brown, then crisp. The surface was bubbling slowly to porousness. Nick pushed under the browned under surface with a fresh pine chip. He shook the skillet sideways and the cake was loose on the surface. I won't try and flop it, he thought. He slid the chip of clean wood all the way under the cake, and flopped it over onto its face. It sputtered in the pan.
>
> —Ernest Hemingway, "Big Two-Hearted River"

To prevent student writing from becoming phony and half-hearted and homogenized, we stress *firsthand observation*. We send them out to see, not the Grand Canyon, but the cities, the neighborhoods, the streets in which they live. We ask them to take in the textures, shapes, and colors that surround them. We ask them to look at the slums, the billboards, the downtown streets of contemporary America. We ask them to write about people—not about the "most wonderful person I have ever met"—but about people the way they are—real, contradictory, human:

> Cora was a good, easygoing woman who worked hard to keep her children in food and clothing, but . . . she was a soft touch for charming down-and-outers like Uncle Charlie and Larry Hickman, a three-hundred-pound sometime bandleader, whose belly flopped up and down when he walked. Hick, a balding man with round dancing eyes, swapped humor and long-winded tales for food, hypnotizing everyone into inactivity as he talked, ate, and refilled his plate. My sister, finally wise to his ways, offered up an amusing prayer at the supper table one night. Our heads were bowed and Hick was

THE CAMERA EYE

Lots of empty buildings and stores, with soaped-up windows.

The alternate-changing time and temperature flashing in a lighted, dot-like pattern on a bank sign.

Wrinkled old, old man looks slyly in littler baskets—he looks lonely.

Awake! the men from the Watchtower are out.

Fredericks of Hollywood: mannikins, platinum blond hair, ratted out, bright red orange, tight-fitting-at-top, flared-at-bottom pants . . . five young boys, about 15, 14, walk abreast, rapping about nothing important (far out, man, like wow) ratty old levis worn by all. "Mr. Big Stuff."

A woman with a baby is being hassled by a drunk; when the light turns green, she shoots across the street in order to lose him.

Fast-talking credit jewelers clad in glove-tight inexpensive suits with white socks, flashy rings, and greasy hair.

Most of the old men wear hats and suits. The old style . . . Bank of America has twelve floors, a bell tower at top. It has Greek-type columns in front. Various designs carved in the rock. The bank has a cop so old he can hardly lock the doors. He carries a dust rag, but he does pack a gun.

Half-empty parking lot and the back of buildings—shows the ugly side of town. This side is not dressed up to appeal to people but left ugly to conserve money.

Billboards: "We load the car, not the price."

The hot, spicy, hunger-grabbing smell of Mexican food . . . and the soft sugary taste of a Mexican pastry as I walk slowly home.

eyeing a chicken leg. "Dear Lord," my sister began, "make us thankful for what we are about to receive—and allow us to fill our plates before Hick fills our heart with lies. This we ask for our stomach's sake. Amen." We fell into uproarious laughter. Maurice and I dropped to the floor, tears streaming from our eyes. It was Marcella who got us back to the table. "You nuts had better come and eat. Hick is already on his second plate."

—Gordon Parks, *A Choice of Weapons*

Observation is the stuff writing is made of. No one can write substantial papers from an empty mind. Only when the student begins to mobilize his resources—his observation, his experience, his reading—can we begin to talk about organization, about structure. True structure is not something that is imposed from without. *True structure is something that we have worked out to give shape to our material.* It *emerges* from the material as we try to do justice to the subject at hand. Structure is *organic* when it emerges from our effort to sort out our data, to resolve the problem at hand, to shed light on the question before the house.

To show what we mean by **organic structure** is the hardest part of teaching composition. To organize a piece of writing means to move from unedited experience toward experience that has been shaped, that is meaningful, that has a point. Autobiographical writing, for instance, may be a mere chronological record of miscellaneous events:

I was one of the thirty girls and two leaders that left for Sebring on a sunny Friday afternoon. . . .

We had almost reached the campsite when we made a wrong turn and got stuck in the mud. . . .

That night we were lulled to sleep by the sounds of baaing sheep, mooing cows and whinnying horses. . . .

The week began with hikes, swimming and singing sessions. . . .

Our last night at Camp Sebring my troop was in charge of the campfire. . . .

Autobiographical writing becomes meaningful when we start to select incidents that *add up*. Something emerges from our experience—over a day, over a week, over the years. A given note recurs. The same thing happens again, and again in a slightly different form, and we begin to see a pattern. As we focus on a recurrent element, a piece of writing acquires the coherence that comes from *thematic* unity:

As we left the bus one by one, we received a few *sordid looks* from some of the people in the community. I guess they thought they were being invaded.

Our second day there we were hiking back from a swimming session when we noticed a girl *stealthily chopping down our sign* with a hatchet.

When we reached our campsite, it had been *ransacked*. But nothing had been taken.

The Camp Director received a *threatening note* saying there would be trouble if we didn't leave.

By this time we were *really scared* and everyone's nerves were on edge including mine. One girl started crying which set off a chain reaction. We sang to keep our minds off our troubles.

We *received so many stares* from the other girls that I came to the conclusion that we were the largest group of Negroes that had ever visited this camp.

The first thing the apprentice writer has to learn is how to be receptive—how to take things in. Our first question as readers is: "What was it like?" But the next question we ask is: "What does it mean?" We wait for the writer to sort things out. We want him to put two and two together so that they will add up to four. The most basic pattern that underlies honest writing is: "Here are the facts—and here is what these facts *show*." "Here is what happened—and here is what I *learned* from the experience."

Once we adopt this perspective, our sample patterns and model passages will often reverse the more conventional patterns. Instead of going from the main point to the examples, we will at least part of the time go *from the examples to the main point*. Instead of announcing a thesis and then marshaling the supporting evidence, we will present the evidence first and then *work toward* a thesis. Instead of giving our students a topic sentence, for them to develop with examples, we will give them a paragraph *without* a topic sentence—asking them: What do these examples add up to? What conclusion do these facts suggest?

Huck Finn's father tries to cheat him and then imprisons him. In order to get away from this drunken "mudcat," Huck must set it up so that everyone will think he has been murdered. This is a boy who, although surrounded by Aunt Sallies who want to "civilize" him, runs off to be himself. He has to protect himself against fraudulent adults like the Duke and the Dauphin. Every time he gets off that raft he is yelped at by dogs and menaced by people.
Conclusion: _____

(Possible answer: Adults are Huck Finn's worst enemies.)

The generalization that occurs at the end of such a paragraph is an *earned* generalization. Such a paragraph follows an **inductive** model: Related details *funnel* into a conclusion. We thus counteract our tendency toward hasty generalization, toward premature abstraction. We first involve the reader in authentic detail, in authentic observation, in authentic reminiscence. When the abstraction emerges at the end, it is as if the reader had collaborated in its discovery. We are *ready* for it, the way we are ready for the term *paternalism* when it emerges at the end of the following paragraph by James Baldwin:

It was an old black man in Atlanta who looked into my eyes and directed me into my first segregated bus. I have spent a long time thinking about that man. I never saw him again. I cannot describe the look which passed between us, as I asked him for directions, but it made me think, at once, of Shakespeare's "the oldest have borne most." It made me think of the blues: *Now, when a woman gets the blues, Lord, she hangs her head and cries. But when a man gets the blues, Lord, he grabs a train and rides.* It was borne in on me, suddenly, just why these men had so often been grabbing freight trains as the evening sun went down. And it was, perhaps, because I was getting on a segregated bus, and wondering how Negroes had borne this and other indignities for so long, that this man so struck me. He seemed to know what I was feeling. His eyes seemed to say that what I was feeling he had been feeling, at much higher pressure, all his life. But my eyes would never see the hell his eyes had seen. And this hell was, simply, that he had never in his life owned anything, not his wife, not his house, not his child, which could not, at any instant, be taken from him by the power of white people. This is what paternalism means.

—James Baldwin, *Nobody Knows My Name*

As our students experiment with inductive patterns, their writing may become less tidy, the overall development of a paper less predictable. But their writing cannot help but gain in interest and in substance. When the student was asked to define an important term, the conservative rhetoric stressed the established logical form, the neat logical arrangement of the three key elements:

Term to Be Defined	Class	Differentiation
An autobiography	is the story of a person's life,	written by himself.
Oligarchy	is a form of government	in which power lies in the hands of a few.
A faun	is a Roman wood god	who is half man and half goat.

Having presented his definition early in the paper, the student could then go on to provide his examples, his supporting evidence. Adopting a more inductive approach, the writer would immerse his readers first in the ambiguities, the problems, a term carried along. He would ask them to participate in the *search* for meaning. Writing about *fairness*, or *fair play*, he could examine a number of test cases, each raising an issue of fair play. He could look for what they seem to have in common. His definition would emerge at the end, presenting the common denominator:

First Test Case:	An honor code states that it is not "fair" to cheat.
Second Test Case:	According to a newspaper story, a mother considered it "fair" to steal food for her starving children.
Third Test Case:	A tennis player considers it "fair" to let his opponent find his footing after stumbling.
Fourth Test Case:	Students consider it "unfair" to penalize a sick student for failure to take a test.
Common Denominator:	Fair play makes us impose limits on competition—and sometimes *suspend* normal limits—in order to assure greater equality of opportunity; it shows our desire to "give everybody a chance."

The most vital kind of writing is not necessarily done by writers who write as if their minds had been made up for a long time. Writing shows signs of life when the reader can feel himself being carried along on a trend of thought. Writing easily becomes dull when a writer merely presents his own point of view, his own patented solution. Writing comes to life when a writer arrives at an acceptable solution through a process of *weighing the alternatives*. He tentatively takes up a proposed solution, gives it the benefit of the doubt, takes it as far as it will go. In the process, he discovers its limitations. He wrestles with its inherent defects, appraises its weaknesses. He works toward an adjusted view that is free from these defects, that is less vulnerable because possible objections have already been considered.

We start to think when someone stops saying "yes" and starts saying "yes, . . . but." A dialogue starts when "on the one hand" is followed by "on the other hand." An argument worth listening to develops when a statement is followed by a counterstatement. To write papers in which something *happens*, students should experiment with the "yes, but" pattern:

Yes: Americans feel they are just as good as the next fellow. They make remarks about people who "put on airs." A political candidate has to show that he can be "one of the crowd."

But: We believe that everyone has a chance to get ahead. We admire the outstanding individual; he is proof that the "American dream" can come true.

Yes: Radicals feel that the media are controlled by the establishment. News about young people and dissenters is distorted. People with too progressive views are fired by the owners of newspapers and television stations.

But: Conservatives in this country often bitterly attack the "left-wing" press. Establishment politicians often complain bitterly about hostile treatment by reporters. The media have had to ward off threats to their independence from Congressional investigations and proposed legislation.

The student learns what it means to think if he becomes involved in the play of *pro and con.* He learns what we mean by a "balanced" opinion —an opinion that is not "opinionated" but that does justice to the actual situation. He learns that we often arrive at a more nearly true picture by a **dialectic** process: We sum up what we think as of now; we formulate a "thesis." The more clear-cut our thesis, the more likely it is to make us aware of exceptions, of complications, of the "other side." We then formulate a counterstatement, an "antithesis" designed to correct the balance. This antithesis may push us too far toward the opposite extreme. If we are lucky, and persevering, we may arrive at a "synthesis" that incorporates the partial truth of both extremes. When writing mirrors a dialectic process, we reach a commitment, but the reader is able to participate in the making of the commitment. The great masters of English prose—Matthew Arnold, George Orwell, James Baldwin—are writers who take a stand, who commit themselves to strongly defined positions. But the intellectual excitement of their prose derives from their reaching these positions as the result of a dramatic confrontation. Their writing helps us understand what Arnold felt when he said:

> That is what I call living by ideas: when one side of a question has long had your earnest support, when all your feelings are engaged, when you hear all round you no language but one, when your party talks this language like a steam-engine and can imagine no other,—still to be able to think, still to be irresistibly carried, if so it be, by the current of thought to the opposite side

of the question, and, like Balaam, to be unable to speak anything but what the Lord has put in your mouth.

The liberal rhetoric of discovery and exploration has its roots in the nineteenth-century stirrings of modernism, in the age of Arnold and John Stuart Mill, of Ibsen and Thomas Hardy. It incorporates assumptions that Northrop Frye has called characteristic of the "modern century": As moderns, we assume that "the dynamic is better than the static, process better than product, the organic and vital better than the mechanical and fixed."[8] As we implement the liberal rhetoric in our programs and materials, the emphasis shifts from writing to **prewriting**, from the structured outline to the *tentative strategy*. We become impatient with the "surface orderliness" of simplified rhetorical patterns. We realize that too often the student formulates "the thesis he defends without adequate study and deliberation"; that too often students are defending opinions "before they have experienced enough and read enough." We begin to feel that "we try too soon to make them frame their thoughts in tightly structured patterns." We surrender the illusion that we "can conquer ambiguity and ambivalence in an opening paragraph." We put more stress on the "observations and fragmented perceptions" that precede orderly presentation. We become more tolerant of the feelings—of love and hate, of frustration and confusion—that complicate what we write even when we deal with "reasoned discourse."[9]

The strength of the liberal rhetoric is its commitment to authenticity, to integrity. It is sensitive to alternatives; it resists shortcuts and fake solutions. But this strength is also a source of potential weakness. When we weigh the alternatives, it is easy for us to become *too* aware of the complications. The more we listen to what is to be said for the opposing view, the harder we may find it to take sides. As Samuel Beckett makes one of his characters say in *Waiting for Godot*: "With folded arms we weigh the pro and con." Openmindedness may finally leave us "stuck in a fuzzy middle ground where opposites may each be partly true, and good and bad embrace in such promiscuous entwinement that it's difficult to shoot the one without maiming the other."[10]

Scepticism does not always function as a mere salutary first step toward clearer vision. It can easily become a dead end. Fully aware of all drawbacks and complications, we may find it hard to decide, to act. Like the donkey Benjamin in Orwell's *Animal Farm*, we may retreat into irony, adopting the stance of the sardonic observer. Satire then masks our sense of isolation. As Bertrand Russell says,

Throughout my life I have longed to feel that oneness with large bodies of human beings that is experienced by the members of enthusiastic crowds. The longing has often been strong enough to lead me into self-deception. I have imagined myself in turn a Liberal, a Socialist, or a Pacifist, but I have never been any of these things, in any profound sense. Always the skeptical intellect, when I have most wished it silent, has whispered doubts to me, has cut me off from the facile enthusiasms of others, and has transported me into a desolate solitude. During the War, while I worked with Quakers, non-resisters, and Socialists, while I was willing to accept the unpopularity and the inconvenience belonging to unpopular opinions, I would tell the Quakers that I thought many wars in history had been justified, and the Socialists that I dreaded the tyranny of the State. They would look askance at me and while continuing to accept my help would feel that I was not one of them.
—Bertrand Russell, *Autobiography, 1914–1944*

A liberal perspective easily becomes *too* skeptical, *too* critical. We then begin to feel a thwarted yearning for commitment, solidarity, effectiveness. We begin to suspect that there are threats and crises that open-mindedness is not equipped to handle. When evil is threatening and imminent, when the great catastrophes build up their thunderheads over the peaceable landscape, we lose patience with the careful examination of the pro and con. When Rome burns, we lose patience with those who tell us that the problems involved in fighting fires are complex and that the causes of fires are diverse.

We then are ready for a more radical rhetoric that shifts the emphasis from the sources of our opinions to their effects. We shift attention from how to find the truth to how to make the truth prevail. We look for writing that is not so much a call to contemplation as a call to action.

THE RHETORIC OF CONFRONTATION

As teachers today, we encounter a radical rhetoric that reflects a disenchantment with liberal values. The militant young, especially, feel that the liberal rhetoric of discussion, of dialogue, "makes nothing happen." Patient inquiry, the balancing of opposites, becomes a *substitute* for action. "Reasonableness" becomes a synonym for ineffectualness, for acceptance of the status quo. Its adherents "argue into the dark," but they can "neither create a new community nor retreat into the old order as an enemy of it, but only provide a critical commentary on both."[11]

When great and present evils cry out for remedy, we look for people who are ready to stand up and speak out. The time is ripe for a radical rhetoric when people who have sought to be fair, who have tried to see "both sides," finally have to choose their side; when people are no longer afraid of being called "simplistic," of being "unable to understand the complexities of life"; when people finally say "No!"; when they stand up and say "Enough!" As Martin Luther King said in his "Letter from Birmingham Jail":

> We have waited for more than 340 years for our constitutional and God-given rights. . . . When you have seen vicious mobs lynch your mothers and fathers at will and drown your sisters and brothers at whim; when you have seen hate-filled policemen curse, kick and even kill your black brothers and sisters; when you see the vast majority of your twenty million Negro brothers smothering in an airtight cage of poverty in the midst of an affluent society; when you suddenly find your tongue twisted and your speech stammering as you seek to explain to your six-year-old daughter why she can't go to the public amusement park that has just been advertised on television, and see tears welling up in her eyes when she is told that Funtown is closed to colored children, . . . when you take a cross-country drive and find it necessary to sleep night after night in the uncomfortable corners of your automobile because no motel will accept you; . . . when your first name becomes "nigger," your middle name becomes "boy" (however old you are) and your last name becomes "John," . . . when you are harried by day and haunted by night by the fact that you are a Negro, living constantly at tiptoe stance, never quite knowing what to expect next, and are plagued with inner fears and outer resentments; when you are forever fighting a degenerating sense of "nobodiness"—then you will understand why we find it difficult to wait. There comes a time when the cup of endurance runs over, and men are no longer willing to be plunged into the abyss of despair.[12]

When we fully open our eyes to an evil such as racism, we conclude that the problem is not basically a lack of information, an inadequate supply of facts, or a breakdown in logic. The basic fault is a failure of our moral imagination. In this situation, the morally committed speaker or writer feels compelled to *bear witness*. He calls attention; he speaks out. He does battle against callousness, apathy, complacency. The rhetoric of the dialogue then gives way and is superseded by a rhetoric of indictment. Its catchwords are COMMITMENT, ENGAGEMENT, RELEVANCE, SOLIDARITY, CONFRONTATION, DEFIANCE. Its goal is not dispassionate inquiry but militant action. Its ideal is not "moderation," or "fairness," but effective impact. As William Lloyd Garrison said in 1831 in speaking out against slavery:

> I am aware that many object to the severity of my language; but is there not cause for severity? I will be as harsh as truth, and as uncompromising as

justice. On this subject, I do not wish to think, speak, or write with moderation. No! no! Tell a man whose house is on fire, to give a moderate alarm; tell him to moderately rescue his wife from the hands of the ravisher; tell the mother to gradually extricate her babe from the fire into which it has fallen;—but urge me not to use moderation in a cause like the present. I am in earnest—I will not equivocate—I will not excuse—I will not retreat a single inch—AND I WILL BE HEARD.

The great strength of a radical rhetoric is its thrust toward *assertion.* "Effectiveness of assertion," as George Bernard Shaw said, is the true test of style. The radical speaker or writer knows that, to be effective, we finally have to cut through the knot. He knows that, in the words of the French painter, "to praise a beautiful thing half-heartedly is an offense"; that to condemn barbarity extenuatingly is collusion. He is impatient with the reservations and qualifications that blunt our purposes, with the scruples and timidities that make the native hue of resolution give way to the pale cast of thought. The strength of the radical writer is his determination that the reader will *get the message*:

> To protest is to play a game. You go to a demonstration, listen to speeches, wave signs, and go home to see if you got on television. . . . We have allowed the form that our protest takes to be defined for us by those whom we protest against. Thus our protest is drained of its power because we do not have the power to make our protest effective. We are no longer outraged at what is being done to us. If we were, we would resist.
>
> To resist is to say, NO! without qualification or explanation. To resist is not only to say I won't go. It is to say, I'll make sure nobody else goes, either.
>
> To resist is to not go to jail when sentenced, but only when caught and surrounded and there is no other choice but death.
>
> —Julius Lester, *Revolutionary Notes*

> As women, we should be aware of how idealization serves oppression. Throughout much of our literature, fanciful constructs of the ideal female, her character and psychology, have obscured the limitations suffered by actual women. Worse, they have encouraged expectations and behavior that only strengthen the real oppression.
>
> —Lillian S. Robinson, "Radical Criticism and the Feminist Perspective"

The major mechanism by which a radical rhetoric pushes toward effective assertion is **polarization**. If we are to take a stand, we must finally suspend debate; we must go beyond the agony of decision to the end result. In order to do so, we must be able to clear away the peripheral and unimportant to lay bare the essential issue. The tendency of the radical rhetoric is to *force* a choice: It narrows down a complex situation to an either-or alternative—of which one is clearly unacceptable or immoral, if not outright despicable:

> For our society faces a choice. Either we become a genuinely integrated
> society, in which the color of a man's skin has no more to do with the way
> other men treat him and feel about him than, say, the color of his eyes or
> his hair, or we will become a genuinely, wholeheartedly, unashamedly racist
> society, like that of Nazi Germany or present South Africa—with perhaps
> our own Final Solution waiting at the end.
>   —John Holt, introduction to *Teaching the Unteachables*

The moral universe of the true radical writer, from John Milton and John Bunyan down to our times, is a room with only two exits, one marked "Right" and the other marked "Wrong." Either we choose full integration or we relapse into Nazism. Either we ban military training for reserve officers from our college campuses, or we embrace militarism, aggression, and war. Either we develop "open classrooms," or we are stuck with "authoritarian" ones.

As positions polarize, disagreement ceases to be primarily an intellectual matter and becomes instead a moral one. In the context of a radical rhetoric, questions are asked *in earnest*. It becomes harder to evade unpleasant facts, to play intellectual games, to "cop out." It becomes harder for people to disagree on basic issues and yet remain on friendly human terms. To "state the arguments for all conflicting opinions fairly" (John Stuart Mill) becomes a dubious luxury, which at worst gives aid and comfort to the enemy.

As a result, the radical rhetoric typically polarizes not only the issues, but also the audience. On the one hand, the radical writer angers, antagonizes, shocks, dismays. He baits the bourgeois; he shakes the pillars of the community. He goads those who have only partial commitments; he besets the indifferent. On the other hand, he provides a rallying point for those ready to share his indignation, ready to be inspired by his sense of mission:

> The rhetorician who wants to break established patterns must often shock,
> must introduce discord and disharmony into the situation. He may realistically
> know that this will gain few adherents among the hostile, but the sad
> fact is that he has probably despaired of most of them at the outset. But such
> rhetoric may be tremendously effective with the other audience, the participants
> or potential participants in the rhetorician's own camp.[13]

In his own camp, the radical writer helps create a powerful sense of **solidarity**, of community, of being part of a larger "movement." Especially in the early stages, the adoption of a radical perspective has a *liberating* effect that can be tremendously exhilarating and elating. We sense this liberation when feelings we have bottled up, that we have kept to ourselves, are brought out into the open and shared with others. There is a tremendous relief when we are finally through bowing and scraping, when we are through being conciliatory and "reasonable." We experience a deep satisfaction when someone finally cuts through the euphemisms and calls a spade a spade:

> I am going to ask you to begin our study of Democracy by considering it first as a big balloon, filled with gas or hot air, and sent up so that you shall be kept looking up at the sky whilst other people are picking your pockets. When the balloon comes down to earth every five years or so you are invited to get into the basket if you can throw out one of the people who are sitting tightly in it; but as you can afford neither the time nor the money, and there are forty millions of you and hardly room for six hundred in the basket, the balloon goes up again with much the same lot in it and leaves you where you were before.   (George Bernard Shaw)

This sense of release, of liberation, is closely related to another characteristic feeling: The audience of the radical speaker and writer experiences a sense of *vindication*. There is a grim satisfaction in seeing others share our defiance, our scorn. It is a lonely business to carry around our own private doubts and disaffections; it is good for the soul to hear the shouts of "Amen!" and "Right on!" We experience this grim sense of finding our own feelings confirmed when we read the poem that Bertolt Brecht wrote upon the arrival of Hitler's new order in Germany:

ON THE BURNING OF BOOKS

> When the new masters announced that books full of harmful
>   knowledge
> Were to be publicly burned and when here and yonder
> Oxen were made to draw carts full of books
>
> To the stake, a poet, hunted from home (he was one of the
>   best)
> Discovered aghast, when reading the list of those burned,
> His own books had been forgotten. He rushed to his desk,
> Furious, and wrote to the rulers:
>
> Burn me at once! he wrote with a frantic pen.
> You cannot do this to me! How can you spare me?
> Have I not always

Recorded the truth in my books? And now
you class me with liars!

This is an order:

Burn me!

A radical rhetoric can offer a sense of identity, a sense of commitment, a sense of pride. It thus has a strong potential appeal for many of
our students. Urging a strong moral stand, it appeals to the latent idealism of youth. It rationalizes and vindicates the sense of alienation felt
by many young people. It mobilizes their sense of injustice. It appeals
to the latent adolescent sense of rebellion.

On the other hand, a commitment to a radical rhetoric raises basic
moral problems of its own. One symptom of these that is of direct concern to the teacher of English is the radical speaker's and writer's use of
language. Aiming at impact, designed to draw attention, a radical style
tends toward **overstatement**. It tends toward habitual overemphasis. We
recognize a radical style by its high concentration on strong, "tough"
words and phrases: Middle-class America is a "wasteland"; administrators try to "castrate" the movement toward student activism; American
undergraduates are the new "dispossessed"; the university is a "whore"
unlawfully joined to government and industry. The government is "corrupt," the military "dehumanizing," our economy "useless," the corpora-
tions "rapacious," the churches "organized hypocrisy," our popular
culture "commercially debauched," the schools "repressive," and marriage a "wretched institution." Like most matters of style, this is more
than just a matter of style. What ultimately identifies the radical, both of
the political left and the political right, is that he appropriates grave
words, solemn words, threatening words, and uses them too cheaply:
*sabotage, treason, disloyalty, perversion, prostitution, class enemy,
flunkey, sadist*; not to mention *corruption, coercion, oppression, exploitation*, and *brutality*. If suburban schools are "jails," what are we going
to call real jails? If undergraduate education in the United States represents "systematic brutality," what are we going to call the German occu-
pation of Poland in World War II? Words like *militarism, imperialism*,
and *fascism* become trivialized and finally serve only as a signal for the
sheep to start chanting "Four legs good, two legs bad."

The great potential weakness of a radical rhetoric is the chronic in-
flation of its verbal currency. There is a price to pay when we make grave
and solemn words the small change of everyday political agitation: A
vocabulary designed to make everybody listen may in the end make sure
that *nobody* listens. People tire of cheap melodramatic titles: "The War
against the Young," "The Student as Nigger," "Murder in the Class-

room." An audience that is constantly bombarded with terms like *rape* and *murder*, rather than becoming more sensitive, may simply become blasé. As the authors of the *Dictionary of Inhumanity* said of the "tough" style encouraged by the Nazi rhetoric,

> A rhetoric that keeps using the floodlights of emphasis finally reaches the opposite of the intended effect: beside the multitude of things flooded by glaring light nothing distinctly visible remains, and only acoustic chaos reigns in language.[14]

The routine verbal extremism, the unremitting polemical stance, of the radical rhetoric is symptom and part of a larger problem. As we study its habitual use of language as a blunt instrument, we confront the classic dilemma of the radical tradition: The means it employs have tended to prove incompatible with the ends it seeks. The means corrupt the ends. The means chosen not only do not accomplish the ends, but defeat them. As Bertolt Brecht said in defense of his generation of radicals of the extreme left,

> We know only too well:
> Even hatred for baseness
> Distorts one's features.
> Even anger at injustice
> Makes for a hoarse rasping voice.
> Yes, we who meant to prepare the soil for kindness
> Could not ourselves be kind.

Here is the modern radical's dilemma: While fighting for humanity, love, and justice, he has found it hard to be himself humane, loving, and just. This is ultimately our reaction to the current radical criticism of our schools, to writers who tell us that the public schools "kill dreams" and "mutilate minds," that teachers are engaged in a "conspiracy to maim the minds of the young." Many of the charges are true, and even the false ones may be well worth pondering. But ultimately the worm turns and we cannot help saying: "You want to make people more open to experience, but you yourself have a closed mind. You want to make people more loving, but you yourself cannot even love your fellow teachers. You want to make people more just, but you yourself are desperately unfair." Young people who are powerfully attracted to a radical style have to face up to a basic paradox. The announced aims of current radical ethics are to reduce the element of competition and aggression and strife in human life. But these aims are proposed and promoted by a rhetoric that is militant and verbally aggressive.

What is missing in the current rhetoric of confrontation comes into focus when we read a writer whose basic honesty keeps him from distorting the truth in order to assure the desired verdict of guilty. Thus, James Baldwin, in *Notes of a Native Son*, talks about his father, a man "indescribably cruel in his personal life" and "certainly the most bitter man I have ever met":

> When he took one of his children on his knee to play, the child always became fretful and began to cry; when he tried to help one of us with our homework the absolutely unabating tension which emanated from him caused our minds and our tongues to become paralyzed, so that he, scarcely knowing why, flew into a rage and the child, not knowing why, was punished. If it ever entered his head to bring a surprise home for his children, it was, almost unfailingly, the wrong surprise and even the big watermelons he often brought home on his back in the summertime led to the most appalling scenes.

And yet Baldwin never lapses into the caricature of the authoritarian father, of the adult as zombie, on whose insensitivity we can unload all the blame for our own lack of fulfillment. He remembers the other side. He remembers how proud his father had been of him when he was little. He remembers the grin of pleasure on the father's face when the son sang before the members of the father's church. He remembers the expression on the father's face when he teased Baldwin's mother. What Baldwin ultimately looks for in his father is this buried humanity, this thwarted human potential:

> There was something else in him, buried in him, which lent him his tremendous power and, even, a rather crushing charm. . . . He was very black —with his blackness and his beauty, and with the fact that he knew that he was black but did not know that he was beautiful. He claimed to be proud of his blackness but it had also been the cause of much humiliation and it had fixed bleak boundaries to his life. . . . In his outrageously demanding and protective way he loved his children, who were black like him and menaced, like him; and all these things sometimes showed in his face when he tried, never to my knowledge with any success, to establish contact with any of us.

The way to a more humane world will have to be led by people who know how to uncover the buried human potential. It will have to be led by those who know how to bring out the best in people rather than the worst in people.

Obviously, teachers vary greatly in how consciously and how overtly they recognize the larger human and political strategies behind their work in composition. Often the larger issues loom in the background as we deal with the tactics of "how to write." In some ways, in fact, the more technical aspects of writing offer us a safe retreat from the "politics" of rhetoric. But in at least one way, a technical view of composition can provide us with a means of seeing different styles of rhetoric in a larger framework. Technically speaking, a conservative rhetoric of order stresses the structure of the *product*. A liberal rhetoric of discovery stresses the integrity of the *writer*. A radical rhetoric of confrontation stresses impact upon the *audience*. With a slight rearrangement of these three emphases, we can make them part of a larger scheme in which we focus in turn on the three major elements of the communication process: the SENDER, the MESSAGE, and the RECEIVER.

When we talk about the writer as the *source* of the message, we stress the need for exploration and discovery. We talk about how to break through the stereotypes; we try to promote authentic observation, honest firsthand experience. We try to demonstrate the process of coming to terms with that experience. We are thus concerned with what gives writing *substance*. Even if we go no further, the writer learns to say to himself: "I learned something from writing this paper—even if nobody else does."

When we analyze the finished *product*, we examine the message for coherence and clarity. We become concerned with communicability, accessibility, intelligibility. We check the message for its internal strength; we shore up the argument; we supply missing links. We focus on *structure*. We ask: "Can this stand by itself? I know what I meant to say, but did I say it?"

When we look for the *receiver* of the message, we become aware of the audience. We begin to worry about persuasiveness, impact, power. We become concerned with the motives, values, and probable reactions of the reader. We become involved in questions of *strategy* and of *style*. We ask: "Is anything I say going to make any difference? Am I making a dent?"

Such an overall scheme suggests a sequence; it suggests priorities. Both the conservative rhetoric of order and the radical rhetoric of impact in their own way put the cart before the horse. The rhetoric of order and clarity, when prematurely imposed on the student, tends to make him straighten and prune something that has not really had a chance to grow. The rhetoric of impact, like any approach that makes the audience the central consideration, must not override our prior concern with the integrity of the message. When it does, persuasion becomes manipulation, argument becomes polemic, writing becomes propaganda. When the three major elements are in some kind of overall balance, a writer writes from his own honest experience and intelligence. He learns to respect the medium through which he works. And he learns how to make himself heard.

THE CREATIVE SPARK

Trying to get real writing from their students, teachers have over the years learned to go beyond external form to what gives writing substance and shape. In the process, there has been a general branching out, an opening up toward what language does as a means of self-expression and human interaction. One major direction of this opening up has been toward social awareness and social relevance. Another major direction has been toward the student's creative and general human potential. Teachers are breaking down the barriers that used to separate composition from "creative writing," or nonfiction prose from "imaginative" literature. We no longer condition our students to think of the writing we expect as something gray, plodding, pedestrian. *Writing and other forms of verbal expression are inherently creative and imaginative.* Imagination and creativity are not luxuries but basic human means of relating to reality and shaping life. We are beginning to heal a traditional split that used to vitiate much of our work! Being imaginative people, we are no longer content with unimaginative ways of dealing with language. Being lovers of poetry, we no longer try to squeeze the poetry from the speaking and writing of our students.

This general movement toward creativity and imagination has been greatly accelerated by a **new pedagogy** that is in full revolt against the traditional academic emphasis on the "training of the mind." A whole generation of educational reformers is rebelling against a too exclusive preoccupation with the intellectual, the cognitive, the conceptual. With John Holt, they object to education that is merely "trying to plant strings of words in children's heads"; they insist that we return language and all other "symbolic manipulation" to the rich context of "sensing, feeling, acting and being." With Herbert Kohl, they insist that we "look for sensibility and feeling" in our pupils "as well as the abilities to perform intellectual tasks."

For the reformer, our most basic task is to free the "natural capacities of the young," allowing them to "develop the creative possibilities provided both by their innate capacities and by their experience."[15] We must learn to respect *individuality*: Children are fortunate when they have a teacher who recognizes perceptions and talents that do not easily "fit into the rigid categories" that we conventionally judge as excellent. We must allow ourselves "to learn from our pupils and to expect the unexpected."[16] We must respect the student's right to be different, to be a person in his own right. We must cherish "the sparks of humanity or independence or originality in children": Stephen, the hero of Jonathan Kozol's *Death at an Early Age*, made drawings that "were not neat and orderly and organized but entirely random and casual, messy, somewhat unpredictable, seldom according to the instructions given, and—in short —real drawings."[17]

English teachers have always believed in imagination, creativity, and individuality. But in practice they have often treated them as a bonus for the gifted few, while the great unwashed labored in the salt mines of alleged fundamentals. Today, we are learning to recognize imagination, creativity, and individuality as a legitimate and necessary part of *all* of English. In our work with oral and written expression, this recognition has two fundamentally important results: (1) We are more and more allowing for a whole *range* of oral and written activities, with the full-length theme only the most finished or most substantial of various kinds of verbal expression. (2) We are more and more relying on literary and other creative materials as *stimulus*, model, or context for the student's speech and writing. We find that a poem or a picture can have "something to say" that leads directly to a student's response; we find that at the same time it can suggest ways of "seeing," of exploring experience.

Looking for alternatives to the formidable 400-word or 500-word theme, we turn first of all to the *limbering-up activities* that help make writing a habit. For years, teachers have reported on the success of **free writing** in breaking up the stiff, solemn "Sunday-Go-to-Meeting" prose of intimidated and inhibited students. They ask their students for "automatic writing"—a stream-of-consciousness kind of prose. The student is asked to keep pen or pencil moving, repeating the same word or slogan even if necessary, but finally, as their minds start wandering, writing down the stray thoughts that come into their heads. S. I. Hayakawa asked students to write "rapidly and continuously . . . without pausing, without taking thought, without revising. . . . In a matter of weeks, student writings, at first so labored and self-conscious, become fluid, expressive, and resonant with the rhythms of the spoken American language."[18] Ken Macrorie's students, asked for free writing, "returned with papers that spoke disjointedly and fragmentarily, but in language often alive. Some natural rhythms appeared, a striking metaphor once in a while, and often a bit of reality that jarred me."[19]

To stimulate the flow of impressions and ideas, hundreds of teachers have asked their students to keep **journals**, in which there is room for random notes, for the trivial as well as the important, for the private as well as the public. At the same time, the journal or log gives students a chance to discover some of the things that writing can do for us: When something special happens, we want to *tell* somebody—even if only our diary. When we are unjustly blamed, we want to explain—if only to our journal. These are some of the same purposes for which we use a letter.

TELLING SOMEBODY

The weather today was wonderful, it was warm outside and the sky was clear, the sun shining, it seemed to make the whole day feel great. So I took a look outside my window and noticed a Blue Jay singing just below my window. He was sitting on a branch and I think he was trying to call for his mate. I could hear the sound he was making. And the way he gave the sound was not like an average person whistle but a short burst of sound. And the sound was something like having a tennis shoe on and rubbing it against the floor, not a high sound or dragging your feet across the floor, but a sound like a normal walk, with a little pressure applied foward. While I was watching I gave the Blue Jay a short whistle and he seemed to have heard my whistle cause he turned his head and looked to both sides. But he still kept on giving a short burst of sound.

L.G.

The Waffle House has good food but some—one in particular —of the waitresses are too snotty for me. This little skinny, boney legged skunk didn't even want to give us silverware when we went in there. I got so disgusted, I just held my peace. I know that a lot of fussing in a public place like that would only bring the police out. I should complain about it to the manager.

To show how little signs of prejudice will seep out: Charles ordered a waffle and he and Pat ordered omelets. They got no syrup to pour on their food even if they had wanted to. (They weren't offered any either.)

This same chick waited on a young white couple. They had about *six* different types of syrup from which to choose.

When checking out, she politely took the bill from the whites, but snatched it from the blacks. That little chick almost got told off and didn't realize it!

When we got ready to go, she and this other white lady were looking at us like they didn't have no sense. Humph, we just acted civilized and walked on off but let me go back again and get the same kind of treatment. I'm afraid I'll give her a piece of my mind!

D.G.

I miss daddy so much. I cried the other night. It seems as if it just happened yesterday. I never knew I could bear so much pain and still live. I'm going back in time to the moment my brother ran in screaming "Daddy was shot in the head". He cried and I almost went crazy—at that very moment it seemed as if the world

was coming to an end. All I wanted was to go back in time and I jumped out of bed without putting on my bra and ran to the car, all I did was scream, cry, and pray. I prayed all the way and I felt like I was losing my mind. I finally came to the hospital where I saw the doctor and my first cousin (the one who was there when he was killed) all they did was shake their heads. I wanted to die. I couldn't stand it. I screamed and they tried to give me something to put me to sleep. All I cried was "God please bring him back", please, please. It was too late. He's gone and he'll never be back. The hardest thing to do was to tell my mother and the rest of the family I loved so much that daddy was gone. I remember the hatred I felt. I was mad at the world. All I pray now is that we meet him some day.   L.H.
—From *Easy Writers*

Sunny Decker, in *An Empty Spoon*, describes how she told students they could write their letters to her if they could not think of someone else to write to. She received and answered real letters:

> I am writing this letter to let you know how I am doing in your class. I know I am failing and I am trying to do my very best to get up. But it seem hard . . .
>
> It is a very hurting feeling when you don't have a mother to cry to when thing are bad. And you two can sit down and make fun of your father . . . I wish I had a mother so when I get married she can say I brought my daughter up and she finished school.
>
> . . . but know I got you where I wont you, and I wont you where I've got you . . . my friend your luck is a thing of the past.
>
> I have a friend with a problem. I can't tell you her name. . . .[20]

As student writing becomes more spontaneous, the native sparkle and humanity as well as the hurt and bewilderment begin to shine through. But as we try to convince our students that "everybody is a writer" and "everybody has got something to say," their getting-the-habit activities will by no means be all unstructured, all free flow. Students bring to us a naïve delight in pattern, in shape; it is part of our job to keep it alive. Students take to the *haiku* because they delight in its simple, predictable three-line form; they catch on to its ability to clear away the debris, to capture some essential impression or feeling:

ROLLER COASTER

> The roller coaster
> Shocking, thrilling as it goes
> I scream all the way.[21]

Students write Aesopian *fables* because they take to the basic scenario —the simple, archetypal situation acted out, followed by the lesson that we can take along:

> Once upon a time there was a pig and a cat. The cat kept saying old dirty pig who want to eat you. And the pig replied when I die I'll be made use of, but when you die you'll just rot. The cat always thought he was better than the pig. When the pig died he was used as food for the people to eat. When the cat died he was bured in old dirt.
> Moral: Live dirty die clean.[22]

Students take to capsule portraits and thumbnail sketches because of the challenge of condensation, which is a challenge of form. They delight in opportunities for **parody**, such as the "updated proverbs" that take a tired old pattern and give it a lively new twist:

> It's a long street that has no parking meter.
> He who laughs last will never be part of a studio audience.
> A watched bus never comes.
> Where there's muck there's headlines.

Something very basic happens as we encourage the creative and imaginative elements in student writing: We begin to read their papers the way we would "literature." We read them with an anticipation of *pleasure*. We expect to be pleased, disturbed, elated, shaken up, moved. Something equally basic happens in the opposite direction: We take imaginative literature off the shelf and read it more the way we read our students' writing—as a response to experience, as a "window upon the world." We present poets and storytellers and playwrights not as exhibits but as fellow mortals—observers, witnesses, people talking. We start to look for poems and stories that combine two key qualities: They are provocative enough to shake students out of routine and apathy, out of a state where our eyes are "clouded over so that we can see neither the beauty nor the ugliness" around us. But they are also "ordinary" enough so that students can relate them to their own experience.[23] We look for writers who can teach our students something about the beauty of ordinary things, the kind of beauty Brecht described in his poem "Of Things That Are Precious":

> Of all works most precious
> Are things of daily use.
> Copper vessels, dented, with smoothed-down rims;
> Forks and knives, their wooden handles worn down
> By many hands—such shapes
> Are the most noble. Also the tiles in front of old houses,
> Ground down by many feet, pebble-smooth,
> With grass in clumps sprouting between—
> These make me glad.

Taking our clue from such writers, we encourage our students to look for the poetry of their own daily lives: the buildings built for a different time and those built for our time; the life histories written in the faces of older people; the pompousness and cleverness of advertisers; the humor and pathos of signs:

SMILE—YOU MAY BE ON RADAR

PAINTINGS CHEAP—ARTIST STARVING

FIGHT SMOG—RIDE A BICYCLE

WELCOME: Parents and other visitors on school business are always welcome in the Chicago Public Schools. Please go directly to the office of the principal.

We thus encourage our students to bring their sensitivity, their creativity, their imagination to bear on the things of every day, on the life around them. Adventure does not lurk only on distant planets, on the Arctic ice, or 20,000 leagues under the sea. It lay in wait for the junior high school student who walked across Harvard Square:

TOILET PAPER A PENNY A PIECE

Anything and everything can happen in Harvard Square. The sky is the limit. It seems that every nut within a eighty mile radius is there.

One day I saw a sight that I swear would pop the eyes out of somebody's head. Coming up from the subway, I noticed—actually I couldn't help seeing—a group of about six girls dressed in the most unbievible fashin. They had levis that were skin tight, and looked like they were painted on. That wasn't too bad since everybody wears tight pants. But thier faces were full of make up, and they looked like they were going on the war path. Lipstick was smeared on their faces in the shape of circles and four lines that when put together looked like something to play tick-tack-toe on. I managed to survive that, but the worst was yet to come.

The part that killed me was these girls about fifteen years old were selling toilet paper. Each girl was armed with one roll of wite Hudson two-ply. The price was a reasonable penny for a piece. They must have been kiding. And to top it all off some Harvard "squares" actually bought some. Apparently they couldn't go home until they sold the whole roll. Good luck to them. Their plea was buy some from the underprivileged children. Personly I thought that the girls and people who bought the toilet paper were mentally unfit. [24]

Getting more technical, we can show our students how imaginative writers use a change in **perspective** to produce an illuminating or provocative effect: It makes us look at a familiar object from a new angle. It shows us an old subject in a new light. By putting Gulliver in Lilliput, Swift magnifies for our astonished inspection his ordinary humanity. By looking at the Lilliputians from Gulliver's height, he makes their intrigues and betrayals the petty squabbles of little men. Taking our clue from such examples of the optics of literature, we can ask our students to adopt different points of view—to see the world from a fresh vantage point, to try to "get inside" a character, to project themselves into a historical situation, to get at the essence of a familiar relationship:

I Am Rain

I am rain
I drop down one by one from the clouds.
I drop on fields to help farmers grow crops.
I drop on hills and roll down waterfalls.
I help people by killing their thirst.
I am rain.

I Am a Rich Man

I am a rich man, a man with lots of money and power. Therefore, I am a man who has authority and gives all sorts of orders which I myself may or may not be able to follow. Since I am a man of authority, I am well known in fields of electrical engineering, political science, government. I have to be the best in these areas or lose the world.

The money I have is "coming out of my ears", if you know what I mean. I have so much I don't know what to do with it. Sure there are lots of people everywhere who could use some of it, but I just can't give it to them, even if it is lying all over the floor.

Who cares I'm rich? I'm rich! I have the whole world at my mercy. I can bend it, break it, crush it, or do with it whatever I want.

What about the poor? I'll give them the crumbs from my table, the leftovers from each meal.

People are just objects to me. If one becomes a red light to try and stop me, I simply switch him off. I can use people. I can buy them. I can control their very lives.

The fools! Why do they humble themselves? Is it because they know what I know? "What is a rich man if he gains the whole world but loses his own life?"

When my bones dry cold and I am waiting to die again, but I am already dead.

POEM

> First the threats
> then
>> the bomb—
>> the radiation
>> changing, maiming, killing
> But after all
>> we were right—
> It said so
>> on the late news
> Our fields are dead, but
>> so are theirs
> We are dying, but
>> so are they
> Who won
>> Why, we did—we clobbered 'em!

My Advice to You, Daughter

Don't hang with the wrong crowd or stay out too late. Just because I'm not around watching you, don't think I don't know what's going on. Don't forget to hang up your clothes and keep your room neat. Even though you don't seem to be dirty, don't forget to shower every night. I know you can wake up in the morning, but don't forget to set your alarm clock. You may be running late, but don't forget to brush your teeth. Don't do this, don't do that, and for God's sake don't forget to lock your door.

Do comb your hair and look neat. Please do study hard every night. Do be polite and smile at everybody. Be ladylike and do the things young ladies do. Do remember your mama here at home loving and wanting the best for you. Do this, do that, and please do say your prayers.

Watch out for those little hot-headed boys that think they know it all. When a boy looks sneaky and sly, you watch out. If one gets too close, have your purse ready and watch out. Even if he seems friendly and kind, be careful and watch out. I know you are a young lady and you like boys, but you never can tell, so watch out. Watch out for this kind, watch out for that kind, and if there's any kind left, watch out.

Mama tells you what she knows and you think about what I've said. Most of all, if you forget some of your do's and don'ts, please remember all the watch out's.[25]

Finally, we draw on those writers who can keep alive the student's fascination with words as words. Many of our students have a quick ear for different *voices*; they love to mimic and parody; they know how to use words as the vehicle of ingenious insult and madcap humor. We try to mobilize this latent fascination with language: We help them become enchanted by a word magician like Dylan Thomas, who is forever setting up gorgeous verbal Christmas trees in the gray backrooms of ordinary experience:

> It was always snowing at Christmas; December, in my memory, is white as Lapland, though there were no reindeers. But there were cats. Patient, cold, and callous, our hands wrapped in socks, we waited to snowball the cats. Sleek and long as jaguars and terrible-whiskered, spitting and snarling they would slink and sidle over the white back-garden walls, and the lynx-eyed hunters, Jim and I, fur-capped and moccasined trappers from Hudson's Bay off Eversley Road, would hurl our deadly snowballs at the green of their eyes.

We try to make students see the power of **understatement**, as used by a writer like Stephen Crane, who knows how to "play it cool" in talking about half-drowned men, ground down by fatigue:

> Of the four in the dinghy none had slept any time worth mentioning for two days and two nights previous to embarking in the dinghy, and in the excitement of clambering about the deck of a sinking ship they had also forgotten to eat heartily. For these reasons, and for others, neither the oiler nor the correspondent was fond of rowing at this time.

We know we can make them appreciate the power of *forceful language* used at the right moment by someone who knows how, as when William Faulkner's Boon finally tells the men getting ready for the hunting trip in the faint starlight before dawn:

> Them that's going, get in the goddamn wagon. Them that ain't, get out of the goddamn way.

We can have our students in turn experiment with style that is more than ornament—style that reveals attitude, style that makes the point, as in the following student experiments with **figurative language**:

> A bug just flew onto my desk. Sometimes I wonder if people aren't kind of like bugs sometimes. Both people and bugs are *always buzzing around with nowhere really to go.*

> Every young man in today's world is usually too busy, too active to think about draft registration. But turn your back, and *just like a leopard stalking its prey*, it's here—you're eighteen.

We can have our students experiment with the alternatives to direct statement, such as the **irony** successfully employed in the following excerpt from an imitation of W. H. Auden's "The Unknown Citizen":

The Unknown Student

. . . he wasn't hip or odd in his views
And his politics never became school news.
Psychological Tests consistently found
He was accepted by his peers and never fooled around.
Popular Ratings conclusively state
That his record collection was kept up to date.
He watched the T.V. and read all the news
Which always became his regular views.
Both Teen Magazine and Consumer Reports show
That he spent his allowance on material blessings
And had everything essential to today's adolescents:
A transistor, A Stereo, a guitar and a Camaro.[26]

We can have students give free rein to their liking for extravagant **word play**, letting it create the kind of absurd universe in which so many of our young people seem to feel at home:

The Snow Also Freezes

. . . A downcast penguin wandered by. It was shivering. Cold penguin.
    "What the hell are you doing at the South Pole?" Joe Gilk asked.
    The penguin pointed mutely at his white front. No studs. Born a social outcast. Born with no studs. Freezing at the South Pole with Joe Gilk. Ice. No studs. Life was hard.
    A blast of cold wind chilled him. He felt his bones. They were cold. He was chilled to the bone. A hopeless feeling passed over him. He raced across the ice and intercepted the pass. He lateraled to a grinning polar bear.
    Hans would know what to do in a situation like this. Good old Hans! Hans would never see the South Pole now. Not after that fight with Leonard's tiger. If he only hadn't agreed to tie one hand behind his back. He should have known that he had just one hand left after trimming his fingernails with the lawnmower. Education was a wonderful thing. Joe Gilk could count. He counted his hands a few times to make sure.

Things really looked black now. He put on his sun glasses, and things looked green again.

"God, it's cold!" he muttered.

"Yeah, it is," muttered God.

Here is the only real "breakthrough" in the teaching of English in the last few decades: *English teachers have come to approach student writing not as judges but first of all as readers.* They show by their response that they value the personal elements in the student's writing—his honesty, doggedness, or wit. They show that they cherish imagination, the free play of the mind that opens up new perspectives. They show that they cherish the telling phrase, word play, verbal mimicry. They also show that they are willing to listen seriously when the time to be serious has come.

What we finally aim at in student writing is an organic balance of the serious and the playful, the objective and the imaginative, the spontaneous and the structured. In some of the most vital writing we read, these elements interact, the way they do in real life. On the one hand, we try to keep from extinguishing the spark, from adjusting the individual to dull mediocrity. We defend spontaneity and vitality against the rigidity of established formulas, the dead hand of routine, the trivia of convention. On the other hand, we try to show that in speech and writing, as elsewhere, anything really satisfying and rewarding involves not merely a freeing but also a channeling of our energies. We become aware of our powers, our talents, when we bring them to bear. There is no chemical substitute for the satisfaction we get from a challenge met, a problem solved, a mission accomplished. A successful speaker or writer derives a basic satisfaction from a job worth doing and well done. As teachers of composition, our job is to set up opportunities for young people to enjoy that satisfaction.

FOOTNOTES

[1]Taylor Stoehr et al., "Writing About Experience: A Report on Freshman English," *College English*, 32 (October 1970), 24–25.

[2]J. Mitchell Morse, "Why Write Like a College Graduate?" *College English*, 32 (October 1970), 1–6.

[3]Peter Marin, review of *This Book Is About Schools*, *Saturday Review*, Mar. 20, 1971, p. 53.

[4]Eugène Ionesco, *Four Plays*, trans. Donald M. Allen (New York: Grove Press, Inc., 1958), p. 31.

[5]Robert B. Heilman, "Except He Come to Composition," *College Composition and Communication*, 21 (October 1970), 232–236.

[6]Richard E. Young, Alton L. Becker, and Kenneth L. Pike, *Rhetoric: Discovery and Change* (New York: Harcourt, Brace & World, Inc., 1970), p. 9.

[7]Ken Macrorie, *Uptaught* (New York: Hayden Book Company, Inc., 1970), p. 33.

[8]Northrop Frye, *The Modern Century* (New York: Oxford University Press, 1969), p. 31.

[9]Margaret B. McDowell, "Honesty in Freshman Rhetoric," *College English*, 32 (March 1971), 673–678.

[10]Heilman, "Except He Come to Composition," p. 231.

[11]Kingsley Widmer, "The End of the Hired Learning," *AAUP Bulletin*, 56 (September 1970), 273.

[12]Martin Luther King, Jr., *Why We Can't Wait* (New York: Harper & Row, Publishers, Incorporated. 1963).

[13]Robert M. Browne, "Counterstatement," *College Composition and Communication*, 21 (May 1970), 189.

[14]Dolf Sternberger et al., *Aus dem Wörterbuch des Unmenschen* (Munich: Deutscher Taschenbuch Verlag, 1962), p. 58.

[15]Louis Kampf, "Must We Have a Cultural Revolution?," *College Composition and Communication*, 21 (October 1970), 245–247.

[16]Herbert R. Kohl, *Teaching the "Unteachable"* (New York: The New York Review, 1967), pp. 13, 47.

[17]Jonathan Kozol, *Death at an Early Age* (New York: Bantam Books, Inc., 1968), pp. 2, 14.

[18]S. I. Hayakawa, "Learning to Think and to Write," *College Composition and Communication*, 12 (February 1962), 5–8.

[19]Macrorie, *Uptaught*, p. 20.

[20]Sunny Decker, *An Empty Spoon* (New York: Harper & Row, Publishers, Incorporated, 1970), pp. 89–91.

[21]Haiku by Linda Blueford, *California English Journal*, 5 (January 1969).

[22]Fable by Barbara (age 11), in Kohl, *Teaching the "Unteachable,"* p. 26.

[23]Lester S. Golub, "A Model for Teaching Composition," *California English Journal*, 5 (December 1969), 21–29.

[24]James Moffett, *A Student-Centered Language Arts Curriculum, Grades K–13* (Boston: Houghton Mifflin Company, 1968), p. 351.

[25]Student writing from *Tracings* (Francisco Junior High School, San Francisco, 1970); *Writers of Tomorrow* (Purdue University, Fall 1970); and *Sophomore Poetry* (Camden High School, Campbell, Calif., 1960).

[26]Paul Cummins, "Teaching Modern Poetry," *California English Journal*.

FOR FURTHER STUDY

A. Study the following sampler of *student writing* from the seventh grade through the first year of college. How do you react to each piece of writing? What kind of student wrote it? What kind of writing is it? How would you respond to it as a teacher?

I'm a Fighter

I'm a fighter. I fight everyone in the house. In fact, I once fought my father. I didn't start it. He didn't start it. My mother started it. As it happened, my mother only lasted five minutes in the fight. My fathers husky and always has been. He weighs two hundred and some pounds. At the time, I weighed 55 pounds. It was a pretty big difference in weight, but I took it like a real tarzan. I tryed to call the operator, but he was coming after me. I put down the phone. I picked up the broom. I started charging his stomach. He grabbed it and took it out of my hand. I ran in to the living room then ran out. I jumped right on his neck. I started scrach-ing, bitting, kicking and screaming all at once. He pulled me off and carried me to my room. Then, he went to his room and locked the door. I ran to the closet took out his clothes, and put them infront of his door. I then told him to get out of the house. He remained inside. He won the fight. I won the argument. While fighting I felt very serious and nervous. I remember my knees clinking together after the fight. The Next day was Sunday. My mother told me, "I didn't know you loved me so much you were willing to fight daddy." I felt very brave. I never knew how I got the courage to fight my father. (probably seeing my mother on the floor.) I'm never afraid of my father. I stand up to take my punishment from him. He never hits me, 'cause he knows I'll hit back.

The hand is the downfall of man
This measly piece of flesh that gives
the signal for life or death
This panting extremity that thrusts
war, poverty and pollution
The instrument of hate, lust envy and war
       Stop!
Lower your filthy fist
Lower the pointer of destruction
       Stop!
Go back
Resume your natural form hand
Be what you are
The human tool of love and peace
The extremity that shows friendship
and affection
The instrument of fortune, beauty,
and resurection

City Child

So maybe I have a
heart of
steel.
SOMEthing pulls me
to the city.
        (give me
        concrete meadows
        with neon flowers
        growing in the
        purple sunshine
        of vapor lights.
Something to satisfy my
steel soul)

I was born in the inner city fifteen years ago. My father was proud of me *then*. I guess I did all the things an average kid did: drop rocks on street cars, break beer bottles, steal dill pickles from the delicatessen, fight, kick dogs, go to matinees, etc. I finally got to school age and was really scared of school, so I used to run home and hide from my mother. But as time went on I became kind of used to school.

When I was six, we moved to the east side. I got into more trouble then than I ever had in my whole life before. Some friends and I threw rocks at a drunk down the street, so he leveled his shotgun and let us have it. I got hit in the right leg, and my friend got hit in the stomach, which put him in the hospital for a few days.

Then we moved out close to the Speedway. That's where I got used to hearing the hardtops running every Saturday night. Nothing much exciting ever happened there except that I got a B.B. gun and shot at the low-flying planes as they taxied in to land at the airport.

The first year after we moved to where we live now, I had only one real friend, my cousin Mike. We did so many mean, unspeakable things that if I sat here all day I couldn't tell you half of them. I started to take drum lessons. I guess I learned fast for my age because in about six months I was playing in the school band. I got my bongos in the eighth grade and fussed around on them a little.

I got my first ticket for speeding and driving without a license. My parents argued an awful lot then, so I ran away from home for eight days and nine nights. It was the best time I have ever had in my whole life. Then I came back.

I guess I want to be a truck driver or an auto mechanic. I like working on engines, transmissions, and almost anything that runs. If I could go to Detroit, I would try to work on the assembly line at General Motors. Or I would try to go to Indiana and become a test driver for road bikes.

I wouldn't get married till I am about thirty. And I won't get involved with any women because I don't want anybody to make up my mind for me that I should get married. After I finish school, I am going to go for about a year's vacation, free from school and parents.

Advice to a Son

Watch for low-flying insects
For they're the ones that, when you're
      yawning, get inside you.
Never get wet, 'cause you'll catch cold
      and sure you don't want that.
Just stay inside and be a good boy,
      'cause then you'll please Mom.
Don't chase girls and drink wine
      'cause I hear they're bad for you.
Just grow up and be a clean-cut American boy
      and get a short haircut.

Black and White

Racial prejudice is not on the decline. Many people like to believe it is, and as long as they keep believing their fantasies and ignore the real root of the problem we'll never achieve true social acceptance. Some people seem to think by forcing integration you will eliminate prejudice. Do you think this is a good idea?

Let me help you answer the question by giving you a few of my first hand experiences on forced integration. I was very lucky to go to the second biggest high school in the United States, with an enrollment over five thousand students. By an unusual coincidence it just happens to be approximately fifty percent white and fifty percent black. The campus is very beautiful with trees of green, purple, red and yellow leaves, bursting with color in the spring and fall. In the middle of the campus there is a square with benches to rest on. You can always spot many birds, squirrels, and strangely spotted butterflies busy at work and play on this square. Strangely enough, I have never sat on one of those benches and a couple of times have had to run by them.

We did have an old cafeteria that was two big rooms. In one room the white pupils sat and in the other the black. The administration put an end to that. Instead of building a badly needed auditorium (as of now we use the gym), they built a new cafeteria. This one has one huge room with only an imaginary line down the middle. It really solved our problem. But now the administration can claim we have true integration.

My old high school is built on a huge block. On each side there is a gate. The four gates were divided among the students as two for white and two for blacks. Well, of course, the administration couldn't have this at their totally integrated high school so now they have closed down two of the gates causing some students a real inconvenience. But the students should realize that even though they might have to walk a few extra blocks it's a small price to pay for a great high school. My sister's boyfriend paid his small price. Right outside one of the gates he was stabbed in the back, missing the spinal cord by a very close margin. The officials claimed that since it wasn't actually done on campus there is nothing they can do about it. They wouldn't even call him an ambulance.

Moving from that high school to college has been a big step for me. Students are free to choose their own friends. No one is crammed down anyone's throat. This new freedom has enabled me to make many new friends of all races. But what about the students leaving that high school who never make it to college?

Unfortunately they are left with a feeling of prejudice that they may never overcome.

A Lot of Growing Up to Do

Although I don't remember my childhood years, I can account for what has been told me by my parents. Since I was the youngest of my family with two older sisters, I was brought up being given everything I ever wanted. My family moved to a small three-bedroom home when I was three. Our house wasn't the quietest place to live. Of course my older sisters both teased me for as long as I can remember. But always mom and dad favored me since I was their "baby." I loved my neighborhood as the years went by until we moved about ten miles away. I was used to the old park with the big slide and the muddy baseball field. But the new home became my favorite. The outside was well kept by my dad, and the inside was kept to perfection by my mom. She always was dad's favorite housekeeper and cook. My life up until the fifth grade was what you would call normal for my age. It wasn't until March of the sixth grade that my life seemed to change abruptly.

My mom had always been sick with a heart condition since she was married. One early morning, I heard her coughing inside my parents' bedroom, so I jumped out of bed to see what the matter was. My father was leaning over my mother trying to pump her heart. I was crying and yelling at my father to call an ambulance. While we waited for one to come, I helped my mother dress. She could hardly breathe. After it had finally come, my sisters got up and asked where everyone was. I was explaining to them what happened when the phone rang. I can still remember the five words dad spoke so clearly to me: "Kathy, she didn't make it."

Facing people I knew on the streets was one of the problems I learned to face after my mother died. We all grew older, each helping around the house. When I was in the ninth grade, my oldest sister got married and moved to the East. So now I was left alone most of the time while my dad and sister worked. I had no mother to watch over me and discipline me. I knew I was still spoiled but too young to realize how much dad still treated me as the "baby." Three years later my father remarried, marrying a young widow with three daughters and a son. My other sister at first lived with us, until she married a year later. My stepmother would not move into our house, so my dad and I had to move all our belongings to her house about two miles away. I can remember crying myself to sleep at night, thinking of the great times I had when it was just the "five of us."

My father remarried to give me a mother, someone who could bring me up as a fine young lady. I never could understand why he did except for this reason, but I didn't let it bother me as long as he was happy. This attitude towards his new marriage had changed absolutely after I had lived in the new house for a year. Having been brought up by my sister for two years, I felt as though I didn't need a mother.

My stepmother and I just didn't get along. She disliked my sisters and myself. At first my father decided to bring me up alone and have my stepmother bring up her children, but this plan didn't work for obvious reasons. You can't have a family living under two rulers. So my stepmother would restrict me in any way she could. I tried hard for years to treat her as a mother, but it was worthless. Everything I said went in one ear and out the other. She was strict with her children, whereas my father did spoil me, so that I was used to being treated leniently. I admit I had a lot of growing up to do, but it was impossible to grow up with her standing over me with evil eyes. My father tried always to make me feel better, knowing I felt uneasy living with a strange family. But it never helped ease the tension which built up inside me.

The problem was that I had already been brought up by my real mother. Then she came along and tried to change my whole way of life. I can remember one incident when we got into a big argument. She disliked my dog and made me give him away. My heart was broken for months, and I resented her for that for a long time. This is why I am away at college right now, to keep peace in my family. Right now my father is alone with their family and I keep in touch with him very often. He knows how I feel about going home, and he understands. Every time I set foot in "her" home, I get jumped on for the littlest things.

I guess to me home life wasn't the best because of my situation. The sad part is that I did grow up, but instead of getting closer to my stepmother, I grew further and further away from her. The fact is that we will never get along only because from the very beginning she resented me as a new daughter, and I sort of resented a "new" mother. She seemed to want my father all to herself and would become very jealous to see the love I received from him.

I will always realize how much my dad loved me to do the thing he did and for my sake mostly. But why did things turn out the way they did in my home? Why did my mother have to "not make it"? Why couldn't I get along with my stepmother, or why did I have to be the "baby" all my life? These questions I may someday answer, but for now I am thankful for my dad and my sisters who love me very much and care for me. My real mother will never be forgotten, but as I continue to grow up and meet new people, I will begin to understand why things happen, and why situations like mine ever exist.

B. Find an article that deals with a teacher's *day-to-day* work with composition. From the article, distill three or four major points of advice for the beginning teacher. How would you support, modify, or challenge the author's recommendations? Choose an article like the following:

Donna Geyer, "Teaching Composition to the Disadvantaged," *English Journal*, 58 (September 1969), 900–907;

Ken Macrorie, "To Be Read," *English Journal*, 57 (May 1968), 686–692;

James P. Moffett, "Coming On Center," *English Journal*, 59 (April 1970), 528–533;

Don M. Wolfe, "Autobiography: The Gold of Writing Power," *English Journal*, 60 (October 1971), 937–946.

C. Find an article about composition that stresses the *creative, imaginative* element in student writing. Discuss and evaluate some of the writing assignments or writing projects described by the author. Choose an article like the following:

Dennis J. Hannan, "Student Poet Power," *English Journal*, 60 (October 1971), 913–920;

Antony Christie, "Making with Words: A Practical Approach to Creativity," *English Journal*, 61 (February 1972), 246–251;

Alan D. Engelsman, "A Piece of the Action," *English Journal*, 61 (February 1972), 252–256;

Gilbert Tierney and Stephen N. Judy, "The Assignment Makers," *English Journal*, 61 (February 1972), 265–269.

D. Find a book about teaching that makes extensive use of *student writing* from classes taught or supervised by the author. Choose a book like Ken Macrorie, *Uptaught* (New York: Hayden Book Company, Inc., 1970); James Moffett, *A Student-Centered Language Arts Curriculum* (Boston: Houghton Mifflin Company, 1968); Herbert Kohl, *36 Children* (New York: New American Library, Inc., 1968); or David Holbrook, *English for the Rejected* (Cambridge University Press, 1964). What are the qualities the author encourages in student writing? (Use detailed illustrations.) How do *you* react to the kind of student writing the author values?

E. As we respond to student writing, we try to keep in mind questions like the following: How does it feel to be a writer? What does the student go through as he puts a paper together? What are some of the things that work for him and against him? What apprehensions, or what expectations, does he have about his audience? The following *writing assignments* will help you put yourself in the student's shoes. Share your writing with others for discussion both of the process that produced it and of the result.

1. Write a *letter* to your teacher. Make it a letter about something you want the teacher to know, or something you want to get off your chest.

2. Pretend you are a social worker or a scientist studying the way people live in America. Write a *report* on the life-style of one family (or other small group of people) that you know well.

3. Write a paper in which you try to fix the boundaries of a large general *term.* Choose one: Where does "power," or "force," end and "violence" begin? At what point does "freedom" end and "oppression" begin? Where, in our society, does "justice" end and "injustice" begin?

4. A writer once imagined how, as a survivor of nuclear war he would be writing a *manual of instructions* for future generations who had lost all the

accumulated knowledge and skills of our civilization. Among other things, he tried to include instructions for making safety matches and a wheelbarrow. He also included whatever parts of Shakespeare he knew by heart. Imagine that you have been given the chance to write a memo for survivors of nuclear war.

5. Do you ever make up imaginary stories to go with faces you see in a crowd, or with pictures you see in a newspaper or magazine? From a newspaper or magazine, clip a *picture that you find interesting or unusual*. Ignore the original caption—make up your own story to go with the picture.

6. To many nineteenth-century Americans, the railroad was a fitting *symbol* of the mighty progress of material civilization. Thoreau, for instance, marveled at the power and punctuality and regularity of the railroad. He saw a symbolic significance in how the train kept to its own track and warned others to keep *off* it. Write about something that you consider symbolic of twentieth-century America.

7. One of the best-known poems by e. e. cummings is his "Portrait" of Buffalo Bill. Write an *epitaph* for a prominent person who died more recently. Follow the form and style of cummings's poem as closely as you can.

Buffalo Bill'
defunct
        who used to
        ride a watersmooth-silver
                stallion
and break onetwothreefourfive pigeonsjustlike that
                Jesus
he was a handsome man
        and what i want to know is
how do you like your blueeyed boy
Mister Death.

8. Novelists create a world of their own whose attitudes and assumptions we are made to share while we are reading the book. How well can you get into the spirit of a *well-known novel* you have read? Write a paper in which you imagine yourself
—on a whaling ship in pursuit of Moby Dick, or
—on a raft with a runaway boy named Huckleberry Finn, or
—on a train, talking to a fellow traveler named Holden Caulfield, or
—on an island with a group of children stranded after a nuclear war, or
—on an island with a group of children stranded after a nuclear war and worshipping the Lord of the Flies.

9. Write a letter in which a *character in a play* tells the story of what happened as seen from *his* point of view. The letter might be from a close friend of Julius Caesar, or one of the citizens who listened to the speech by Mark Antony, or a servant in the castle of Macbeth, or Juliet's nurse.

10. The moving picture camera can capture at first apparently unrelated scenes and help us put them together in a pattern—to bring out a theme, to make a point, to create a mood, to stir the audience. By yourself, or as a group project, prepare a *script* for a short movie. If you have access to the necessary equipment, go ahead and produce the picture.

The Relevance
of Literature

Whatever else English teachers do, they teach imaginative literature. An English teacher is a person who on any given day might take a poem to class, or assign a short story or a play. The poem does not have to be an immortal classic; the play does not have to be by Sophocles. Imaginative literature as taught by English teachers ranges over the whole creative, imaginative use of language—from the nursery rhyme to the sonnet by Shakespeare.

Let us look at a poem that an English teacher might take to class:

Seed said to Flower:
You are too rich and wide.
You spend too soon and loosely
That grave and spacious beauty

I keep secret, inside.
You will die of your pride.

Flower said to Seed: Each opens, gladly
Or in defeat. Clenched close,
You hold a hidden rose
That will break you to be
Free of your dark modesty.[1]

What does such a poem do? What does it do that story, novel, and play do on a larger scale, and with somewhat different means? First, *the poem makes us share in experience.* A miniature drama is enacted on the small stage set by the poem. It is as if we had been walking along and—look! we see by the side of the road something like a puppet stage on which a seed is talking to a flower. The poem puts a frame around a happening. We stop to take it in. We pay attention. Where the stage may have been dark, where there may have been only grey routine, there are signs of life. What happens when we read a poem is similar to what happens when we listen to a kindergarten girl hopping and skipping and reciting a rhyme, or when we look at an impressionist painting. Like the other creative arts, imaginative literature beckons to us, saying: "Be alive. Share more fully in the drama of life."

Second, *the experience of literature engages our full attention as human beings.* It is not just information, to be stored and retrieved. It does not just appeal to the recording, registering part of our minds. It is not just something that we could report to the census taker, to become part of a quantitative measurement. More than our intellect is engaged— our senses, our emotions. The poem makes us see and hear and feel. There is something to watch and to marvel at. We hear voices of warning and of threat ("You spend too soon and loosely"; ". . . a hidden rose, that will break you . . ."). There is a contest, a conflict, for us to take sides in: We are made to feel the apprehension that keeps us from letting go, the fear that keeps us from making ourselves open. But we are also made to fear the restrictions that hem us in, turning our protective covering into a cage, our fortress into a prison. We thus feel and react as well as think: WE become involved.

Third, *the poem imposes a pattern upon experience.* The motions we observe are not merely arbitrary, disoriented, chaotic. A pattern of expectation is set up and then satisfied. The pendulum swings one way: "Seed said to flower . . ." Then it swings back the other way: "Flower said to seed . . ." It is as if a shuttle train had first passed through one way—and then returned. Similarly, a note is struck—and then echoed:

"rich—wide—spend—soon—loosely—spacious—free." And again: "se-cret—clenched—close—hidden—dark." It is as if a network of syno-nyms and near-synonyms held the poem together. These patterns are not merely decorative, "stuck on"—they are part of a larger pattern of the kind we find in human experience. There is attack and defense, as-sertion and rebuttal. First, one part to the contest makes its plea, then the other. There is a balance: The opponents are fairly matched, since we listen gravely to warnings against pride—but equally gravely to warnings against repression. There is in the poem some of the drama of life—but selected and arranged in such a way that we can follow, that we are ready for what comes next. We thus experience the pleasure to be derived from **form**—from things that fall into place, things that have a direction, things that hang together. Here as elsewhere, literary experience is not "raw" experience but experience that has been ordered, shaped, bal-anced, formed.

Fourth and last, *the poem has meaning.* Though we cherish the poem as poem, we can translate what it says into a prose statement. Though the poem engages our senses and our emotions, we can intellectually sum up what it all means. The poem is not really about flowers but about peo-ple. The protected, encapsuled seed and the opening, lavish flower are symbolic. There are two views of the world in contention, and the poem is weighted in the direction of the second, which "has the last word." There is an appeal to our fear of what is stifling, of what boxes us in. We are encouraged to break out. There is a plea for freedom, for unfolding, for liberation. The reason the poem is not identical with its prose meaning is that in the actual poem the meaning is *acted out.* In reading imaginative literature, we *live through* the experience in which human meanings exist and take shape.

The reason we teach literature to young people is that it makes them branch out emotionally and intellectually. It takes them beyond their own narrow range of observation, outside of what is already familiar. It does so not by providing impersonal information, but by involving them in experience that appeals to their senses and feelings as well as to their minds. It promotes the kind of imaginative understanding of life and people that takes us beyond overt behavior to an understanding of motives and aspirations. Ideally, imaginative literature helps our students become more sensitive, more capable of sympathy, more aware of the range of human possibility.

If this broadening and humanizing potential is to be realized, our teaching will have to stress the human relevance of literature. We have to make sure that dry analysis or a dusty, fact-oriented method does not come between us and the richness and variety of life that literature has to offer. The final test of what we do is whether our students can share in the basic satisfactions that literature has to offer: the heightened sense of life' as we participate imaginatively in a fuller range of experience; the feeling of heightened clarity as some limited aspect of human life comes into focus; the feeling of solidarity as we discover our roots in our common humanity. Whatever we bring into our teaching from literary history or literary criticism has to be judged by how it helps us to achieve these goals.

TOWARD A NEW LITERARY HISTORY

We study literary history as a means of understanding who we are. Reading the great writers of the past, we begin to see where we come from. We begin to see what has shaped our consciousness, what has shaped the categories that help us think. Literature is one of the means by which man records his sense of himself and of his world. It is closely related to art, music, and architecture, and to the institutions and traditions that shape our lives. When we relate literary history to the history of the other creative arts, and to the history of ideas and institutions, we begin to see literary style as the reflection of a "life style." We see literary history as a central part of the history of our common culture. We then teach the literature of the past because its legacy is with us today, because it plays a role in the way people today think and feel and act.

At the same time, when we study literature from a historical perspective, we cease to be mere prisoners of an inherited cultural tradition. We become aware of a larger range of human possibility. In reading the literature of other times and places, we try on *alternative* life styles. As we respond to the way different kinds of literature reflect, illuminate, and shape experience, our horizons broaden, our sympathies are enlarged.

Ideally, literary history makes us aware of the "presence of the past." To teach the great works of the past in this spirit, we have to make them seem as contemporary and topical and alive as the living literature of our own current culture. We have to make possible a kind of imaginative reconstruction that makes our reading a living experience rather than an inspection of literary monuments. In this task of imaginative reconstruction, traditional literary history, because of characteristic built-in biases and limitations, too often failed.

First, traditional scholarship too often led the student *away from* rather than *into* the literary text. The standard procedure of the traditional scholar was to provide "background," to establish the context in which the literature was written. Introducing an author to students meant extensive preliminary treatment of his biography and of his social, economic, and cultural milieu. The student who wanted to read Wordsworth's "Tintern Abbey" was first taken to Cumberland, to Cambridge, to France, to Germany, and to the Lake Country. He became acquainted with the poet's parents, his sister, his friends, his wife. Often, the background material proved so extensive that the student was trusted to read "Tintern Abbey" for himself, between classes. Teachers learned the hard way to resist the endless detours proposed by conventional literary historians and to concentrate instead on the actual reading of major selected works. They learned to select works so fully imbued with the life of their times that they created their *own* context. They learned to select related works that provided background for each other.

Today, we no longer get the student ready for *Oedipus Rex* by the introductory lecture on Greek politics and religion. Instead, we make the student pay careful attention to what attitudes toward priests, gods, and kings are acted out in the play itself. We have learned to use historical knowledge "from the inside out rather than from the outside in."[2] We have learned that "history is as much *in* our literary texts as our texts are in our history."[3]

Second, conventional literary scholarship relied heavily on a dry, *fact-oriented* method. In the graduate schools where many teachers of literature were trained, literary study often meant a kind of historical scholarship taken over from the German universities and influenced by late nineteenth-century **positivism**. Dealing with a subject that would seem to call above all for imagination, for empathy, the positivistic scholar concentrated on what could be rigorously verified. In the words of Jacques Barzun, he applied "the literal part of the historical method—the part that stops short of intuition and imagination. . . . Whatever was not factual and 'shown,' whatever was imaginative and readable, was unscholarly."[4] Much literary scholarship dealt with details of chronology, cases of disputed authorship, identification of an author's sources. Who are the real authors of major anonymous medieval poems? Was a poem published in 1637 or 1639? How are earlier treatments of the Hamlet theme related to each other and to Shakespeare's play? Who were the possible historical models for some of Chaucer's pilgrims? Were some of the minor poems ascribed to Chaucer (or plays ascribed to Shakespeare) really written by him, or partly by him, or wholly by someone else? Getting embroiled in these and similar questions, the student was led, first, from the major works to much minor and obscure stuff, and much of the time away from literature altogether into the study of city ordinances, publishing registers, parish records, business letters, and bills of sale. To many a frustrated student, the scholar's prized discoveries—

controverted dates of composition, obscure sources, variant texts—
came to seem mere dust and ashes.

Third and last, conventional literary scholarship suffered from absurd
overspecialization. Literature was chopped up into periods firmly
separated by the conflicting interests and prejudices of their respective
specialists. As a result of rigid compartmentalization, no one was ultimately responsible for what history is all about: major, profound historical
shifts, major historical continuities through the centuries. The traditional
organization of literary studies in the colleges and universities sliced
through major historical relationships the way a butcher's knife slices
through meat. As a result, the student often failed to gain a feeling for the
basic and continuing concerns of literature. Teachers trained in traditional programs went out into the schools with a mass of historical detail
but without a clear rationale, without a sense of what gives literary history its relevance and vitality.

Literary history serves the teacher's purposes when it is the servant
rather than the master of literary study. To overcome the limitations of
traditional scholarship, the teacher must learn to approach the literature
of the past first and last as a *reader*—a reader who laughs and cries, who
cheers and objects, who is filled with foreboding and with sudden joy.
Historical knowledge pays off when it helps us read: Words have meaning in a contemporary setting; patterns of behavior have contemporary
implications. A sense for the historical context, for the historical moment,
gives us a feeling for what reactions, what interpretations, might have
seemed natural to the writer and his contemporary audience. *A contemporary audience brings to a play or a novel certain patterns of expectation*—which the author fulfills or bends to his own purposes.

Historical training equips the teacher to direct attention to those
elements of a work that can help the student "get into the spirit of the
thing." Historical training should help the teacher answer the question:
"How might this have looked to a contemporary reader (or spectator)
reasonably well attuned to the author's language and intentions?" For
instance, is Hamlet, as Coleridge and his fellow romantics claimed, "endlessly reasoning and hesitating," indecisive, irresolute? Or did the romantics, looking in Hamlet for a kindred spirit, overemphasize the dreamy,
talky side of Hamlet's nature? To get into the spirit of the play, should
we correct the balance and see Hamlet as a brilliant, active, even impetuous Renaissance prince—tested and ultimately defeated by tragic
developments that cut short his career?

Awareness of the play's historical context could in several ways
lead us to opt for the latter alternative. First, the play was not the first
of its kind. It was not the first **tragedy of revenge** ever written: Certain

features of such a play had become familiar to playwright and audience. Elaborate manipulations and delays, plottings and counterplottings, were to be expected *in this kind of play*. They were not necessarily caused by the indecisive, vacillating temperament of the hero; rather, they were suited to test the mettle of a forceful and determined protagonist. Most basically, the play, and the revenge, had to occupy a certain length of time.

If Hamlet had killed the villainous Claudius in the first act, the play could not have served its basic purpose: to keep the spectators of a "large, cheap, and popular" commercial theater entertained for the expected period of time.[5] The audience was ready to see the plot proceed through a number of familiar steps: The crime had to be discovered and the criminal's guilt confirmed. Formidable obstacles in the avenger's path had to be overcome. Finally, the avenger would turn the tables on his enemies, executing his revenge in an ingenious and spectacular way, making sure the punishment would more than pay for the crime.

In *Hamlet*, the reported nightly wanderings of the dead king's ghost bring the first hints of foul play. ("I'll speak to it though Hell itself should gape/And bid me hold my peace.") Like Hieronimo in Kyd's *Spanish Tragedy*, Hamlet distrusts the first accusation brought against the alleged murderer. He feigns madness to be better able to confirm the ghost's charges: "The Devil hath power/To assume a pleasing shape. . . . I'll have grounds/More relative than this." Hamlet stages the ingenious play-within-the-play in order to test the king's conscience. When the king's guilt has been confirmed, Hamlet lets pass his first opportunity when he sees the king, unguarded and at his mercy, saying his prayer. If the king were to die with his soul in a state of grace, the punishment would not fit the crime:

> Up, sword, and know thou a more horrid hent.
> When he is drunk asleep, or in his rage,
> Or in the incestuous pleasure of his bed—
> At gaming, swearing, or about some act
> That has no relish of salvation in 't—
> Then trip him, that his heels may kick at Heaven
> And that his soul may be as damned and black
> As Hell, whereto it goes.
>
> (Act III, Sc. 3)

Hamlet jumps at his second opportunity when he stabs the person hiding behind the curtain in his mother's room—who turns out to be Polonius rather than the king ("I took thee for thy better"). In the meantime, the king's counterplotting is beginning to put formidable obstacles in Hamlet's path: the trip to England, and the enmity of Laertes, who holds Hamlet responsible for the deaths of Polonius and Ophelia, Laertes's father and sister.

From the point of view of the spectator, there is *no hurry*. We want to savor the story: Hamlet's "madness" has already made the defenders uneasy; the prince is playing cat-and-mouse with the flunkeys and hangers-on of the corrupt king; the chief villain will be punished in good time. Hamlet has a passionate nature, a cruel wit, a flair for mimicry and high drama—all of which the leisurely pace of the revenge tragedy allows him to display brilliantly.

Just as the play as play fits its historical context, so does the verbal style: The Elizabethan playgoer was bound to expect from his tragic heroes a grand rhetorical (even theatrical) manner. Hamlet's self-denunciations are not the ruminating soul-searching of the introvert. They are rhetorical; they are passionate outbursts in which he spurs himself to action—the way an impetuous, excitable person would:

> O what a rogue and peasant slave am I! . . .
>
> . . . Am I a coward?
> Who calls me villain? . . .
>
> . . . it cannot be
> But I am pigeon-livered and lack gall
> To make oppression bitter, or ere this
> I should ha' fatted all the region kites
> With this slave's offal.
>
> (Act II, Sc. 2)

These self-denunciations lead naturally into equally passionate, equally vigorous denunciations of the intended victim of revenge: "Bloody, bawdy villain!"

It is the brilliant, passionate side of Hamlet's nature that gives true tragic force to what has happened to him: The brilliant, beckoning world of his adolescence and young manhood has come to an end. He has learned the ghastly truth, and he has assumed the terrible burden of the avenger's duty. His passionate nature has been deeply wounded by his disillusionment; his cruel wit is a weapon with which he strikes back at the world that has fatally wounded him. He has of late "lost all my mirth":

> . . . . indeed it goes so heavily with my disposition that this goodly frame, the earth, seems to me a sterile promontory; this most excellent canopy, the air, look you, this brave o'erhanging firmament, this majestical roof fretted with golden fire; why, it appeareth nothing to me but a foul and

pestilent congregation of vapors. What a piece of work is a man, how noble in reason, how infinite in faculties, in form and moving how express and admirable, in action how like an angel, in apprehension how like a god: the beauty of the world, the paragon of animals; and yet to me, what is this quintessence of dust?

(Act II, Sc. 2)

To read Shakespeare in his historical context, we need to weigh equally strongly the two sides of the paradox that pervades much of the literature of his time: the glorious promise of good and the potent force of evil.

When we teach Shakespeare, the universality of his themes and the sheer force and beauty of his language tend to make us forget that we *are* dealing with literary conventions, with a period style. Our most basic job in dealing with the literature of the past is always this: To approach conventions and styles that have come to seem merely quaint or arbitrary or "artificial" to the modern reader and to bring them back to life—to show that in their time they were living and changing as a means of giving shape to things that mattered and still matter. Thus, we take students to the poetry of **courtly love**, not because it is one of the objects on display in the literature museum, but because love is not likely to go away as a basic human need. The humble, long-suffering lover of the medieval romance and of the love sonnets of the Renaissance did not merely dance out a strange minuet to whose significance we have lost the key. As we watch Chaucer's lovers in *Troilus and Cressida*, we begin to see the human meaning of the ritual of reluctance, of "disdain," required of the lady. We begin to understand the ritual of humility, of "service," required of the man. Love, with Chaucer, is something tender and vulnerable—it must be protected from the sniggers of a callous world, from the cynicism bred by casual conquest, from the damage done by blurted-out ugly words. The lady must have time to become aware of the man's good intentions, "his truth and clean intent." The man must have time to learn to take love seriously: He shows his genuine interest by being willing to wait; he shows his respect for her by doing her bidding. He *talks* to her—sometimes in the tone of playful banter, but more often with the painful intensity of the lover, who, against his own original frivolous intentions, has come to care more deeply than he ever did before or ever will again. The implied message from the courtly lady to the male is something like this: "If you love me, learn to be considerate, learn to be tender, learn to show respect. Unlearn your patronizing airs, your fashionable callousness, and then your love will grow. Come to know me, learn to listen to me, take me seriously as a person, and our love will be a beautiful coming together of body and soul." If we learn to be patient enough, receptive enough, we may for a time, Fortune willing, triumph over sorrow and fear, and experience as much joy as the human heart is capable of, "as muche joie as herte may comprende."

What strikes us about the convention of courtly love is its pervasive influence, its staying power, its ability to affect through the centuries in many contradictory ways the way people in the Western world have thought, talked, and acted about love. As C. S. Lewis said in *The Allegory of Love*, "humanity does not pass through phases as a train passes through stations":

> French poets, in the eleventh century, discovered or invented, or were the first to express, that romantic species of passion which English poets were still writing about in the nineteenth. They effected a change which has left no corner of our ethics, our imagination, or our daily life untouched, and they erected impassable barriers between us and the classical past or the Oriental present.[6]

This late in the day, we see the courtly heritage in our everyday vocabulary of romantic love: The girl expects the boy to talk (if not to feel) an overpowering, once-in-a-lifetime passion. She expects to be put "on a pedestal." She expects him to be "serious" about love. While the modern sexual revolution tends to make love "cool," casual, detached, biological, much of our popular entertainment and popular culture, reinforced by much of the most powerful literature of the past, stubbornly clings to the medieval ideal of a beautiful, deep, ennobling, and lasting passion in which our emotional nature finds its true fulfillment and realization.

At the same time, the convention of romantic love illustrates powerfully a major principle of development in our literary and cultural history: Ours is not an ossified tribal culture in which established rituals are passed on from generation to generation. *Ours is a culture in which powerful influences generate strong countertrends, in which dominant patterns are broken or modified by strong countercurrents.* In the words of Lionel Trilling, our culture "is not a flow, nor even a confluence; the form of its existence is struggle, or at least debate—it is nothing if not a dialectic."[7] Much "modern" literature is animated by a *rebellion* against the idealizing, romanticizing literary treatment of love. For centuries, the idealized woman had been indoctrinated into thinking of herself as more ethereal, more sensitive, more refined than man. She had learned to feel that men are of a coarser grain, until a woman like Sue Bridehead in Thomas Hardy's *Jude the Obscure* found herself incapacitated for the coarser side of life. Here is the paradox that Ibsen's Nora rebels against in *The Doll's House*: When the idealized, romanticized woman looks with a sober eye at her true social and economic position, she finds that she is elevated in poem and song but treated as an inferior in prosaic fact. She finds herself shut off from any effective share of responsibility in business, church, and state. Her "most sacred duty" is to be a wife and mother and not to meddle in a man's world except to be decorative, to entertain men in the interludes between business, and to do poorly paid work that turns out to be a dead end. Nora no longer wants to be her husband's "sweet little song bird," with whom he has never had a serious talk, "never sat down in earnest together to get to the bottom of a single thing," and who is not even trusted with the key to the mailbox, let alone seriously consulted in decisions that most gravely affect her own life and those of her children. Writers like Ibsen and Thomas Hardy and G. B. Shaw and D. H. Lawrence are "modern" in their groping attempts to put the relationship between the sexes on a new footing, to invent a new language of the emotions, to create new patterns of partnership.

The tradition of romantic love is only one example of a literary **convention** that helps us understand who we are, that continues to be a powerful force in our culture. In the more recent past, we take our students to a writer like Hemingway because his reportorial, "bare-facts" stance and his terse, taciturn heroes bear witness to one of the great traumas of modern man: *his disillusionment with language, his distrust of words.* Hemingway's generation had marched into World War I to the accompaniment of high-minded oratory about decency, duty, love of country, loyalty, heroism, dedication, and culture. But the realities of war made a mockery of the established idealistic rhetoric; they provided the supreme example of man's beautiful words belied by his ugly performance. Western man, who for decades had talked of progress and civilization, saw these edifying phrases turn hollow as gallant men died in the mud of blood-spattered and foul-smelling trenches, with whole divisions slaughtered in futile attacks, as if "healthy young men had become hateful in the sight of Europe." In the words of Ezra Pound,

> There died a myriad
> And of the best, among them,
> For an old bitch gone in the teeth,
> For a botched civilization,
>
> Charm, smiling at the good mouth,
> Quick eyes gone under earth's lid,

For two gross of broken statues,
For a few thousand battered books.[8]

Hemingway's heroes are taciturn because they are weary of big words. In Hemingway's short story, "Soldier's Home," Krebs, home from the war, has "acquired the nausea in regard to experience that is the result of untruth or exaggeration." The stay-at-home bourgeois vocabulary of work being honorable, of having an aim in life, of being "a credit to the community," of loving one's father and mother, goes by him like the wind. Though he likes girls, "he did not want to have to do any courting. He did not want to tell any more lies."[9]

Hemingway's characters are part of a generation that has acquired a deep-seated suspicion of rhetoric, of beautiful and edifying claptrap— a generation determined to hold on to a few simple realities, without "all this talking." A whole generation of European and American writers scorned cheap words. When they did use words, they more often than not used them for the sardonic comment, the deflating remark. In turn, they found it difficult to verbalize love, tenderness, devotion, awe. Much of Hemingway's work in fact is an attempt to establish new values untainted by the hypocrisies of conventional language.

For a long time, modern literature in our schools meant twentieth-century literature of the post-World-War I generation. Its pervading negativism, its corrosive satirical bent, its suspicion of contentment and happiness and innocence—all these are part of our historical legacy, a legacy powerfully reinforced by the reaction of later generations to the disasters of later wars.

Ideal love, Puritanism, romantic utopianism and Victorian "realism," modern disillusionment and alienation—these are part of our *general cultural history*. We can best come to sense their power and understand their inner dynamics through the study of literature because they are not merely intellectual "ideas" or social "forces." They are rooted in how people think and feel, how they sift and interpret and shape experience, how they order their contradictions and pattern their lives. Literary history helps us understand our identity by tracing some of these major strands; it fascinates us by tracing their interplay, their evolution. The giants of our literary tradition—Chaucer, Spenser, Milton, Whitman, Lawrence—are writers who rewrite the great myths to make them viable in a changing world. The most fascinating figures of our tradition—John Donne, Emily Dickinson, G. M. Hopkins, Henrik Ibsen, Dylan Thomas —are the great nonconformists, the great innovators, who react against the prevailing fashions of their time, who turn the tide, who set a new pattern. The excitement in teaching literary history results from our reconstructing the great struggles for the minds and souls of men.

Traditional historical scholarship, through its retreat into specialization and antiquarianism, by and large failed to do justice to the larger
historical drama. Discouraged by the bit-facts unearthed by much conventional "research," put off by the elaborate scaffoldings erected around
the literary monuments by historical scholars, many teachers in the fifties
and sixties followed the swing to an entirely different kind of literary
study, critical rather than historical in emphasis. The new critical emphasis provided a much needed counterweight to the prevailing preoccupation with "background" material: Attention shifted from the historical framework to the literary work itself. Though in time the new
approach developed its own kind of specialization and isolation, it made
possible and necessary a fresh look at what literature basically is and
does.

THE NEW CRITICISM AND AFTER

Modern literary criticism made its influence felt in the classroom and in
textbooks by insisting on the close reading of the actual literary text.
The traditional historical approach had concentrated on *preparing* the
reader for a fuller appreciation—by study of setting, authorship, sources,
and currents of which a work was part. Under the influence of the **New
Criticism,** the emphasis in literary study shifted to close firsthand analysis.
College textbooks like those by Cleanth Brooks and Robert Penn Warren
made the student go to the literary text for definite answers about its
structure and form. Survey courses shifted from a fast-paced inventory
of literary history to the close reading of selected major works. Period
courses received increasing competition from courses in the literary
genres: the poem, the short story, the novel, the play. Here, interest
centered clearly on the formal features of literature rather than on the
biographical context, the intellectual and cultural milieu. The short lyric
and the short story became phenomenally popular as objects of study and
teaching, being perfect objects of close, comprehensive analysis. In the
short stories of Hemingway, Faulkner, and Joyce, the teacher could explore details of language and structure while at the same time relating
them to the central situation or conflict that gave unity to the whole.

The new critical approach put a premium on **explication,** on detailed
interpretation of how a given poem or story "works." In dealing with a
poem, R. P. Blackmur said, "criticism must be concerned, first and last
—whatever comes between—with the poem as it is read and as what it
represents is felt." We become suspicious when a critic too early and too
fast leaves the actual work behind; we expect him to maintain above all
"a sense of continuous relationship, of sustained contact" with the work

under discussion.[10] Ideally, the student following in the footsteps of the New Critic would learn to *read*. He would learn to cooperate with the writer—follow the pattern of a work without interference from preconceptions. He would learn to yield the author's right of way, to become, in Virginia Woolf's phrase, his "fellow-worker and accomplice."

Though ideally promoting an open and receptive firsthand relation with literature, the New Criticism in practice made teacher and student approach literature with certain characteristic expectations. Analysis focused on what sets literature *apart* from ordinary communication: its more deliberate structure, its denser texture, its more finished form. Mere impressionistic "appreciation" gave way to a detailed study of form as the "unique structural means" without which the elements that go into art "would remain nothing but experience, neither beauty nor esthetic truth." Literary form "has been the great contemporary concern, and contemporary criticism has taught us that if we neglect art in its technical actualities, we are not talking about art at all, but about something else—life as the artist has lived it, or life as the critic would like it to be."[11]

This focus on the unique technical means of literary expression had a far-reaching effect on what works, and what authors, were considered worthy of critical attention. The values by which the modern critic judged literature reflected his preference for works that were rich and difficult enough to make close, formal analysis rewarding. *Typically, the modern critic required in a literary work of the first rank concreteness, complexity, inclusiveness, and wholeness.* Each of these requirements deserves detailed explanation and illustration.

The modern insistence on **concreteness** was in part a reaction against a tradition of versified abstraction and facile rhetoric. As the poet explains that life is real, life is earnest, and the grave is not its goal, we long for a kind of poetry that will get its teeth more firmly into experience. As the Memorial Day speaker eulogizes the happy dead, assured of their country's gratitude, we long for something more real, if only, as in MacLeish's "Memorial Rain," for the rasp of the wind, the minutely shifting sand, the first thin spurts of the relaxing, loosening rain. With MacLeish in "Ars Poetica," we ask for images rather than ideas, for things rather than meanings:

> A poem should be palpable and mute
> As a globed fruit
>
> Dumb
> As old medallions to the thumb
>
> Silent as the sleeve-worn stone
> Of casement ledges where the moss has grown—

> A poem should be wordless
> As the flight of birds. . . .
>
> A poem should be equal to:
> Not true
>
> For all the history of grief
> An empty doorway and a maple leaf
>
> For love
> The leaning grasses and two lights above the sea—
>
> A poem should not mean
> But be.[12]

One of the most persistent themes in modern criticism has been that a poem should not deal in abstractions but in sights, sounds, textures, feelings. *Presentiment*, for instance, is a mere intellectual construct, a verbal entity that maps out a certain area of experience. Its dictionary definition rates barely a nod of recognition: "A feeling that something, especially of an unfortunate or evil nature, is about to take place." The most striking thing about a poem on the same theme is the completely different manner in which it engages our attention:

> Presentiment is that long shadow on the lawn
> Indicative that suns go down;
> The notice to the startled grass
> That darkness is about to pass.
>
> (Emily Dickinson)

The dictionary definition is abstract. We intellectually take note of it; we check it off, as it were. The poem is visualized and felt. We *watch* the shadow on the lawn; we *feel* the premonitory shudder that presentiment implies. We identify with the "startled grass"; we sense the approaching darkness. We become *involved*; we participate in the experience. The poem takes the abstract concept and restores it to its full life in concrete three-dimensional experience.

A novel does not merely *tell* us things; it acts them out so that we can imaginatively live through what develops on the novelist's stage. As John Ciardi said, one of the basic principles of good writing

> is to let action speak for itself. A good novelist does not tell us that a given character is good or bad (at least not since the passing of the Dickens tradition): he shows us the character in action and then, watching him, we know. Poetry, too, has fictional obligations: even when the characters are

ideas and metaphors rather than people, they must be *characterized in
action*. A poem does not *talk about* ideas; it *enacts* them.[13]

A century earlier, Coleridge had included among the essential requirements for poetry "that it be sensuous, and by its imagery elicit
truth at a flash; that it be impassioned, and be able to move our feelings
and awaken our affections." The modern critic made the requirement
for the concrete sensuous image a basic article of faith. He taught a
generation of readers to be suspicious of authors who provide a built-in
commentary of their own, who "explain" their intentions, who point the
"moral of the tale."

Next to concreteness, the modern critic required complexity as a
test of great literary art. Many former terms of critical praise acquired
unfavorable connotations: Regularity, symmetry, smoothness, and ele-
gance came to seem undemanding and simpleminded. Tennyson's slow,
lush verse came to seem facile. Poe's breathless rhythms and multiple
rhymes earned him his modern reputation as the "jingle-poet." Modern
critics turned to what was angular, complicated, incongruous; they
were impatient with anything that was too predictable, too easily reduced
to a formula. They found what they were looking for in poets like G. M.
Hopkins, who preferred

> All things counter, original, spare, strange;
> Whatever is fickle, freckled (who knows how?)
> With swift, slow; sweet, sour; adazzle, dim.[14]

To some extent, at least, the requirement for complexity in great
art is independent of stylistic fashion and changing critical preference.
The great memorable lines do not follow a simple "tedúm-tedúm-tedúm"
pattern that puts the reader to sleep. They show the inversions, the
breaks, the changes in tempo that complicate and enrich the underlying
rhythm:

> Lét me not / to the marriage of true minds /
> Admit impediments . . .

> If thou didst ever hold me in thy heart
> Absent thee / from felicity awhile /
> And in this harsh world draw thy breath in pain
> To tell my story . . .

> The holy time is quiet as a nun,
> Bréathless with adoration: / the broad sun
> Is sinking down in its tranquillity . . .

Without complication, there is no challenge. Without challenge, it becomes hard to hold our attention. In the search for challenging, attention-arousing complexity, modern critics rehabilitated much that earlier critics had condemned as obscure, extravagant, or farfetched. They turned to the **metaphysical** conceits that critics like Dryden and Johnson had rejected. In "The Ecstasy," John Donne says of the two lovers

> Our eye-beams twisted, and did thread
> Our eyes upon a double string.

To the conventionally logical mind, the picture of eyes threaded like buttons on a string is at once too prosaic and too grotesque to furnish an appropriate expression for the close communion of the lovers, looking as in a trance into each other's eyes. The modern critic, by contrast, admired the ability of the poet to bring together the jostling elements of experience without the euphemisms and simplifications imposed by conventional good taste.

The modern distrust for superficial smoothness and simplicity did not mean a denial of the "rage for order," of the shaping, controlling forces that impose literary form. The critic merely turned against *static* order. To be truly satisfying, order should be *achieved* order; it will be the more satisfying if it has been imposed upon resistant materials. The most deeply gratifying art does not simply project serene calm; it involves us in struggle and diversity. Without the struggle, there is no feeling of triumph, of accomplishment. The order of great art is that of richly, even chaotically vital experience brought under control. As Robert Penn Warren said about poetry, a poem "is a motion toward a point of rest, but if it is not a resisted motion, it is a motion of no consequence."[15]

To the modern critic, complexity of style is merely the most tangible expression of the inclusiveness of literary art. Henry James had insisted that "the province of art is all life, all feeling, all observation, all vision. . . . it is all experience." He had ridiculed those who would fence in the artist by putting up little signs warning him not to step on the grass or not to bring dogs into the public gardens. To him, it was "the essence of moral energy" to "survey the whole field."[16] Robert Penn Warren said that "other things being equal, the greatness of a poet depends upon the extent of the area of experience which he can master poetically."[17] For W. K. Wimsatt, as for others, complexity of form was merely the external manifestation of a work's "maturity or sophistication or richness or depth, and hence its value."[18]

Modern criticism led teachers to a crucial "opening out" of the concerns of literature; it led them to extend the range of poetry beyond the conventionally poetic. The modern critic insisted that "fine poetry can derive from the roots of common life—that poetry does not dwell apart in some rarefied realm called Beauty."[19] Most teachers were ready to surrender the view that poetry should achieve beauty by limiting itself to subject matter inherently "poetic": flowers, May mornings, young love. By presenting to our students a poem like "Auto Wreck" by Karl Shapiro, we can show that the poet does not *have* to write about flowers. He may write about the pulsing red light of the ambulance, the policemen hosing off the pavement spattered with blood, the tightened throats and sickly smiles of the passers-by:

> Its quick soft silver bell beating, beating
> And down the dark one ruby flare
> Pulsing out red light like an artery,
> The ambulance at top speed floating down
> Past beacons and illuminated clocks
> Wings in a heavy curve, dips down,
> And brakes speed, entering the crowd.
> The doors leap open, emptying light;
> Stretchers are laid out, the mangled lifted
> And stowed into the little hospital.
> Then the bell, breaking the hush, tolls once,
> And the ambulance with its terrible cargo
> Rocking, slightly rocking, moves away,
> As the doors, an afterthought, are closed.[20]

Finally, though the modern critic stressed the rich and complex ingredients of literature, he at the same time aimed at demonstrating the **wholeness** of a successful work. He emphasized the interconnectedness of its parts. Rather than exhibit, with Matthew Arnold, beautiful passages as "touchstones" of great poetry, he looked for the multiple connections and cross-references that made the poet's creation a tightly structured, fully controlled whole. The modern critic asked readers not to look at poetic effects as ornaments—as decorative details *added* to a basic design, as embellishments added to the basic structure as frosting is to a cake. Each detail served the total effect: In drama, "the central point of view emerges from the total interaction of every aspect of the play." In a poem, "the meaning resides in the interaction of every element—image, statement, rhythm, rhyme—every element which goes to make up the whole poem."[21]

Modern critics were happy when they could show how details of imagery or of rhythm were organically related to the poet's overall intention. Thus repetition becomes functional, carries meaning, in G. M.

Hopkins' plodding repetition of the "have trod" in a line devoted to the treadmill effect of man's toil:

Generations have trod, have trod, have trod.

When Hopkins talks about "the dearest freshness déep dówn things," we feel a similar organic relation between sound and sense: The insistent equal stress on "déep dówn" seems to reinforce the word *deep*. It gets us *deeper down* into things than a more regular, more normal iambic line could. Modern critics tried to show that such correspondences are not merely accidental and incidental. In a truly great poem, such features as rhyme and meter are not merely mechanical, external, but are often in some larger way significant.

In looking for the means by which the poet achieves concreteness, complexity, and inclusiveness, *the New Criticism stressed the special uses to which language is put in literary art*. It concentrated on what makes creative language richer than ordinary workaday talk: metaphor, symbol, irony, paradox, ambiguity. To the modern critic, these were not merely optional poetic devices. They were the key to what literature essentially is and does.

Typically, the New Critic looked in the language of literature for ways of conveying a deeper significance than a mere prose meaning. He looked for the ways literary language could express a consciousness more finely attuned and more fully integrated than the stereotypes and stock responses of ordinary, "practical" man. In dealing with **metaphor**, for instance, the critic stressed the difference between the familiar metaphors of ordinary speech and the bolder, more complex, more connotative metaphors of imaginative literature. Poetic metaphor is not merely a more vivid, a more pictorial way of saying what could be said more abstractly. Even if it were, it would make language that much more concrete and complex, giving it more bite. However, beyond rendering idea as image, metaphor brings into play emotions and attitudes. When Hamlet says, "What should such fellows as I do crawling between earth and heaven?" the word *crawl*, associated with insects or vermin, projects Hamlet's feelings of disillusionment and disgust.

Metaphor is the natural language of the feelings whenever ordinary language has become too neutral, too colorless, too functional:

My love is of a birth so rare . . .

A hard tin bird was my lover . . .

My love—thy hair is one kingdom . . .

> All in green went my love riding
> on a great horse of gold . . .

Such metaphorical language *stretches* the ordinary resources of communication. It enables us to express emotional states for which there is no ready-made verbal tag, to communicate feelings enriched by complex associations and cross-references.

The New Critic was dissatisfied with the kind of metaphor that merely carries through an "apt" analogy in neat, predictable fashion. In the Petrarchan tradition, for instance, an extended metaphor often merely traces in detail the full implications of one basic analogy: The lover is a ship lost at sea. The wind is his sighs, the rain his tears. The clouds are the dark disdain of his beloved. The drowned pilot is the lover's reason, overruled by cruel, desperate fashion. Shakespeare's metaphors, by contrast, are often technically "mixed" metaphors. In a much analyzed passage, Shakespeare uses the familiar analogy between the approach of age and the tree in autumn:

> That time of year thou mayst in me behold
> When yellow leaves, or none, or few, do hang
> Upon those boughs which shake against the cold,
> Bare ruined choirs, where late the sweet birds sang.
> (Sonnet 73)

In the last line, the comparison is complicated and enriched by a further analogy between the defoliated tree and the choirs of abandoned churches, now in ruins, where the choristers used to sing as sweet birds used to sing in the foliage of the tree. The prevailing emotion of sadness and regret is thus reinforced by an image evoking a special kind of nostalgia, of beauty, of awe.

In the religious poems of John Donne, rich "metaphysical" metaphors give expression to complex, contradictory emotions clustering around the basic paradoxes of Christian doctrine. When Donne calls Death "slave to fate, chance, kings, and desperate men," when he exclaims, "Death, thou shalt die," he is "turning the tables" on Death. Our ordinary human fear of death is tempered by the orthodox hope of immortality. Fear and despair are balanced by a strong counteremotion of triumph, of disdain. In the sonnet, "Batter My Heart, Three-Personed God," Donne concludes,

> Yet dearly I love you, and would be loved fain,
> But am betrothed unto your enemy:
> Divorce me, untie or break that knot again;

> Take me to you, imprison me, for I
> Except you enthrall me, never shall be free,
> Nor ever chaste, except you ravish me.

Ravish is a bold and paradoxical word to use in an orthodox religious context. As a central metaphor of the poem, it balances two powerful conflicting forces. One of these is man's *fear* of an overpowering, crushing God, "imprisoning" man in His love. The other is man's *yearning* for an overpowering experience of God that would put an end to backslidings and uncertainties.

Next to metaphor, **symbol** is the most prominent of the devices carrying the rich added freight that the modern critic looked for in literary language. To the literal meaning of a work—"the meaning accessible to everyday practical habits of thought"—symbolic analysis adds the level of symbolic meaning, with symbols taken to "constitute a richer, fuller affective language than the language of rational discourse." [22]

Modern criticism showed little interest in the kind of "obvious," clearly functional symbol that meets the eye of the uninitiated. Such are the symbolic props in the tradition of realistic drama: In Ibsen's *Hedda Gabler*, Hedda's pistols throughout symbolize the explosive, destructive potential of her rebellion against middle-class society. They symbolize her fatal inability to fit into the mold. The modern critic has typically looked for symbols surrounded by a richer, more ambiguous aura of implication. In Melville's *Moby Dick*, the white whale is at times, like the sea, serene and peaceful. At times, like the sea, it is wrathful and destructive. The whale thus becomes symbolic of the basic ambivalence of life: Its two-faced quality of serene beauty and overpowering, destructive violence. Students often ask which of the many conflicting interpretations of *Moby Dick* is the "right" one. No interpretation *can* be right that, like Captain Ahab, sets out to destroy one of the complementary principles, that is unable to accept, with William Blake, both the tiger and the lamb.

The rich, ambiguous symbol has attracted the modern critic because if offers a challenge to the interpreter. Among his favorite authors have been writers like Yeats and Joyce. These use a symbolic language that is to some extent private and obscure. Here the critic must "read" the symbol by studying its recurrence in typical contexts or by tracing it to sources in the author's reading and experience. In poems by the later Yeats, "the blood-dimmed tide," the "dolphin-torn" and "gong-tormented sea," the "salmon-falls" and "mackerel-crowded seas," are opposed to the world of art and intellect. The sea thus becomes symbolic of anarchic sensual existence, at the opposite pole from the poet's ideal of order, "ceremony," form.

Symbolic analysis grew in popularity because it was in keeping with a feeling shared by many readers: There is in great literature something more than meets the eye. There is something deeper, more profound than is grasped by hurried, practical-minded people. The basic question for the symbol-conscious reader is: How can we be sure of the symbolic intentions of the author? Symbolic interpretation is most convincing when it sees the symbol as *part of a larger whole*, when the symbol fits organically into a larger context. In discussing Robert Frost's "Stopping by Woods," we can show how *the rest of the poem* bears out our interpretation of the central symbol:

> Whose woods these are I think I know.
> His house is in the village, though;
> He will not see me stopping here
> To watch his woods fill up with snow.
>
> My little horse must think it queer
> To stop without a farmhouse near
> Between the woods and frozen lake
> The darkest evening of the year.
>
> He gives his harness bells a shake
> To ask if there is some mistake.
> The only other sound's the sweep
> Of easy wind and downy flake.
>
> The woods are lovely, dark and deep,
> But I have promises to keep,
> And miles to go before I sleep,
> And miles to go before I sleep.[23]

Here the critic may discover in the dark loveliness of the woods a symbolic hint of the peacefulness and dark tempting beauty of death. This interpretation is supported by many details *in the poem*: the woods are associated with darkness, hostile to activity, and with snow, hostile to life. They are remote from farmhouses, villages, and other centers of human life and endeavor. They are associated with the ceasing of motion, of purposeful forward movement. Their attraction is an alternative to the keeping of promises and implied commitment to the future. The silence, the "easy wind," the "downy flake," the dark depth of the woods—all point toward rest, sleep. At the same time, the reader is hearing echoes of a literary tradition. Before Frost, Keats had been "half in love with easeful death/Called him soft names in many a mused rhyme." Whitman had heard whispered in the darkness "the low and delicious word death. . . . laving me softly all over,/Death, death, death, death, death."

Looking at the symbol in context, we learn to let the poem or story establish its own symbolic implications. We become wary of ready-made symbolic equivalences imported into a poem or story from the outside. Frost's poem is simple enough to make possible a clear opposition between a life of activity and obligations on the one hand and the tempting loveliness of rest on the other. As a work of literature becomes more complex, the broad antitheses and dichotomies of the symbol-seeker may lead us to oversimplify. It is true, for instance, that in Hawthorne's "Young Goodman Brown" the nocturnal forest lives up to its familiar associations with wilderness, lurking Indians, and Satanic forces. But it is misleading to stipulate in the story too sharp an antithesis of day and night, and of town and forest, to correspond to a sharp dualism of Good and Evil. We gather from the story that Quaker women are whipped through the streets *in broad daylight*, while the night may be starlit and calm. The night could have been devoted to calm sleep, pure and sweet, in the arms of Goodman Brown's wife, but he chose to pursue his "present evil purpose." The point of the story is Young Goodman Brown's discovery of evil, not in places where it is conventionally reputed to exist, but in "church, bed-chamber, street, field *or* forest"—in the early morning sunshine as much as in the secrecy of the night. The pervading irony of the story is that the devil is "not as black as he is painted." On the contrary, he is a master of all the urban civilities; indeed, clad in grave and decent attire, he "had an indescribable air of one who knew the world, and who would not have felt abashed at the governor's dinner table or in King William's court, were it possible that his affairs should call him thither." Young Goodman Brown discovers that Good and Evil are paradoxically intermingled everywhere in human life. He finds himself united with the pious and the dissolute alike in "a loathful brotherhood" by "the sympathy of all that was wicked in his heart." Unable to accept this discovery, he allows it to become an obsession—an obsession that makes him shrink from his fellows, making him "a stern, a sad, a darkly meditative, a distrustful, if not a desperate man." Here as elsewhere, the teacher must make sure that he sees how the symbol serves the story. He must take care not to make the story serve the symbol.

Metaphor and symbol are both basic means of restoring a rich imaginative dimension to the language of literal, logical, practical speech. A third means is **irony**, which became a third major preoccupation of readers influenced by the modern critical tradition. In its most predictable, everyday use, irony *exposes*: It points to the bare ugly rear of the motion-picture palace with the profusely ornamented facade. It points to the warlike preparations of the statesman talking peace. The modern critic looked in imaginative literature for a more mature kind of irony—a kind of irony that does not simply debunk. Irony came to be looked upon as one of the principle ways in which the poet brings together the jostling, warring elements of experience. In a complex and mature attitude, there may be a mingling of tenderness with intellectual awareness, or of pity with laughter. We do not always simply approve or condemn. We approve with grave private reservations after agonizing over the pros and cons; we condemn reluctantly. In the words of Cleanth Brooks,

> Very many, and, indeed, nearly all mature attitudes represent some sort of mingling of the approbative and the satirical. Frequently, the more complex attitudes are expressed, and necessarily expressed in varying degrees of irony.[24]

Irony so defined makes it possible for us to recognize the imperfections of beauty or of goodness without being soured on such beauty and goodness as does exist. Sentimental literature tries to simplify experience by filtering out whatever would keep us from feeling intensely tender, intensely loving, and intensely righteous. Cynicism simplifies experience by making us accept ugliness and corruption once and for all as the norm, as what is to be expected. "Mature" literature is neither sentimental nor cynical; it makes it possible for idealism and scepticism to exist in a state of fruitful tension, to exist as part of a larger dialectic.

Like other modern critical preferences, the search for a literature marked by a bracing, mature kind of irony leads us to the first half of the seventeenth century, to the plays of Shakespeare, to the metaphysical **wit** of poets like John Donne and Andrew Marvell. In Shakespeare's plays, Lear has his fool. Antony has his Enobarbus. Hotspur, who sets out to "pluck bright honor from the pale-face moon," is answered by Falstaff:

> Honor pricks me on. Yea, but how if honor prick me off when I come on? How then? Can honor set to a leg? No. Or an arm? No. Or take away the grief of a wound? No. Honor hath no skill in surgery, then? No. What is honor? A word. What is in that word honor? What is that honor? Air. A trim reckoning! Who hath it? He that died o' Wednesday. Doth he feel it? No. Doth he hear it? No.'Tis insensible, then? Yea, to the dead. But will it not live with the living? No. Why? Detraction will not suffer it. Therefore I'll none of it.
>
> (*Henry VI*, Part I; Act V, Sc. 1)

However, the shrewd comments of Enobarbus do not simply invalidate the greatness of Antony. Falstaff does not simply and conclusively have the last word. In *Romeo and Juliet*, we have in the lovers all the hyperbole of idealized love:

> Oh, she doth teach the torches to burn bright!
> It seems she hangs upon the cheek of night
> Like a rich jewel in an Ethiop's ear—
> Beauty too rich for use, for earth too dear!

(Act I, Sc. 5)

If this were all, we would soon be rudely brought back to earth by the leer of the cynic who mutters to himself: "*I* know what he climbed up to the balcony for!" But at this point we have, in the play itself, already heard all the obscene jokes; what is more, we have already seen glimpses of that violent, unheeding world that hems in and shortens young love. Thus, when we hear the "haw, haw!" of the sophomoric reader, we can only say, "We know all that! We know that souls inhabit bodies; we know that the same relationship that inspired Romeo's lyrical raptures provides Mercutio with the materials for endless bawdy jests. But will you not treasure both the tenderness of Juliet and the exuberance of Mercutio—will you not treasure the beauty and gallantry that flower forth in this grim and violent and earthy world?" Shakespeare's work predisposes us to accept with Robert Penn Warren "a scale of excellence based, in part at least, on degree of complication." The good poem "must, in some way, involve the resistances"; it must "come to terms with Mercutio."[25]

The fourth and last major preoccupation of the New Criticism was **ambiguity.** Modern criticism has typically been attracted to literature that can be read and interpreted in more than one way, that is pregnant with multiple meanings. Thus, in the short stories of Hawthorne or of Kafka, we have a sense of disturbing and perplexing questions being raised to which there are no simple answers. Is Young Goodman Brown's vision a hallucinatory distortion of reality, or is it the symbolic expression of a genuine insight into human nature? Are the good people of Salem ensnared by the devil's wiles as Goodman Brown thinks they are? The story does not say. It's something for the reader to think about, something to test his own view of human motives. Was Faith, the pure and sweet young wife, in the forest on that fateful night, or is Goodman Brown obsessed by a Calvinist suspicion of sin? Hawthorne won't tell. Perhaps Calvinism is an evil dream that like other evil dreams contains a large share of human truth.

Modern critics labored to show the multiple meanings lurking in the richly suggestive and allusive language of Shakespeare, or of Donne and his contemporaries. William Empson, for instance, tried to show that the puns and paradoxes we find there are more than examples of ingenious verbal humor, that often they are the poet's way of hinting at his central intentions. A pun may be the poet's way of pointing to a crucial relationship. It may be his way of "reconciling" or "uniting" two ideas that in the normal use of language are contradictory but that to a more profound insight are in an essential way connected. Thus, when the clown in *As You Like It* puns on the *faining* (desiring) and the *feigning* (pretending, deceiving) of lovers, Empson feels that Shakespeare is getting at an underlying truth. The lover pretends with a purpose, that is, motivated by desire. Lovers are frivolous in the way they lie and cheat, but they do so in the service of a goal they sincerely pursue.

In recent years, the New Critic's emphasis on the technical or formal means employed by imaginative literature has caused him to be accused of **formalism**, of a lack of concern for the vital meanings that give literature human relevance. But at least ideally, the New Critics were not studying literary form as an end in itself: Rather, they were trying to show how form *serves* meaning, how poetic language shapes and orders life. The basic theoretical weakness of the New Criticism was that its account of how literature "orders" or "integrates" experience was too often strained or unconvincing. The New Critics made large claims for literature as a special kind of insight. They turned to literature for a true synthesis of the jostling elements of experience, seeing, with I. A. Richards, the "reconciliation of disparates" as one of the chief virtues of poetry. They quoted with approval T. S. Eliot's description of Donne as constantly amalgamating disparate experience, constantly forming new wholes of what in the ordinary man's experience is chaotic and fragmentary. According to Eliot, what to us seems disconnected and irrelevant—love, Spinoza, the smell of cooking—is absorbed by the poetic sensibility into a previously unperceived order.[26]

Brooks, in *The Well-Wrought Urn* (1947), used Donne's "Canonization" as a crucial example of the "welding together" of the discordant and contradictory. In the poem, the lover rejects secular fame and wealth for earthly love the way the saint rejects them for divine love. But throughout the poem, the religious metaphors *serve* the earthly theme; the central paradox is that the lovers reject the world not for the spirit but for the flesh. It is doubtful that the poem in any valid sense brings the world of the saint and that of the lover closer together. After years in which Donne was considered the archetype of a unified poetic sensibility, this more sceptical view seems to be gaining ground:

> Even among Donne's friendliest critics in recent years there has been a growing perception that (to use Douglas Bush's words in *English Literature*

in the Earlier Seventeenth Century) . . . "Donne's fragments of experience remain fragments," and "his sensibility is not unified but multiple."[27]

Some of the most powerful literature seems to rivet our attention by giving us a heightened sense of the divided loyalties, the contradictory commitments that we are capable of; by involving us fully in our most basic and inescapable existential dilemmas. Modern literature (and, for that matter, much of the great literature of Renaissance England and classical Greece) often finally leaves us with the Sphinx-like riddles of existence unresolved. The broken-mirror effects of the modern literature of the Absurd bring us to a higher sense of the confusions and mysteries of life rather than pointing toward a possible order. Literary form—pattern, "order," rhythm—is then at least in part ceremonial rather than functional. Like music, like the dance, it expresses our *need* for order; it reaffirms our *desire* to cherish and promote it insofar as it is possible to do so in a disordered, perplexing world. With some modern poets, at least, form becomes an antidote, rather than a solution, to the complexities of life. In the Byzantium poems of Yeats, there is a vision of a pure art, a "golden handiwork," taking us beyond "the unpurged images of day," "the fury and the mire of human veins." In Yeats's poems, "ceremony," "artifice," describe a kind of art releasing us from the "bitter furies of complexity" of an anarchic, sensual world.

Teachers today can look back over several decades in which the now-waning influence of the New Criticism dominated textbooks and courses. What has been the practical effect of this influence on the way we teach literature? The New Criticism greatly increased the technical know-how of teachers. It kept lecturing them about how a poem means, about how form carries meaning, about how the technical features of literature communicate. Its net effect, parallel to that of modern linguistics on our teaching of language, was to make our teaching of literature less amateurish. Over the years, however, the trend toward a more rigorous, more demanding teaching of literature proved a mixed blessing. The critic aimed at making students respond more fully to what literature had to offer. But in practice he often succeeded in making literature seem *difficult* and obscure. It often seemed that literary enjoyment was not to be had without special technical equipment. To become a good reader seemed to require above all arduous, and often discouragingly dry, technical training. Taught to prize technical sophistication, teachers equated first-rate literature with the work of writers like Henry James, William Faulkner, James Joyce, Wallace Stevens, e. e. cummings, and Dylan Thomas. They tended to look down on the kind of literature that speaks most directly to the "common reader": the great realistic novel in the tradition of George Eliot and Thomas Hardy; the novel of ideas by

George Orwell and Aldous Huxley and Ralph Ellison; the social drama of Henrik Ibsen, G. B. Shaw, and Arthur Miller. As a result, students too rarely came to think of poetry and fiction as something they could hope to relate to their own experience without the assistance of a critical priesthood mediating between them and the author.

The strong analytical slant of modern criticism tended to make the literary experience too technical and remote for the beginner; and it tended to make that experience too *dry* for the initiate when he finally got there. G. M. Hopkins' "The Windhover" is more than a challenging subject for intellectual analysis. It is a poem that stirs the heart with wonder and loveliness and ecstasy. Jonathan Swift's portrait of the Yahoos is not a drily intellectual commentary. It glows with the savage indignation of a writer profoundly disturbed by the obscene, fawning, predatory brutishness of men that constantly defeats their potential for sane and humane living. A generation of teachers of literature was taught to think rather than to emote, to explicate rather than to act out. They had to learn on their own how to liberate the powerful emotional potential of literature, so that their teaching of it would be impassioned and alive.

When our students started to ask for relevance rather than aesthetics, for commitment rather than aesthetic distance, teachers trained in conventional literary analysis found it difficult to rise to the challenge. One result was a renewed interest in critical tendencies that seemed to relate literature more directly or more single-mindedly to basic human concerns. Sensitive to charges that we have treated literature too much as a thing apart, we have come to give an attentive second hearing to critics who closely link the study of literature to politics, to psychology, to anthropology. We have come to reconsider the role of literature in the life of the individual and of society. In part, this reorientation has merely reinforced a long-range shift from the formalism of the orthodox New Critics to a strong interest in the larger cultural functions of literature. But in part, it has also made English teachers more willing to reconsider approaches that they long tended to consider as extraliterary and beyond their ken.

THE RELEVANCE OF LITERATURE

Whatever the original intentions of the New Critics, they created a tradition that focused on form and technique. Literature was not to be confused with life. It had its own laws of being; the proper function of the critic was to explore what made literature different, separate, unique. This orientation worked against teachers whose major interest was in the intentions of the author and the response of the reader. In spite of warnings to the contrary, many teachers continued to feel that what really matters about a poem or a play is what it *does* for the author and for the audience. They were ready to look at literature as more directly a response to basic human needs, as a way of dealing with basic human problems. They were ready to look at literature as a form of human behavior, serving needs and purposes similar to those served by other social and cultural phenomena.

Both inside and outside the established academic criticism, there have long been strong countertrends that encouraged readers to look for a writer's personal and social agenda. As Lionel Trilling observed in *The Liberal Imagination*, "emotions and ideas are the spark that fly when the mind meets difficulties."[28] Kenneth Burke, in *The Philosophy of Literary Form*, called literature part of our "equipment for living." He looked at literary creation as governed by "strategies" aimed at satisfying basic psychological or social needs. He looked for the vital "function" of a work, assuming "that the poem is designed 'to do something' for the poet and his readers."[29]

If we ask how literature serves basic human purposes, we can start by looking at *literature as a social document and as a political act*. We can look for an expression of the writer's social consciousness. While Chaucer was writing about the loves of knights and ladies, his contemporary Langland wrote about the people who "sweated at their labor, winning wealth that the worthless wasted in gluttony"; about "prisoners in pits, and poor folk in their hovels" charged with children "crying out for food." He told the warlords and landowners of medieval England not to torment their tenants, to "let Mercy fix the taxes":

> Never bully your bondman; it will be better for you;
> Though he be your underling here, happen in heaven
> He'll have a better seat, above you in bliss, . . .
> For in the charnel churchyard a churl is hard to know
> Or a knight from a knave there.[30]

The most direct way to establish the relevance of literature is to examine closely a writer's relation to society. For many decades, critics influenced by **Marxist sociology** have focused attention on the writer's economic and social motives. How does he relate to the historical forces shaping his society? How does he identify with, or reject, his social class? The Marxist critic takes his cue from Marx's dictum that the intellectual superstructure reflects underlying material, that is, economic, realities:

> The ideas of the ruling class are in every epoch the ruling ideas: i.e. the class which is the ruling material force of society is at the same time its ruling intellectual force. The class which has the means of material production at its disposal has control at the same time over the means of mental production, so that thereby, generally speaking, the ideas of those who lack the

means of mental production are subject to it. The ruling ideas are nothing more than the ideal expression of the dominant material relationships, the dominant material relationships grasped as ideas.[31]

Once the ideal superstructure is thus anchored to material reality, we can apply to it the characteristic standards and values of Marxist social analysis. In the Marxist universe, the ultimate criterion of value is "socially useful work." Man is "a social being who should be active for the welfare of others." The program for the writer, as for other artists, is "to sing the song of the new man with the authentic voice of the people." That voice will eulogize "the ideals and the purity of the people," who day by day will have rid themselves of their "shortcomings."[32]

When applied in a doctrinaire manner, this perspective yields familiar results: No matter how genteel or "disinterested" literature may seem on the surface, the bourgeois writer will be found to be writing in the service of his class. He serves political ends: to justify the ways of capital to man; to divert the attention of the exploited from their grievances; to discredit the forces working for change. The "progressive" writer, by contrast, identifies with the exploited masses and exposes the rapaciousness of monopoly capital. A central task of the critic is to show how a given writer fits into this framework: Kafka, for instance, "fits in" if we read his work as a record of the emptiness of the lives of the "ruling imperialist classes."

American teachers of literature have by and large found it difficult to swallow the rigid formulas of the party-line critic, and doctrinaire ideological criticism has played only a minor role in the teaching of literature in this country. But its *indirect* influence has been very strong. Over the years, it has helped end the school tradition of treating literature as a genteel pastime, as part of the "cultivated" person's accomplishment, and perfectly harmless in political and ideological terms. It has helped remind teachers that literature is fully rooted in the social, political, and cultural history of its time. John Milton was trying to mobilize good men in the fight for justice, exhorting them not to do "the work of the Lord negligently," glorying, even in defeat, in the vision of Samson at Gaza pulling down the roof of the temple on the enemies of the true faith. Shakespeare often speaks as an advocate of the Tudor monarchy, painting the tensions of late feudal history, and the gory accidents of English dynastic succession, as tending toward a larger ideal order, in which

The heavens themselves, the planets and this center,
Observe degree, priority and place.
                    (*Troilus and Cressida*, Act I, Sc. 3)

Literature has something to do with what men most passionately care about, and one of their most basic concerns is their relation to the larger social order. We read with grave attention books that are truly "books for our time"—books that make us examine, with grave apprehension, the world into which we were born. Among the books most seriously read by young people are those that give us a picture of the world in which we live.

To understand the power of literature, the student must have the experience of being carried away by an author's eloquence, of being moved to indignation or compassion. Thus, every student should at some time encounter the literature of **social protest** of the thirties. In John Steinbeck's *The Grapes of Wrath*, we ponder the picture of an economic system out of control, no longer either understood or mastered by its prophets, unable to distribute the fruits of skill and labor and choking on its own plenty. We live through Steinbeck's account of a system brutally impersonal in its operation and brutalizing those that make their terms with it; frustrating the need for meaningful, productive work; baffling the impulse toward kindness. We remember the words of a writer who knew how to tell the complacent and the callous that "in the eyes of the people there is the failure; and in the eyes of the hungry there is a growing wrath."[33]

Similarly, every student should at some time encounter the literary record of modern man's traumatic encounter with the gloomy totalitarian ideologies of the twentieth century. In the experience of André Gide, Stephen Spender, and Richard Wright, we find played out the pattern of ideal aspirations betrayed, of generous impulse exploited and perverted by crude force and low cunning. George Orwell, in *Animal Farm*, wrote with biting scorn of a totalitarian mentality stifling all criticism, branding all dissent as treason, making impossible all fair judgment of the relative merits of conflicting policies, drowning all thought in the mindless chant of "Four legs good—two legs bad." Orwell gives voice to a generation of long-since-silenced victims when he castigates the obscene vilification of former heroes of the revolution, the abject glorification of the all-wise leader, the paranoid search for a capitalist under every bed, the squealing of meretricious hacks rationalizing the zigzags of the party line. He writes the epitaph of all made-to-order literature when he mimics the court poet's anthem:

> Friend of the fatherless!
> Fountain of happiness!
> Lord of the swill-bucket! O how my soul is on
> Fire when I gaze at thy

Calm and commanding eye,
Like the sun in the sky,
Comrade Napoleon![34]

In the literature of our own time, the impetus of social criticism has been powerful in the black writer's attempt to come to terms with his role in American society. A book like Ralph Ellison's *Invisible Man* reflects the young Negro's turning away from an older generation of leaders that had preached patience and humility, that had insisted on the need for presenting to the complacent white the flattering facade of the humbly grateful liberated slave. There is in the book a black anger at the white man's thoughtless, lazy assumption of superiority. ("So I was not so highly developed as they! What did he mean? Were they all Ph.D.'s?")[35] There is a blazing consciousness of the Negro's centuries-old record as a victim of callousness, injustice, and condescension. One way English teachers can pay their dues as members of society is to read and ponder with their students poems like Arna Bontemps's "A Black Man Talks of Reaping":

I have sown beside all waters in my day.
I planted deep, within my heart the fear
That wind or fowl would take the grain away.
I planted safe against this stark, lean year.

I scattered seed enough to plant the land
In rows from Canada to Mexico,
But for my reaping only what the hand
Can hold at once is all that I can show.

Yet what I sowed and what the orchard yields
My brother's sons are gathering stalk and root,
Small wonder then my children glean in fields
They have not sown, and feed on bitter fruit.[36]

The literature of social protest or of **black identity** is a literature of commitment; it asks us to share the aspirations of the author. But much other literature turns out to be *indirectly* relevant in social or political terms because of the way it challenges or contradicts the commitments of teachers and students. No one who teaches literature in today's classrooms can pretend that great books exist in a vacuum. A book like Mark Twain's *The Adventures of Huckleberry Finn* is not simply "a great novel by a great author." It is a human document written by a great author who was ahead of his time and yet inevitably *of* his time. Mark Twain was partially emancipated from, and partially caught up in, the cultural traditions and institutional patterns of his society. On the one hand, Mark

Twain has Huck break through the established legal and political view of the slave as property, as object. Huck, in the course of the novel, establishes strong *personal* relations of friendship and loyalty with Jim, the escaped Negro slave. Huck makes the basic break with racism: He recognizes the fellow human as a human being, capable of true fellow-feeling and moral choice. On the other hand, the author's comic genius does exploit Jim's wide-eyed ignorance and superstition. Jim can't see how the many-wived biblical kings could be considered wise ("I reck'n de wives quarrels considable . . . would a wise man want to live in de mids' er sich a blim-blammin' all the time?"). Jim can't see why Frenchmen "doan' talk de same way we does": "Is a Frenchman a man?" "Yes." "*Well*, den! Dad blame it, whe doan' he *talk* like a man? You answer me *dat!*"

The comic treatment of Jim willy-nilly reinforces the cultural stereotype of the "backward" Negro. Jim is treated condescendingly, and amused condescension helps us keep people in inferior positions by making us feel that in some important ways they really *are* inferior. In addition, Jim's basic appeal to our sympathy is his self-sacrificing devotion to his white friend. Whatever the sentimental value of the loyal black companion for a white audience, in effect Jim subjects himself "to domination by a child to the extent of allowing himself to be led deeper and deeper into slave territory and further and further away from freedom on the Illinois shore."[37] The student who objects to Jim's naïveté and submissiveness is paying us the compliment of taking literature seriously, of reading it with an awareness of its moral and social implications.

Between a period of intense social consciousness in the thirties and the cry for relevance of the seventies, many teachers have seemed to turn their backs on literature as politics. Experience had taught many to be wary of the ideological critic: It is only one step from examining a work for its social relevance to examining it for its conformity to one particular social doctrine. In doctrinaire ideological criticism, the writer is judged according to an ideal not of his own creation. His achievement is measured against a quota not set by himself. The critic ceases to be first of all a reader, a spectator; he becomes a censor. Clearance is withheld for Mother Goose until it is established that the child needs fantasy, fairy tales, and nonsense verse to help him "escape the narrow frame of ego-centric interests and feelings" by participating "with concern in the lives of imaginary people and animals."[38]

Nevertheless, ideological critics, like moralistic and religious critics before them, have found that creative impulse is not easily harnessed for ideological purposes. To be truly a writer, the poet or novelist must follow where his human loyalties and artistic integrity will lead. Even when an author is committed to a definite ideology, in proportion as he is a true artist his work will prove too big for its ideological frame. In the plays of Bertolt Brecht, a committed socialist and proletarian writer, there is a sense of irony, of openness to human possibilities, that is often at odds with the single-minded political message their author preaches. In the ideological framework of Brecht's play, Mother Courage is the haggling, profiteering petty-bourgeois trader who follows the armies of the Thirty Years' War in her trader's wagon, pulled at one time by a horse, then by herself and her children, and finally by herself as the sole survivor. She tries to live off war while hoping to save her own children from its clutches; and she learns that he "who wants to sup with the devil needs a long spoon." But to Brecht's dismay, Mother Courage as the central character of the play acquired a tremendous vitality of her own: Audiences saw her as the spokesman of the martyred common people, who have no stake in the glorious wars fought by their leaders but who have nowhere else to go ("I'd rather have peace and be ruined"). Her wagon, intended as a symbol of corrupt profit, became a symbol of life that goes on in spite of incredible hardship. The most powerful thing in the play turned out to be the mutual loyalty of Mother Courage and her crippled deaf-mute daughter, who gives her life to save her mother. What Mother Courage really learns is that war, no matter how elevated its declared ideological or religious motives, brings out the worst in men; that it kills the just and the unjust; that History is a murderous abstraction. Like her creator, Mother Courage knows too much to be a true believer: "The Poles here in Poland should have stayed out of it, but instead of keeping the peace, they keep interfering in their own internal affairs. . . . The reason he had to throw them in jail was that they did not want to give up their oppressed condition: If someone does not want to be liberated, he doesn't kid around."[39]

In a world torn by revolution and war, teachers of literature have by and large managed amazingly well to steer clear of the "messy" facts of contemporary history. In this effort, they have been helped by a traditional definition of humanistic culture as dealing with timeless values, independent of changing social circumstances and narrow political boundaries. In recent years, many forces have combined to make that traditional separation of culture and politics hard to maintain. New kinds of politically or socially engaged literature are enjoying a tremendous vogue: the political drama of Bertolt Brecht and Peter Weiss; the "convict literature" of Jean Genêt or Eldridge Cleaver; the angry black rhetoric of writers like LeRoi Jones. We find new kinds of political awareness in middle-class students and teachers; we encounter critical or hostile students from social strata long excluded by elitist definitions of culture.

Teachers have often resisted a sociological perspective on literature because the sociological critic seems to tell only one part of the story. A view of man as a social animal easily becomes one-dimensional. It often focuses on the part of the iceberg that shows above water. Literature is deeply involved with man's social relations; but it is also a record of his private thoughts and feelings, an expression of his private self. *To balance a sociology of literature, we need a psychology of literature.* Modern views of imaginative creation have indeed been profoundly influenced by schools of modern psychology whose view of man is based at least in part on the record he leaves of himself in song, story, drama, myth, and ritual. Imaginative literature is often probing, confessional, revealing; it enables us to probe the depths below the social surface. In great literary art, we sense something that matters more deeply than a mere tale, more lastingly than mere entertainment. One way of substantiating this feeling is to trace in literature the **symbolic action** by which the writer tries to deal with his psychological "burdens." We will then search in literature for patterns of alienation and rejection, of attraction and repulsion, of a new identity emerging from the integration of warring psychological elements. With a critic like Kenneth Burke, we will look in literature for strategies for rationalizing or disguising guilt or weakness, for rituals of self-acceptance and self-justification.

There is a large share in imaginative literature of what to the narrowly practical person seems idle, fantastic, irrational. The literary artist is someone more sensitive than his fellows. Often he seems profoundly disturbed or even possessed, seized by Plato's "divine madness." It therefore seemed logical to apply to literature the kind of **depth psychology** developed by Freud and his followers. Freud had rediscovered for modern man the repressed chaotic forces lurking behind the facade of respectability, hiding under the thin veneer of civilization. As Lionel Trilling said in his essay on "Freud and Literature,"

> The Freudian psychology is the only systematic account of the human mind which, in point of subtlety and complexity, of interest and tragic power, deserves to stand beside the chaotic mass of psychological insights which literature has accumulated through the centuries . . . the human nature of the Freudian psychology is exactly the stuff upon which the poet has always exercised his art.

As Trilling pointed out, the romantic tradition in literature had always been "passionately devoted to a research into the self." To Blake, to Shelley, the affective, emotional forces in man were the source of truth and beauty. The analytical understanding, the "false secondary power," was the enemy that narrowed and distorted our vision of life. The romantic rebellion against the practical, the conventional, the merely rational can be formulated in Freudian terms: "Again and again we see the effective, utilitarian **ego** being relegated to an inferior position and a plea being made on behalf of the anarchic and self-indulgent **id**."[40]

In the literature of our century, an obsessive theme has been the emotional aridity of contemporary life. In T. S. Eliot's *The Waste Land* as in James Joyce's *Ulysses*, the basic quest is the search for the healing waters in the land where "the dead tree gives no shelter," the land of "empty cisterns and exhausted wells." With a writer like D. H. Lawrence, the central problem of modern man becomes that of coming to terms with his instinctual self. The ideal becomes a new integration of the personality. We search for a life in harmony with the "dark forces" of the soul that our mechanistic civilization tends to destroy. We try to revive our lost capacity for tenderness, for fulfillment.

The kind of psychological dynamics investigated by Freud and his followers helps us explain our feeling that much powerful literature engages us at levels deeper than that of its literal action. In Shakespeare's *Hamlet*, the surface action takes place on the familiar level of dynastic rivalry and intrigue: a usurped throne, the rightful heir threatened, plot and counterplot. On the surface, Hamlet's actions and reactions can be plausibly, even cogently, explained as conforming to his conscious standards and ideals. His filial piety toward his murdered father, his determination to avenge the murder, his plans for ascertaining the truth about his father's death—these are all "rational" motives acceptable to the conscious ego. But all the while we have evidence of a deeply disturbed mind. Hamlet cruelly mistreats Ophelia, a naïve, pious, innocent girl he has "ruthlessly jilted" and now torments with "coarse familiarity and bandying of ambiguous jests." He speaks to his mother with intense loathing and "almost physical disgust" at her conduct, which to him is "rank and gross." He uses language expressing intense sexual revulsion as he accuses the queen of living

> In the rank sweat of an enseamed bed
> Stewed in corruption, honeying and making love
> Over the nasty sty.
> (Act III, Sc. 4)

Hamlet's "bitter misogyny," his "repulsion against women in general, and Ophelia in particular," makes us realize that under the surface of dynastic rivalry a more primitive, a more personal drama is acted out: What festers in Hamlet's mind, under an overlay of "respectable" conscious motives, is poisoned love—the son's hurt and resentment at the gradual withdrawal of the all-enveloping mother love of his childhood; the thwarted natural affection, heavily tinged with sensuality, that the son feels for his mother; his jealous rage at the male adult (the mother's husband) who shares his mother's bed and seems the successful rival for her love.

When the psychoanalytic critic strips the play of its surface complications, Hamlet is revealed as the eternal Oedipus who as a child "bitterly resented having had to share his mother's affection even with his own father, had regarded him as a rival, and had secretly wished him out of the way." The basic **Oedipus complex** of thwarted love and jealous resentment, repressed by an education imposing "adult" moral standards on the impulses of the child, lives on in the unconscious part of the mind. Disguised, repressed, it continues to war against the conscious, adult part of the personality, causing an intense inner turmoil, a "tortured conscience," whose true nature is hidden from Hamlet himself, but which "finds its echo in a similar conflict in the mind of the hearer."

The basic ambiguity of the play, which has a paralyzing effect on Hamlet, lies in the double role that Claudius plays in the eternal triangle of the Freudian family: Claudius is the father-substitute, the hated rival for the mother's love. But Claudius, in murdering Hamlet's *real* father, has also acted out the son's own secret parricidal impulses. In slaying Claudius, Hamlet would slay a part of himself.[41]

The critic indebted to psychoanalysis encourages us to read literature "with a lively sense of its latent and ambiguous meanings, as if it were, as indeed it is, a being no less alive and contradictory than the man who created it."[42] We thus become more sensitive to the ambivalence and depth of literature that deeply engages our emotions. On the debit side, we may discount too drastically the "surface" level of theme and form. The surface structure of a poem or play may become mere "disguise," which the critic must interpret the way the psychoanalyst interprets the dream. Freudian criticism powerfully reinforced the modern critic's dislike for the obvious, his tendency to prefer esoteric explanations to commonsense observation.

Freudian criticism tended to be dogmatic, and its categories easily became clichés: the ever-present phallic symbols, the young-male-as-Oedipus, the fear of inadequacy, the universal failure to "relate." A rival school of psychoanalysis seemed to offer critics a perspective more richly responsive to the full range of imaginative literature: An alternative way of making us "sensitive to the tap-roots below"[43] is to adopt the **analytical psychology** of C. G. Jung. We then see the underlying significance of literature not so much in the expression of the individual subconscious as in *a preconscious level of experience common to the race.* Poetic intuition then becomes an avenue to a deep-seated preconscious, prerational knowledge. To the Freudian view of poetry as intensely personal and subjective, Jung opposed a view of the poet as "objective and impersonal—even inhuman":

> The specifically artistic disposition involves an overweight of collective psychic life as against the personal. Art is a kind of innate drive that seizes a human being and makes him its instrument. . . . As a human being he may have moods and a will and personal aims, but as an artist he is "man" in a higher sense—he is "collective man"—one who carries and shapes the unconscious, psychic life of mankind.[44]

Jung distinguished between literature clarifying or heightening materials from conscious human experience and literature that draws on "a strange something that derives its existence from the hinterland of man's mind," rising in its enormity or grotesque foreignness from timeless depths, giving expression to primordial experiences "that rend from top to bottom the curtain upon which is painted the picture of an ordered world." With the conscious ego swept along as on a subterranean current, such literature expresses something "not clearly known and yet profoundly alive." It expresses the **myths** of the race, the **archetypes** that live in the collective unconscious. Jung felt Faust lived as a primordial image in the German soul:

> The archetypal image of the wise man, the saviour or redeemer, lies buried and dormant in man's unconscious since the dawn of culture; it is awakened whenever the times are out of joint and a human society is committed to a serious error. When people go astray they feel the need of a guide or teacher or even of the physician. These primordial images are numerous, but do not appear in the dreams of individuals or in works of art until they are called into being by the waywardness of the general outlook. When conscious life is characterized by one-sidedness and by a false attitude, then they are activated—one might say, "instinctively"—and come to light in the dreams of individuals and the visions of artists and seers, thus restoring the psychic equilibrium of the epoch.[45]

Literature, like all art, thus meets the deep-seated spiritual needs of society or of the age; it draws on the "healing and redeeming forces of the collective psyche that underlies consciousness."[46] In the words of R. P. Blackmur,

> By intuition we adventure in the pre-conscious; and there, where the adventure is, there is no need or suspicion of certainty or meaning; there is the

living, expanding *prescient* substance without the tags and handles of conscious form. Art is the looking-glass of the pre-conscious, and when it is
deepest seems to participate in it sensibly.[47]

Many critics thus found in the Jungian analysis of mythical significance a new way of relating literature to "the momentum of the whole
human enterprise." They set out to demonstrate that underlying the
technical and conceptual aspects of a work is a level of symbolical action
through which forces greater than ourselves press into and transform our
experience. Thus, we see a critic like Francis Fergusson, in *The Idea of a
Theater*, accept Jung's view of myth "as a way of ordering human experience" and as a way of "understanding and representing human
experience . . . prior to the arts and sciences and philosophies of modern
times." We see him search for dramatic art "popular, traditional, and
ritualistic," and "based upon a uniquely direct sense of life." We see him
find such art in the plays of Sophocles and Shakespeare, written for a
theater "which had been formed at the center of the culture of its time,
and at the center of the life and awareness of the community," there fo-
cusing "the complementary insights of the whole culture."[48]

Like the Freudian approach, criticism focused on archetype and
myth, and treats much (too much) of the actual structure and texture of a
work as mere surface, as **rationalization**, as disguise. It exploits hints and
ambiguities that to the naked eye seem merely incidental. Thus, Fergusson, in discussing *Oedipus Rex*, states that "no one who sees or reads the
play can rest content with its literal coherence." The "suggestive mystery
of the Oedipus myth" is not to be solved by a literal acceptance of Sophocles's theological and didactic purpose. It will slowly come into focus,
"like repressed material under psychoanalysis," as we respond to the
deeper "rhythm" of the play. The true action of the play is not the attempt
by Oedipus to solve a fateful challenge to his wisdom, authority, and self-
reliance. It is rather the consummation of his "quest" for his true nature
and destiny. In trying to find the slayer of Laius, he "finds himself." This
element in the play links it with rites and ceremonies circling around
individual growth and development, **initiation**, passage from one stage of
life to another. At the same time, the play presents the "tragic but perennial, even normal, quest of the whole city for its well-being." The "overall aim" which "informs" the play is "to find the culprit in order to purify
human life":

The figure of Oedipus himself fulfills all the requirements of the scapegoat,
the dismembered king or god-figure. The situation in which Thebes is presented at the beginning of the play—in peril of its life; its crops, its herds, its

women mysteriously infertile, signs of a mortal disease of the City, and the disfavor of the gods—is like the withering which winter brings, and calls, in the same way, for struggle, dismemberment, death, and renewal. And this tragic sequence is the substance of the play.[49]

From the overt theological message of the play, with its drama centered on the relationship between man and god, the critic thus takes us to the pretheological, ritualistic past, where our interest is in the perennial rites of the tribe. We thus presumably reach a "deeper" level than that reached by the Chorus in the concluding lines of the play:

> Men of Thebes: look upon Oedipus.
>
> This is the king who solved the famous riddle
> And towered up, most powerful of men.
> No mortal eyes but looked on him with envy,
> Yet in the end ruin swept over him.
>
> Let every man in mankind's frailty
> Consider his last day; and let none
> Presume on his good fortune until he find
> Life, at his death, a memory without pain.[50]

A whole school of cultural anthropology has assumed that in the myths and rituals of primitive tribes we can catch a glimpse of something more profound, something in an obscure way more meaningful, than we find in the consciousness of rationalistic, conceptual Western man. Here we can look for man still intuitively relating to his world, his intuition not yet trammeled by the restricted and isolated analytical understanding. This anthropological perspective proved powerfully attractive to academic critics who were ready to move beyond the formalism of the New Critics but who were wary of the narrow doctrinaire formulas of Marxist sociology and Freudian psychology. Thus, in the theory of literary **genres** developed by Northrop Frye, we look in age-old literary forms for the underlying ritual patterns which examples of the type act out. We trace the historical tradition of **comedy**, for instance, to prehistoric rituals deeply anchored in the collective experience of humanity.

At its most profound level, comedy then appears as a "ritual of death and revival" that celebrates the "victory of summer over winter." Comedy is the final phase of a larger "sacrificial ritual" of which tragedy is the initial phase:

> This is the ritual of the struggle, death, and rebirth of a God-Man, which is linked to the yearly triumph of spring over winter. The tragic hero is not really killed, and the audience no longer eats his body and drinks his blood,

but the corresponding thing in art still takes place. The audience enters into communion with the body of the hero, becoming thereby a single body itself. Comedy grows out of the same ritual, for in the ritual the tragic story has a sequel. Divine men do not die: they die and rise again. The ritual pattern behind the catharsis of comedy is the resurrection that follows the death, the epiphany or manifestation of the risen hero.[51]

Comedy tends through struggle toward "festival"—toward the sense of renewal, of renewed natural vitality, expressed in the final marriage, dance, or feast. A familiar element of Shakespeare's comedies, anchored in pagan folk ritual, is the theme of the "green world." We find it by leaving behind court and city to join the fairy world of *A Midsummer Night's Dream* or the Forest of Arden in *As You Like It*. In the **pastoral** idyll of *As You Like It*, the exiled courtiers live carelessly in a world of shepherds and shepherdesses, shunning ambition and "living in the sun":

> Under the greenwood tree
>   Who loves to lie with me,
> And turn his merry note
>   Unto the sweet bird's throat,
> Come hither, come hither, come hither.
>   Here shall he see no enemy
> But winter and rough weather.

Theirs is a civilized, literary version of an age-old primitive drama: Its theme is "the triumph of life over the waste land, the death and revival of the year impersonated by figures still human, and once divine as well."

In the more realistic comedy of Molière or Ben Jonson, the theme of "youth will have its way" or "young love conquers all" is a realistic "foreshortening" of the older death-and-resurrection pattern. The struggle and rebirth of a divine hero has shrunk into the "triumph of a young man over an older one" competing for the same girl. Life, vitality, are symbolized by the young lovers. The eccentric, laughable **humor** characters—the miser, the hypochondriac, the hypocrite—are the forces that hinder the progress of the comedy toward the final marriage. As the hero gets closer to the heroine, opposition is gradually overcome. The audience has been on the "right side" from the beginning; other characters in the play come over to the side of the young hero. A fortunate discovery of the heroine's true identity may help make her "marriageable," make her an accessible object of desire. The plot can thus proceed to act out a wish-fulfillment pattern. The play ends in a general atmosphere of "reconciliation"; we experience a sense of renewed social integration. The forces of life and youth have triumphed over neurotic obstruction and restrictive social norms.

Myth-and-ritual criticism has strongly appealed to English teachers, since the "prerational image of human nature and destiny" found in myth and ritual is a fascinating study in itself. The major problem is to know when to stop: Much myth criticism moves too glibly from the actual work to abstractions about life cycles and prehistoric patterns of existence. At times, the teacher has to choose between the say-so of the critic and the plain sense of a passage. Thus, Northrop Frye says early in his discussion of *Lycidas*, Milton's elegy on the death of Edward King, his fellow poet "unfortunately drowned in his passage from Chester on the Irish Seas":

> King is given the pastoral name of Lycidas, which is equivalent to Adonis, and is associated with the cyclical rhythms of nature. Of these three are of particular importance: the daily cycle of the sun across the sky, the yearly cycle of the seasons, and the cycle of water, flowing from wells and fountains through rivers to the sea. Sunset, winter and the sea are emblems of Lycidas' death; sunrise and spring, of his resurrection. . . . The imagery of the opening lines, "Shatter your leaves before the mellowing year," suggests the frosts of autumn killing the flowers, and in the great roll-call of flowers towards the end, most of them early blooming flowers like the "rathe primrose," the spring returns.[52]

However, the *overt* meaning of Milton's opening lines is that the poet is *disturbing* the "season due" of the plants mentioned, plucking berries and leaves contrary to their usual life cycle, "*before* the mellowing year," for a special ceremonial purpose: Regardless of the cyclical rhythms of nature, the laurels, myrtle, and ivy are needed for the symbolic crowning of the dead poet. Similarly, the flowers with which the speaker in the poem strews the imaginary hearse help to "interpose a little ease"; they serve their familiar ceremonial function that *cuts short* their usual, natural cycle of life. The poet's own life has been prematurely cut short, contrary to what we might consider a natural cycle of youth, maturity, and age. We are reconciled to the abrupt loss by his role in a larger spiritual cycle of rebirth and redemption, turning our natural grief into rejoicing.

In practice, myth criticism has powerfully reinforced the modern tendency to look for hidden meanings and to engage in uncontrolled symbolic analysis. For instance, modern critics have typically found Coleridge's "The Ancient Mariner" too pat in its overt moralistic message. The stated moral of the poem is that redemption for the parched soul lies in our capacity for spontaneous love of our fellow creatures. The mariner alienates himself from nature by killing the albatross, the bird of good omen. This deed brings unspeakable agony for him and his companions. But he is finally redeemed when in the moon-lit night he watches the water snakes moving in the ship's shadow:

> Within the shadow of the ship
> I watched their rich attire:
> Blue, glossy green, and velvet black,
> They coiled and swam; and every track
> Was a flash of golden fire.
>
> O happy living things! no tongue
> Their beauty might declare:
> A spring of love gushed from my heart,
> And I blessed them unaware:
> Sure my kind saint took pity on me,
> And I blessed them unaware.
>
> The selfsame moment I could pray;
> And from my neck so free
> The Albatross fell off, and sank
> Like lead into the sea.

The message of the poem is well summed up in the final stanzas:

> He prayeth well, who loveth well
> Both man and bird and beast.
>
> He prayeth best, who loveth best
> All things both great and small;
> For the dear God who loveth us,
> He made and loveth all.

This theme is close to the heart of the romantic's message. It is also most profoundly relevant to the brutalities and callousness of our own time, to a world haunted by the specter of gutted cities and silent springs. Nevertheless, modern critics have again and again tried to explain the poem's power by a symbolic surcharge more or less dimly felt. They have found in the poem an archetypal pattern of rebirth and regeneration. They have found a theological pattern in which the shooting of the albatross is parallel to Original Sin. They have found a philosophical pattern which makes the sun symbolic of the drily analytical understanding, the moon symbolic of the beneficent, all-integrating imagination. They have found a biographical pattern which makes the poem a ritual for the redemption of the drug to which Coleridge was addicted.

Even if these themes were indeed hinted at by Coleridge, it is hard to see how they could be more profound or more powerful than the overt, stated theme. They would at best be secondary, peripheral, affecting the response of an occasional knowing reader.

In looking for the human relevance of literature, *we ultimately have to trust the clues provided by the author himself for the benefit of the common reader.* These clues may at times be ambiguous or contradictory, reflecting vital tensions or existential dilemmas. Nevertheless, our students must come to feel that they can learn to read these clues for themselves, without going to the commissar, the psychoanalyst, or the anthropologist for the correct analysis. Much of the action of the greatest literature is anchored in common life and traceable to generally understandable human motives. Macbeth is persuaded of the need for effective action, unhampered by "womanish" scruples. But he finds that there is something in him stronger than his own "tough" talk, something that makes him turn against his own deeds and makes him shudder at the consequences of his own acts. Othello is a great and good man, but he finds that his reason is no match for the destructive fury of his anger once it is fully aroused. Our most basic need in the teaching of literature is for an approach that encourages our students to look for such basic human meanings for themselves.

THE THEMATIC APPROACH

Writers are human beings recording their personal vision of experience. A poem or a play in its own way reflects the author's "scrutiny of life," his "view of the world and his conception of the powers that move it."[53] As we see a play or a story unfold, we feel that things are falling into place, that things have meaning. Sometimes that meaning is acted out in familiar surroundings, in a realistic setting: In Arthur Miller's *Death of a Salesman*, Willy, coming rapidly to the end of his rope, is blundering about in a dark backyard trying to plant seed. He engages in a gesture of hopeful preparation for the future when there is no future, nor hope. He clings to something that suggests open space and freedom, when he is actually being ground down by a jostling, competitive society. Willy is everybody's neighbor; he is every boy's uncle. But just as often, literature acts out its meaning in a setting that is strange, far away, romantic, taking us to the neverland of dream and desire. W. K. Wimsatt, Jr., says of Keats's "La Belle Dame Sans Merci" that literally it is

> about a knight, by profession a man of action, but sensitive, like the lily and the rose, and about a faery lady with wild, wild eyes. At a more abstract level, it is about the loss of self in the mysterious lure of beauty—whether woman, poetry, or poppy. It sings the irretrievable departure from practical normality (the squirrel's granary is full), the wan isolation after ecstasy.[54]

When we focus our teaching on the human meaning of literature, we emphasize **theme**. In the thematic study of literature, we try to make students see how literature reflects and shapes human life. We ask them to look at the writer as a fellow mortal who bears witness to the conditions and predicaments of mankind. Our laughter, our tears are then not mere physical reactions to an artificial stimulus. They are part of our common involvement in what it means to be alive.

To lead young readers to a perception of theme, we try to find literary materials where setting, plot, character, or mood have their own fascination—but where yet a theme naturally, organically, emerges from these "surface" elements. Events then are not isolated or accidental but seem to have a more general significance. Characters are not merely superficially colorful but make us understand something about how people think and feel. A setting does not merely lend local color but mirrors some outside force that shapes or limits our lives.

When we first read a good story, we may be carried along by our interest in the action. John Steinbeck's short story "Flight," for instance, keeps us in grim suspense as the boy, Pepé, is hunted down in the mountains after he has killed a man in a fight. But though this is basically the story of a human being hunted to his death, we cannot help becoming involved with Pepé as a person: This is the story of a boy who *wanted to be a man*. We see him spend hours practice-throwing the long, heavy knife he inherited from his father. We see him proudly going on a man's errands for his widowed mother:

> "Adiós, Mama," Pepé cried. "I will come back soon. You may send me often alone. I am a man."

We see him trying to act like a man when finding himself suddenly in a man's world:

> "I am a man now, Mama. The man said names to me I could not allow."

We see the boy die like a man when he finally turns to face his pursuers:

> It was a long struggle to get to his feet. He crawled slowly and mechanically to the top of a big rock on the ridge peak. Once there, he arose slowly, swaying to his feet, and stood erect. . . . There came a ripping sound at his feet. A piece of stone flew up and a bullet droned off into the next gorge. The hollow crash echoed up from below. Pepé looked down for a moment and then pulled himself straight again.
>
> His body jarred back. His left hand fluttered helplessly toward his breast. The second crash sounded from below. Pepé swung forward and toppled from the rock. His body struck and rolled over and over, starting a little avalanche. And when at last he stopped against a bush, the avalanche slid slowly down and covered up his head.[55]

This is a story of initiation, of growing up. A boy is trying to find his identity, the direction of his life. The story raises questions that concern us all: In growing up, do we "find ourselves," or do we only find the values of our culture, or of a group? Are individual pride and bravery remnants of an archaic, anachronistic life style no longer appropriate to a crowded urban world, where men have to "adjust," to "make allowances," for the sake of common peace and survival? How many people accept values not really made for them? (Steinbeck describes Pepé as a "gentle, affectionate boy.")

A strong thematic emphasis does not rule out a concern with form. Whatever human meaning a poem or a story has reaches us through its language, its form, its structure. We are concerned with *what* literature means—and *how* we know. Looked at from this point of view, many familiar categories cease to be criteria that we apply to a work from without. **Unity**, for instance, in a short story like Stephen Crane's "The Open Boat," is not an external, ready-made standard by which we judge the writer. The unity of Crane's story is what gives it its *impact*. It focuses our attention on what really matters, on what is central to the story. We observe the four shipwrecked men in their lifeboat; we follow their conversation, their efforts. As we do so, we again and again return to details, events, and comments that direct our attention to a central issue: man's relationship to nature, of which the shipwrecked sailors' struggle with the elements is a small but revealing example. Again and again we are led back to the idea that, contrary to man's confident expectations, "Nature does not regard him as important." She is serenely indifferent amid the struggles of her creatures. The ironic discrepancy between man's hopes and the indifference of nature is mirrored in a hundred incongruities and *non sequiturs*. The shipwreck, like the accident that is always expected to happen to other people, was "apropos of nothing." The boat the four shipwrecked men find themselves in is absurdly small contrasted with the "wrongfully and barbarously" tall waves. The sea is wildly picturesque, but the men are hardly in the mood to appreciate its savage splendor. The comfortable safety of the water birds enrages the men threatened with extinction by elements that to the birds are home. The call, on the men rowing the boat, for sheer raw physical exertion is beyond all that is reasonable. The surf keeping the boat from reaching the shore already clearly within sight seems a preposterous and abominably unjust obstacle to offer to the men's revived hopes. In the end, the injured captain, who seemed the most likely candidate for drowning, makes it to the shore. The oiler, the strongest swimmer and at first "ahead in the race" after the boat is swamped, drowns. The correspondent is at first immobilized by a current but then by sheer luck able to swim on and swept by a lucky large wave clear of the dangerous overturned boat.

The story ends with the ironic survival, not of the virtuous, nor even of the fittest, but merely of those who happen to survive. The oiler drowns because nature, who has small pity for the weak, does not really care for the strong either. Man's judgments and expectations seem strangely out of place in Crane's amoral, unthinking, **naturalistic** modern universe. Man's values are indeed man-made; they bind him with his fellows in gallant brotherhood of the victimized, but they find no echo in the unheeding cruelty of nature.

The unity of this story results from the author's single-minded preoccupation with his central theme. It reflects the naturalistic writer's grim determination to make us face the sober truth. Unity here is functional, organic; it is not a mere technical device or technical effect. Similarly **conflict** is not a mere technical term useful in tracing the plot development of drama. A dramatic conflict involves motives, persons, institutions; it raises *human* as well as critical questions. How real is the conflict? How avoidable? How does it engage our sympathies? How does it appeal to our moral judgment? Such questions guide us in setting up the distinction between **melodrama** and a mature play. Melodrama deals in polar opposites: The villain serves to focus our hostilities; he is there to be hissed and booed. The heroine becomes the object of our admiration; she is there to be wept over and agonized about. A mature play pits its hero against a more worthy, more formidable antagonist. There is a real conflict because there is something to be said for the other side. As A. C. Bradley says in discussing Hegel's theory of tragedy,

> the essentially tragic fact is the self-division and intestinal warfare of the ethical substance, not so much the war of good with evil as the war of good with good. Two of these isolated powers face each other, making incompatible demands. The family claims what the state refuses, love requires what honour forbids.[56]

Thus, Antigone's loyalty to her dead brother conflicts with Creon's demand for loyalty to the state. The conflict is more than a stage conflict in which we complacently identify with those representing purity, motherhood, and the flag. Instead, it brings into play conflicting parts of our own being.

Arthur Miller, in *The Crucible*, deals with a subject that would seem to invite melodramatic treatment: the witch trials of Salem, with their modern parallels in witch hunts directed at political heretics. But Miller resists the temptation to make the Puritan ministers and judges mere contemptible villains. Instead, they are men of varied and believable temperaments. They are animated by pride of scholarship, belief in authority, horror of heresy, and consciousness of injured merit. It would be *too easy* (and catastrophically misleading) to write them off as laugh-able hypocrites or monuments to human stupidity. When John Proctor, Miller's hero, finally confronts Danforth, the Puritan judge, he is not facing a small man, a spiteful man, a prevaricating man, or a forger of records. He faces a man who is determined to do justice, who is deter-mined to make the truth prevail, and who will hang the enemies of truth for the greater glory of God:

> DANFORTH [*realizing, slowly putting the sheet down*]. Did you ever see anyone with the Devil?
> PROCTOR. I did not.
> DANFORTH. Proctor, you mistake me. I am not empowered to trade your life for a lie. You have most certainly seen some person with the Devil. [PROCTOR *is silent*.] Mr. Proctor, a score of people have already testified they saw this woman with the Devil.
> PROCTOR. Then it is proved. Why must I say it?
> DANFORTH. Why "must" you say it! Why, you should rejoice to say it if your soul is truly purged of any love for Hell!
> PROCTOR. They think to go like saints. I like not to spoil their names.
> DANFORTH [*inquiring, incredulous*]. Mr. Proctor, do you think they go like saints?
> PROCTOR [*evading*]. This woman never thought she done the Devil's work.
> DANFORTH. Look you, sir. I think you mistake your duty here. It matters nothing what she thought—she is convicted of the unnatural murder of children and you for sending your spirit out upon Mary Warren. Your soul alone is the issue here, Mister, and you will prove its whiteness or you cannot live in a Christian country.[57]

The central conflict of Miller's play commands our grave attention because it dramatizes and heightens a conflict that is basic to our relation-ship with society and that admits of no easy solution: The individual's independent moral sense asserts itself against the official, public norms of righteousness, backed by the collective power of society. The basic pattern of the play derives from a conflict that is part of our own predica-ment.

One way to make sure that our preoccupation with technical detail does not obscure the vital meanings of what we read is to organize our study of literature around *thematic units*. Here are some examples of materials for extended thematic groupings:

(1) MAN AND NATURE
    Daniel Defoe, *The Adventures of Robinson Crusoe*
    Jack London, "To Make a Fire"
    Stephen Crane, "The Open Boat"

John Keats, "Autumn"
Dylan Thomas, "Fern Hill"
Robinson Jeffers, "Hurt Hawkes"
D. H. Lawrence, "Snake"
Henry Thoreau, *Walden*
William Faulkner, "The Bear"
William Blake, "The Lamb," "The Tiger"
(2) MAN AND THE MACHINE
Emily Dickinson, "The Train"
Stephen Spender, "The Express"
E. M. Forster, "The Machine Stops"
Charles Dickens, *Hard Times*
Carl Sandburg, "Chicago"
(3) MAN AND SOCIETY
Robert Frost, "Mending Wall"
Walt Whitman, "Crossing Brooklyn Ferry"
Robinson Jeffers, "The Purse-Seine"
W. H. Auden, "The Unknown Citizen"
Henry Thoreau, "On Civil Disobedience"
Sophocles, *Antigone*
Arthur Miller, *The Crucible*
(4) BLACK IDENTITY
Joseph Conrad, "An Outpost of Progress"
Eugene O'Neill, *The Emperor Jones*
Frederick Douglass, *Autobiography*
Richard Wright, *Black Boy*
James Baldwin, *Notes of a Native Son*
Lorraine Hansberry, *A Raisin in the Sun*
Poems by Langston Hughes, Gwendolyn Brooks, Robert Hayden, Helene Johnston
Poems by young black poets: Nicki Giovanni and others
(5) THE FEMININE IMAGE
Elizabethan love sonnets
Elizabeth Barrett Browning, "How Do I Love Thee?"
Henrik Ibsen, *The Doll's House*
G. B. Shaw, *Arms and the Man*
Tennessee Williams, *The Glass Menagerie*
Katherine Anne Porter, "The Jilting of Granny Weatherall"
Prose by Margaret Mead, Simone de Beauvoir
Poems by Sylvia Plath, Gwendolyn Brooks, and others
(6) ALIENATION
Willa Cather, "Paul's Case"
Franz Kafka, "Metamorphosis," "The Judgment"

Shirley Jackson, "The Lottery"
J. D. Salinger, *The Catcher in the Rye*
T. S. Eliot, "The Love Song of J. Alfred Prufrock"
Albert Camus, *The Stranger*
Allen Ginsberg, "Howl"
Samuel Beckett, *Waiting for Godot*

(7) VISIONS OF THE FUTURE
Current science fiction
Ray Bradbury, *The Martian Chronicles*
George Orwell, *1984*
Aldous Huxley, *Brave New World*
William Golding, *Lord of the Flies*

Emphasis on major themes keeps us from teaching literature as an inventory of literary techniques. It keeps us from teaching metaphor and irony and symbol as if they were what poetry is all about—with content optional. Even when we try to make students more aware of *how* the writer shapes his material, we can use groupings that combine attention to technique with a thematic focus. Modern studies of fiction, for instance, have paid much attention to **point of view**. They have investigated the perspective adopted by the author, the vantage point from which he surveys people and events. We can show why point of view *matters* by teaching a unit dealing with different perspectives toward one central theme, such as the nature of evil, or the disasters of war.

Some writers make us watch evil as though we saw it happening for the first time. They thus break through the film of familiarity; they make us ponder afresh its symptoms, its causes, its remedies. Stephen Crane, in a story like "The Blue Hotel," assumes the stance of the businesslike, unsentimental reporter. We watch, like helpless spectators, how the Swede, a stranger passing through a small Western town, arouses first wonder, then hostility, and finally deadly violence in the townspeople by his erratic actions. Before we know it, before our astonished eyes, he lies dead on the floor of the saloon, under the cash register with the ironic legend: "This registers the amount of your purchase." Other writers use the opposite strategy: They give us the inside story—they have the agent of evil take us into his confidence. They make him reveal to us, with frightening plausibility, the motives behind his actions. Thus, Browning, in "My Last Duchess," makes us share the cold, unforgiving enmity that comes from injured pride. Nelson Algren, in "A Bottle of Milk for Mother," involves us in the confused allegiances and blocked views that explain the "senseless violence" of the juvenile delinquent in the big city.

In teaching imaginative literature, we try to maintain an organic balance between form and theme, between medium and message. The human message of literature does not come to us as bare intellectual generalization. It takes concrete shape through image and symbol; it unfolds through narrative; it is acted out in the fruitful tension of dramatic opposites. To read a poem or a play, we have to respond fully to image, metaphor, symbol, pattern, structure. We have to let our emotions, our sympathies, our loyalties become fully engaged. But ultimately, literature plays a basic role in the student's liberal education because it is, in the largest sense of the term, a learning about life. Its beauty and power are organically linked to the insight it offers into human life. Taught in this spirit, literature ministers directly to the intellectual and spiritual needs of the adolescent. In his moments of confusion and self-pity, he may think of himself as adrift without bearings in a world not of his making. In a psychedelic world of changing sensations, literature acts out for him the patterns that men have created to make sense of their world, to explain to themselves who they are.

FOOTNOTES

[1]Jon Swan, "The Opening," *The New Yorker*, Apr. 2, 1960.

[2]Robert E. Spiller, "Is Literary History Obsolete?" *College English*, 24 (February 1963), 348–351.

[3]Roy Harvey Pearce, "Literature, History, and Humanism: An Americanist's Dilemma," *College English*, 24 (February 1963), 364.

[4]Jacques Barzun, "The Scholar-Critic," in *Contemporary Literary Scholarship: A Critical Review*, ed. Lewis Leary (New York: Appleton 1958), pp. 4–5.

[5]G. E. Bentley, "Shakespeare and His Times," in Leary, *Scholarship*, p. 58.

[6]C. S. Lewis, *The Allegory of Love: A Study in Medieval Tradition* (New York: Oxford University Press, 1958), pp. 1, 4.

[7]Lionel Trilling, *The Liberal Imagination: Essays on Literature and Society* (New York: Doubleday & Company, Inc., 1953), p. 20.

[8]Ezra Pound, "Hugh Selwyn Mauberley," *Selected Poems* (New York: New Directions Publishing Corporation, 1949), p. 64.

[9]Ernest Hemingway, *The Short Stories of Ernest Hemingway* (New York: Charles Scribner's Sons, 1938), pp. 145–153.

[10]R. P. Blackmur, *Language as Gesture: Essays in Poetry* (New York: Harcourt, 1952), pp. 390, 385.

[11]Mark Schorer, Josephine Miles, and Gordon McKenzie, *Criticism: The Foundations of Literary Judgment*, rev. ed. (New York: Harcourt, 1958), p. ix.

[12]Archibald MacLeish, *Collected Poems: 1917–1952* (Boston: Houghton Mifflin Company, 1954), pp. 40–41.

[13]John Ciardi, "Robert Frost: The Way to the Poem," *Saturday Review*, Apr. 12, 1958, 13–15.

[14]H. W. Gardner, ed., *Poems of Gerard Manley Hopkins*, 3rd ed. (New York: Oxford University Press, 1948), p. 74.

[15]Robert Penn Warren, "Pure and Impure Poetry," *The Kenyon Review*, 5 (Spring 1943), 251.

[16]Henry James, "The Art of Fiction," reprinted in Schorer, et al., *Criticism*, pp. 52, 54.

[17]*Kenyon Review*, 5, p. 250.

[18]W. K. Wimsatt, Jr., "The Structure of the 'Concrete Universal' in Literature," reprinted in Schorer, *Criticism*, 400–401.

[19]Louis L. Martz, "The Teaching of Poetry," in *Essays on the Teaching of English,* eds. Edward J. Gordon and Edward S. Noyes (New York: Appleton, 1960), p. 244.

[20]Karl Shapiro, *Poems 1940–1953* (New York: Random House, Inc.)

[21]Martz, "Poetry," in Gordon and Noyes, *Essays*, p. 256.

[22]Frederick A. Pottle, "Modern Criticism of *The Ancient Mariner*," in Gordon and Noyes, *Essays*, p. 265.

[23]Edward Connery Lathem, ed., *The Poetry of Robert Frost* (New York: Holt, Rinehart and Winston, Inc., 1969), p. 275.

[24]Cleanth Brooks, *Modern Poetry and the Tradition* (Chapel Hill: University of North Carolina Press, 1939), pp. 28–29, 39–45.

[25]*Kenyon Review*, 5, p. 251.

[26]T. S. Eliot, "The Metaphysical Poets," in *Selected Essays: 1917–1932* (New York: Harcourt, 1932), p. 247.

[27]Merrit Y. Hughes, "The Seventeenth Century," in Leary, *Scholarship*, p. 73.

[28]Trilling, *Liberal Imagination*, p. 16.

[29]Kenneth Burke, *The Philosophy of Literary Form: Studies in Symbolic Action* (Baton Rouge: Louisiana State University Press, 1941), p. 89.

[30]William Langland, *Visions from Piers Plowman*, trans. Nevill Coghill (London: Phoenix House, Ltd., 1949), pp. 15, 50, 56.

[31]Karl Marx and Frederick Engels, *The German Ideology, 1845–46* (New York: New World-International, 1967), p. 39; quoted in Lillian S. Robinson, "Dwelling in Decencies: Radical Criticism and the Feminist Perspective," *College English*, 32 (May 1971), pp. 880–881.

[32]James G. Kennedy, "The Two European Cultures and the Necessary New Sense of Literature," *College English*, 31 (March 1970), 576–587.

[33]John Steinbeck, *The Grapes of Wrath* (New York: The Viking Press, Inc., 1939), p. 477.

[34]George Orwell, *Animal Farm* (New York: Harcourt, 1946), p. 78.

[35]Ralph Ellison, *Invisible Man* (New York: Random House, Inc., 1952), p. 169.

[36]Arna Bontemps, ed., *American Negro Poetry* (New York: Hill and Wang, Inc., 1963), pp. 75–76.

[37]Donald B. Gibson, "Mark Twain's Jim in the Classroom," *The English Journal*, 57 (February 1968), 196–199.

[38]Kennedy, "Two Cultures," p. 586.

[39]Bertolt Brecht, *Mutter Courage und ihre Kinder* (Frankfurt am Main: Suhrkamp, 1961), pp. 37–38.

[40]Trilling, *Liberal Imagination,* pp. 44, 47.

[41]Ernest Jones, "Hamlet Psychoanalysed," reprinted in Laurence Lerner, ed., *Shakespeare's Tragedies* (Baltimore: Penguin Books, Inc., 1963), pp. 47–64.

[42]Trilling, *Liberal Imagination*, p. 48.

[43]Blackmur, *Language as Gesture*, p. 398.

[44]C. G. Jung, *Modern Man in Search of a Soul* (New York: Harcourt, 1933), pp. 194–195.

[45]Jung, *Modern Man*, pp. 180–181, 197.

[46]Jung, *Modern Man*, p. 198.

[47]Blackmur, *Language as Gesture*, p. 398.

[48]Francis Fergusson, *The Idea of a Theater* (New York: Doubleday, n.d.), pp. 26, 14–17.

[49]Fergusson, *The Idea of a Theater*, pp. 27–52.

[50]Sophocles, *The Oedipus Cycle: An English Version*, trans. Dudley Fitts and Robert Fitzgerald (New York: Harcourt, 1949), p. 78.

[51]Northrop Frye, "The Argument of Comedy," reprinted in Leonard F. Dean, ed., *Shakespeare: Modern Essays in Criticism* (New York: Oxford University Press, 1957), pp. 79–89.

[52]Northrop Frye, "Literature as Context: Milton's *Lycidas*," reprinted in C. A. Patrides, ed., *Milton's* Lycidas: *The Tradition and the Poem* (New York: Holt, Rinehart and Winston, Inc., 1961), pp. 200–211.

[53]Edmund Wilson, *Classics and Commercials* (New York: Farrar, Straus, 1950), pp. 43–45.

[54]Wimsatt, "Structure of the 'Concrete Universal,'" in Schorer, *Criticism*, p. 400.

[55]John Steinbeck, *The Long Valley* (New York: The Viking Press, Inc., 1956), pp. 45–70.

[56]A. C. Bradley, *Oxford Lectures on Poetry* (New York: St. Martin's Press, Inc., 1959), pp. 71–72.

[57]Arthur Miller, *The Crucible* (New York: Bantam Books, Inc., 1959), p. 135.

FOR FURTHER STUDY

A.   The following poems were written by students and published in a
college literary magazine. Examine each poem to see how it reflects and
shapes experience. What is the role of concrete image, metaphor, symbol,
irony, point of view? What are the patterns that help organize each poem?
How are they related to patterns existing in life? What is the theme of each
poem? How do you react to each poem?

1.
Colored dots that flit
She's staring into the aviary
In her mouth then in theirs
Feeding the birds
Stuffing peanuts in
She has a ripped dress
Beneath the arm on the left side
And she is alone

Except for the sad eye of a bird
And people who brush beside her
Like paper bags
Her life is
She has peanuts
And the birds are whispering
"Come through the wire."
                                        —Joan Eyles

2.
Marianne comes.
I move a coat for her.
She sits.
False lashes,
Black fringe
Like the powdered wrinkles
On her cheeks.
I watch her white nails,
Her too-wide teeth,
Her silver-green eye shadow flashing.
The waitress brings her soup.
"Latin men destroy, she says.
Have you noticed that?
They have used me
Since I am flesh,
See I am flesh."

My crab salad sandwich drips.
                                        —Jan Zalenski

3.   I ask,
                 You say, "No."
            I plead,
                 You say, "Maybe."
            I beg,
                 You say, "All right."
            What could it possibly be worth to me now?
                                        —Trudy Robben

4.   What I liked was that her
                      sheets were clean
                  her cupboards ordered
                           each ailment in
            Alphabetical
               Biological
                  Chronological
                     ORDER
            Quite naturally,
                  When she entertained her
                        glasses were cold
                      her liquors ranked
                           each Bacchus in
            Liturgical
               Metaphysical
                  Numerical
                     ORDER
            Efficiently labelled,
                  The several rooms divided
                      herself categorically
                           each part filed
                  IN THE STUDY FILE
            Drawer 1 : A through K
            Drawer 2 : M through R
            Drawer 3 : S through Z
            Drawer 4 : MISCELLANEOUS
                              I
            was neatly filed here next to
                        LOVE
                        —Paula Truesdell

5.   I have lain
                  in the broad lap
                        of the wise woman
                  and later sought
                        the high narrow hip
                  of the laughing girl.
                  Throwing the dream covers
                              off

slow and warm
I got up
    to find you
smiling wisely.
—Henry O. Johnson

B.   The following is a poem by Emily Dickinson with a range of reactions that a teacher might obtain from a class of high school seniors or
college freshmen. As a teacher, how would you react to these student responses? Which do you like best? Which least? Why?

Because I could not stop for Death,
He kindly stopped for me;
The carriage held but just ourselves
And Immortality.

We slowly drove, he knew no haste,
And I had put away
My labor, and my leisure too,
For his civility.

We passed the school, where children strove
At recess, in the ring;
We passed the fields of gazing grain,
We passed the setting sun.

Or rather, he passed us;
The dews grew quivering and chill,
For only gossamer my gown,
My tippet only tulle.

We paused before a house that seemed
A swelling of the ground;
The roof was scarcely visible,
The cornice in the ground.

Since then 'tis centuries, and yet
Feels shorter than the day
I first surmised the horses' heads
Were toward eternity.

1.   Emily Dickinson writes about death in a calm and uninhibited way, as though
it were just one of the occurrences of everyday life. Her presentation of death
is simple, not magnified as is quite often the case. First, death calls whether or
not one is ready. There is no hurry, though; there is time to view life's passing
incidents. Miss Dickinson talks about passing a school where children are playing, about passing fields of gazing grain, and about the setting sun. All of these

things are part of one's everyday life, things one remembers most vividly. In the fifth stanza, she talks about a house, conveying to us that the home is probably the most significant part of one's life. Although death arrives, these things will be present in one's mind for an eternity.

2.   When I read the poem I get the idea that someone is near death. The person has led a good life and has probably retired. He is waiting for death to catch up with him. Before death arrives, the person takes an imaginary ride in a carriage and takes in the highlights of his life. He passes a school where children play, and this reminds him of his own youth. He also passes a field of grain, which reminds him of his days as a farmer or of the time when he was working to earn a living. Finally, death catches up with him, as the setting sun indicates. The person is buried, the mound being the symbol of a cemetery. The pause near the mound is probably the funeral service held for him.

3.   The poet regards Death as a person always present in the background of life. Death knows "no haste," because once he has made his claim upon a person the only goal is immortality. There is no hurry, the carriage of Death always leads to the one goal. The carriage passes children playing happily. Even though Death is in the background, life, carefree and gay, will continue for them. Other things that are not disturbed by the thought of Death are "fields of gazing grain," for they remain serene. The setting sun symbolizes the "twilight" or ending of life. The house that seemed a swelling of the ground is the last sight which reminds the rider in the carriage of life on earth. He takes a last look at these objects but still moves slowly, though deliberately, toward eternity.

4.   The poem gives an impression of calmness and serenity. After the writer has been "kindly" picked up by death for immortality, their progress is slow and orderly, as if there were no rush or limit on time. As soon as she enters the chariot, her labor and her leisure—all worldly ambitions, pleasures, and pursuits—are ended, and she is devoted entirely to death "for his civility." The journey past the various scenes could represent her life in retrospect; the children could represent her youth, the fields of grain could mean maturity or the middle years of her life. The pause at the "swelling in the ground" symbolizes to me the fact that they pause by her grave long enough to leave her material body on earth in the customary manner. Only her spirit accompanies the driver of the chariot on through the centuries of immortality into eternity.

5.   I don't particularly like this poem by Emily Dickinson. It feels like sand running through my toes. I am sure I can't say why she mentions playing children, gazing grain, and a setting sun. Perhaps these are the things she loves best. The lightness of the poem reminds me of a woman riding home and casually remarking about the things she sees that impress her. The last stanza leads me to believe that she knew what it would feel like after death. She thinks she'll know when she is approaching death, because she'll experience some sequence of emotions, or see some particular sequence of objects. I feel as if I were running after the carriage with Emily Dickinson in it and hollering to her to tell me what she means. But she keeps going slowly on toward something mysterious, saying casual things that I don't quite understand. I'm not going to guess at what she means. Maybe she doesn't mean anything. Maybe the poem is as light as it feels.

C.   Of the following plays, select the one you know best: Arthur Miller, *Death of a Salesman* or *The Crucible*; Tennessee Williams, *The Glass Menagerie*; Thornton Wilder, *Our Town*; Bertolt Brecht, *Mother Courage*; Eugene O'Neill, *The Emperor Jones*; Samuel Beckett, *Waiting for Godot*. For the play you choose, write *three* different versions of a short (two-page) review. Each time impersonate a different kind of critic. For instance, you might write versions by a Marxist critic, a Freudian critic, and an anthropological critic.

D.   In literary or professional journals, find three full-length discussions of *one* of the following much-analyzed short stories: Hawthorne, "Young Goodman Brown"; Kafka, "The Country Doctor"; Shirley Jackson, "The Lottery"; William Faulkner, "A Rose for Emily"; Ernest Hemingway, "The Killers"; James Joyce, "The Dead." As fully as you can, identify each critic's characteristic assumptions, preoccupations, and approach. Which seems to you the most instructive or helpful from the point of view of a teacher? Why?

E.   The articles listed below deal with crucial issues for the teacher of literature: the relationship between theme and form, between intellectual analysis and emotional involvement, and between established literary values and the actual reading interests of students. Prepare a critical review of one of these articles. Describe as fully and fairly as you can the author's personal stand; support your own reactions. Choose one of the following, or a more recent similar article recommended by your instructor: Louise M. Rosenblatt, "Pattern and Process—A Polemic," *English Journal*, 58 (October 1969), 1005–1012; Deanna Tressin, "Toward Understanding," *English Journal*, 55 (December 1966), 1170–1174; G. Robert Carlsen, "The Interest Rate Is Rising," *English Journal*, 59 (May 1970), 655–659; Stanley Bank, "A Literary Hero for Adolescents: The Adolescent," *English Journal*, 58 (October 1969), 1013–1020; Charles Clerc, "On Spirit Booster Literature," *English Journal*, 56 (December 1967), 1255–1262; Arthur Daigon, "Literature and the Schools," *English Journal*, 58 (January 1969), 30–39; Gladys Valcourt Gaumann, "A Year of Utopias," *English Journal*, 61 (February 1972), 234–238, 251.

F.   The following statements deal with issues that concern teachers of literature. How do you react to each statement, and why? What examples, evidence, or arguments could you present pro and con? How would you formulate your own position on what is involved?

1.   If the English class, in its very nature, deals with the strongest feelings that human beings have, the usual English teacher, by some magic, or miasma, or

blanket dilutes these feelings so that the English class generally becomes the model of propriety. Strange, when the creators of English literature have not been known for either the sanity or the sanitary characteristics of the values they lived by. The things that are conjectured about Shakespeare would turn your hair, but he's a decent chap in the English class. Some unkind things have recently been said about that other English staple, the late Robert Frost, meaning that literary men are human beings too. But all our heroes have a bit of the villain in them and something of the fool, and one function of the English class is to assess the relationships of the hero-component, the villain-component, and the fool-component in human beings.

—Abraham Bernstein, "Cultural Clash, Crash, and Cash"

2. Most English professors are quite defensive *vis-à-vis* writers and poets. They try to establish themselves as a different breed with different standards and objectives. Reading poetry and writing it are said to be totally different activities. But while reading poetry is not the same thing as writing it, and the same men will not reach the top in these two fields, the two activities *are* related to each other. A graduate training program for literary scholars ought to recognize this and get the prospective scholar to try his hand at the art which he will be criticizing. Many would not perform very well, but that is not the point. Nobody should get a Ph.D. in English who has not *tried* to write a sonnet.

—Christopher Jencks and David Riesman, "Where Graduate Schools Fail"

3. Suddenly, classroom dramatization has been re-discovered. I have watched classes come alive when they wrote scripts from stories or from their imagination and worked them up for a broadcast over a P.A. system or tape-recorded them for playback to the class. I have watched youngsters spontaneously dramatize plays that are under study. I have observed one class become cinematographers and write, direct, and film their own motion picture. What does this add to the class? At least it breaks up the lethargy and boredom of students. Perhaps, it gives them some poise. It provides a chance to use language in patterns predetermined for them. And it certainly leaves them with significant memories of English classes for years to come. Over and over I have run into individuals who went to old West High School in Minneapolis during the late twenties and early thirties. One of their cherished memories is of their class in Shakespeare when the class was taught completely through dramatizations of the plays.

—G. Robert Carlsen, "English Below the Salt"

4. My Shakespeare students didn't know how to read drama as if it were primarily two persons talking to each other with tension—responding, confronting, or not responding in a significant way. So I asked each student to write a one-page drama in which persons with real voices said real things that counted for them, and the whole added up in some way. They did this. I was astonished, and so were they. Some of the little plays had to be published in a literary supplement to the campus newspaper, and dozens had to be posted on a bulletin board in the corridor of the building where I held class. Knots of students from other classes and departments collected around the posted papers.

I can remember months later many of the dramas—the one about the girl introducing her new roommate to her old roommate now clerking in a department store and pregnant with illegitimate child, the one about the boy who angrily moved out of the dorm because he had to live three students in a room and joyously found freedom in a town apartment where he was living three in a room, the one about the young man arguing in a bar with his friend about his inability to decide what to do about the draft—he thought the war immoral but was not a pacifist.

None of the dramas have been sustained, complex artistic works. But they exhibit many of the devices employed by Shakespeare and other professionals—irony, interruption, play on words, alliteration, metaphor, careful and accurate differentiation of dialects, change of voice within one man's speech as he moves into different situations, etc. Whether or not they succeed as dramatic sketches, these one-page workouts help students read Shakespeare as a playwright and appreciate his range and command.

—Ken Macrocrie, *Uptaught*

Chapter 6

English in a
Pluralistic Society

Mass Culture and the Mass Media—Popular Culture and the Native Tradition—
Multi-ethnic America—The Culture of Minorities

At one time, English teachers lived in a stable, protected world where the rules were known, where there were lasting values, and where established classics made up the cultural heritage. Today, we see everywhere the opening up of that closed and protected world, a branching out, a rediscovery of the world outside. No English teacher is an island: Like it or not, we are asked to ponder the relationship between literature and politics. English studies and consumerism, standard English and white supremacy, composition and the electronic media. We are becoming more aware of the larger social, political, and cultural implications of what we do. Whether we teach James Baldwin's *Notes of a Native Son* or Eldridge Cleaver's *Soul on Ice* is in part a literary choice, but it is also a political choice. Whether we assign Whittier's *Snow-Bound* or Ginsberg's *Howl* has something to do with whether we see it as our job to preserve the heritage or to promote a counterculture.

We can no longer look at our subject as a self-contained subject-matter specialty: English is our national language, the common bond in a nation of immigrants, a key agent in the historical process of assimilation and Americanization. Literature is the arena where value systems take shape, are perpetuated, are challenged and redefined. In teaching American English, and in teaching imaginative literature, we help define our national culture. In the past, our definition of that culture has often been too narrow, too exclusive. To relate our subject authentically to the society of which we are a part, we need a broader, a more pluralistic definition of American culture. Specifically, we need to recognize, to bring in, major strands that English teachers in the past have tended to slight or to ignore.

As English teachers today we are rediscovering American *popular* culture—its reflection in mass entertainment and the mass media, its relation to the counterculture of the young, its relation to an authentic, native American literary tradition. We are rediscovering the *immigrant's* America—bilingualism and biculturalism as pervading facts of American life; the ethnic American's view of the American experience. We are discovering the culture of *minorities*—linguistic and cultural diversity resulting from the existence of a Spanish-American and a black American community, whose relations to mainstream culture are complex and in a state of flux.

MASS CULTURE AND THE MASS MEDIA

As long as anyone can remember, *English teachers have looked upon culture as the possession of a cultivated élite*. They carried on a tradition of educated taste whose watchwords were EXCELLENCE, DISTINCTION, ORIGINALITY. They deplored the trite and the obvious; they strove to rise above the sentimentality of the philistine; they rejected the epic vulgarities of the arts of the masses. They helped establish and perpetuate an approved canon of cultural objects which were, in Susan Sontag's words, "undefiled by mass appreciation." They subscribed to publications whose pundits deplored the taste of "middle-brows" and of the "mass audience." By and large, "serious" art and literature meant art cut off from the public at large by its stylistic sophistication and thematic complexity, and ennobled by its lack of commercial potential.

Today, this **élitist** tradition of academic culture is everywhere being challenged. It is being leavened and democratized by a more anthropological view of culture as rooted in the experience of a whole people. The serious arts, when not moribund or peripheral, are parts of a larger whole. As teachers, we cannot just be "keepers in the museum of high but irrelevant art, training a few in the next generation to be keepers in their turn."[1] We have to break out of our self-imposed isolation. It is true that in order to understand American culture we should read Franklin and Melville and Emerson and Thoreau. But these very classics themselves had sturdy roots in the common life of their own time. To understand contemporary American culture, we need to look at Hollywood movies and the rituals of Rotarians, at *Gone with the Wind* and *Uncle Tom's Cabin*, at gospel music and the rhetoric of Baptist preachers. In recent years, this necessary discovery of **popular culture**, of folk culture, has made tremendous strides. Where we once sniffed at "mass culture," we have come to discover something authentically American in comic strips and Humphrey Bogart movies, in folk blues and rock lyrics, in Burma Shave ads and Alka Seltzer commercials, in the lore of the outlaws of the West.

The revolt against the narrow exclusiveness of "high culture" gathered momentum in the middle sixties when highbrow critics began to tell us that "there are other creative sensibilities besides the seriousness (both tragic and comic) of high culture and of the high style of evaluating people. And one cheats himself, as a human being, if one has respect only for the style of high culture, whatever else one may do or feel on the sly." Thus,

> the affection which many younger artists and intellectuals feel for the popular arts is not a new philistinism (as has so often been charged) or a species of anti-intellectualism or some kind of abdication from culture. The fact that many of the most serious American painters, for example, are also fans of "the new sound" in popular music is *not* the result of the search for mere diversion or relaxation; it is not, say, like Schoenberg also playing tennis. It reflects a new, more open way of looking at the world and at things in the world, our world.[2]

Tiring of the endless sour polemics against our "commercially debauched" popular culture, readers began to agree that the person "who insists on high and serious pleasures is depriving himself of pleasure; he continually restricts what he can enjoy." The ability to branch out beyond the austere confines of high culture "makes the man of good taste cheerful, where before he ran the risk of being chronically frustrated"; it is "good for the digestion."[3]

At first gingerly and apologetically, intellectuals began to experiment with new attitudes toward billboards, country music, and the picture tube. They learned to relish, rather than to judge, some of the garish, flamboyant, extravagant elements of the popular culture around them. They rediscovered Buster Keaton and King Kong; they even began to develop a kind of connoisseur's interest in the corny, the vulgar, and just plain awful. Mass entertainment, good and bad, teaches us something about the imaginative life of urban societies and about people as they are. Much popular art has its own kind of meaning, its own kind of interest:

> Who can listen to a program of pop songs, or watch "Candid Camera" or "This Is Your Life," without enduring a complicated and complex mixture of attraction and repulsion, of admiration for skill and scorn for the phony, or wry observations of similarities and correspondences, of sudden reminders of the raciness of speech, or of the capacity for courage or humor, or of shock at the way mass art can "process" anything, even our most intimate feelings. . . . All this is deeply related to hopes, uncertainties, aspirations, the search for identity in a moving society, innocence, meanness, the wish for community and the recognition—far down—of an inescapable loneliness. It is a form of art (bastard art if you want to call it that) but vulnerable, mythic and not easily explained away.[4]

Once we stop holding popular culture at arm's length, we discover much that is fascinating to the teacher of language and literature, much that is grist for the English teacher's mill. We discover an inexhaustible live teaching aid in the capsule drama of the **comic strip**, where we see acted out irony and parody, doubletake and repartee, topical allusion and deadpan humor:

Turtle: I'm taking a survey of all the human bean's who live in the swamp.
Pogo: Ah—a survey of the *denizens*.
Turtle: No—just them what *lives* here.

Charlie Brown (while Linus is sucking his thumb and holding on to his security blanket): This writer says that children are remarkably observant . . . He says that children are much more aware of what is going on around them than adults think they are . . . I'm rather inclined to agree with him, aren't you?
Linus: Huh?

Pogo (trying to make polite conversation with Mrs. Hopfrog, whose baby carriage is occupied by a big jar of water with her little tadpole swimming in it): Look at it this way, Miz Hop Frog, the boy there got *promise*!
Mrs. Hopfrog: Not much *frog*-promise, Pogo, apparently he wanna ree-main a fish.
Pogo: But he *already* got nostrils . . . ain't many fish got nostrils . . . You look at it the right way, *whales*, the champeen fish, got nostrils . . . nothin' wrong with bein' a whale—How 'bout *that*?

Mrs. Hopfrog: Son, if my tad grow up to be a whale, I'll be the Mother-of-the-Year for a century!

Marryin' Sam (reciting his prospectus for the eight-dollar wedding): "Fust—Ah strips t' th' waist, an' rassles th' four biggest guests!! Next— a fast demon-stray-shun o' how t' cheat yore friends at cards!!—follyed by four snappy jokes—guaranteed t' embarrass man or beast—an'— then after ah dances a jig wif a pig, Ah yanks out two o' mah teeth, an' presents 'em t' th' bride an' groom—as mementos o' th' occasion!!—then —Ah really gits goin!!—Ah offers t' remove any weddin' guest's ap- pendix, wif mah bare hands—free!! Then yo' spread-eagles me, fastens mah arms an' laigs t' four wild jackasses—an'—bam!!—yo' fires a gun!!— While they tears me t' pieces—Ah puffawms th' weddin' ceremony!!"[5]

In popular literature, we can often see basic literary processes at work that may be obscured in highly sophisticated and self-conscious literary art. We can observe some of the basic functions that storyteller and bard served through the ages before high culture and popular culture went their separate ways. Modern **science fiction**, for instance, is a major modern genre, comparable in its popularity and topical relevance to the travel literature, the untold accounts of real and imaginary voyages, of the centuries after Columbus.

The most basic effect of science fiction is to revive our sense of *wonder.* The basic stance of the science fiction writer is to turn to us and to say: "Assume for the time being that . . ."; "Suppose . . ." As Isaac Asimov says,

> Suppose tobacco is outlawed and adultery accepted. Suppose robots do the world's work and humanity lives in enforced and resented leisure. Sup- pose some men can live for centuries while other men cannot. Suppose an intelligent form of life visits our planet and suppose they (or we) happen to be good to eat?[6]

For the writer, the creative delight is in working out this at first "unlikely" supposition and making it come out likely, real, plausible. For the reader, one major effect is that he encounters familiar things but sees them in a new light. He sees things that are in some ways routine— only they are no longer routine. They are fascinating, challenging, new as the result of being put in a different context, to be looked at from a new perspective. They are combined according to new rules, put to new uses:

> "The humans warred against the invaders, using bullets, ordinary bombs, and gases. . . . 'Ammunition' they were called. The humans fought each other with such things."

"And not with ideas, like we do now, father?"

"No, with guns, just as I told you. But the invaders were immune to the ammunition."

"What does 'immune' mean?"

"Proof against harm. Then the humans tried germs and bacteria against the Star beings."

"What were those things?"

"Tiny, tiny bugs that the humans tried to inject into the bodies of the invaders to make them sicken and die. But the bugs had no effect at all on the Star beings . . . these newcomers were vastly more intelligent than the Earthlings. In fact, the invaders were the greatest mathematicians in the System."

—Arthur Feldman, "The Mathematicians"[7]

In the living room the voice-clock sang, *Tick-tock, seven o'clock, time to get up, time to get up, seven o'clock!* as if it were afraid that nobody would. The morning house lay empty. The clock ticked on, repeating and repeating its sounds into the emptiness. *Seven-nine, breakfast time, seven-nine!*

In the kitchen the breakfast stove gave a hissing sigh and ejected from its warm interior eight pieces of perfectly browned toast, eight eggs sunnyside up, sixteen slices of bacon, two coffees, and two cool glasses of milk.

"Today is August 4, 2026," said a second voice from the kitchen ceiling, "in the city of Allendale, California." It repeated the date three times for memory's sake. "Today is Mr. Featherstone's birthday. Today is the anniversary of Tilita's marriage. Insurance is payable, as are the water, gas, and light bills."

Somewhere in the walls, relays clicked, memory tapes glided under electric eyes.

Eight-one, tick-tock, eight-one o'clock, off to school, off to work, eight-one! . . . Outside, the garage chimed and lifted its door to reveal the waiting car. After a long wait the door swung down again . . .

Nine-fifteen, sang the clock, *time to clean.*

Out of warrens in the wall, tiny robot mice darted. The rooms were acrawl with the small cleaning animals, all rubber and metal. They thudded against chairs, whirling their mustached runners, kneading the rug nap, sucking gently at hidden dust. Then, like mysterious invaders, they popped into their burrows. Their pink electric eyes faded. The house was clean.

—Ray Bradbury, "August 2026"[8]

Much science fiction deals with basic recurrent themes that grip us at a level deeper than mere surface entertainment. One of the central topics of science fiction and science fiction films is threat, challenge, disaster, which, as Susan Sontag said, "is one of the oldest subjects of art."[9] The monstrous threat, the superhuman challenge—the Martian invaders, the runaway mutation, the rival life form—these shake us out of our insipid daily lives. They confront us with some of our most basic fears; they arouse us to a renewed sense of the precariousness of human existence.

At the same time, much science fiction material symbolically acts out basic processes by which we arrive at *group identity and moral self-justification*. The adversary to be fought is often monstrous, freakish, "excluded from the category of the human. The sense of superiority over the freak conjoined in varying proportions with the titillation of fear and aversion makes it possible for moral scruples to be lifted, for cruelty to be enjoyed. . . . In the figure of the monster from outer space, the freakish, the ugly, and the predatory all converge—and provide a fantasy target for righteous bellicosity to discharge itself."[10] The resulting sense of group identification and group loyalty can produce a vision of a collective life "which uses the cosmic emergencies of science fiction as a way of reliving a kind of wartime togetherness and morale, a kind of drawing together among survivors which is itself merely a distorted dream of a more humane collectivity and social organization."[11] In the scientist-hero of much science fiction material, we can see a nostalgic modern archetype of a person engaged in meaningful, challenging work, a kind of work that is fascinating and at the same time personal and psychologically satisfying. We can see acted out the old dream of science as the means by which man achieves control, becomes master of his fate; and we can see acted out the old fear of the uncanny, superhuman power that the scientist's magic gives to those willing to abuse it.

Comics, science fiction, the comedy classics of the silent screen, the formulas of the classic television Western and of the situation-comedy serial, modern documentary photography as it flourished in the now moribund large-circulation popular magazines—all these provide the English teacher with areas for exploration and experiment. When English teachers first move into these areas, they often do so in a proper, detached, and scholarly manner: They set out to develop "critical appreciation"; they promote **visual literacy**; they read about film aesthetics and the built-in messages of the media. But the major benefit to be derived from openness to popular culture is not critical or theoretical. In fact, we turn to popular culture for a *counterweight* to the overly critical, theoretical, and detached spirit of much of the academic enterprise. During the last decade or two, popular culture has had a pervasive leavening influence not just on the content of what we teach, but on the *mood* in which we teach, the *tone* we set in the classroom, the *spirit* in which we deal with language and literature.

Our renewed interest in popular culture has helped us bring back to our teaching the gusto and vitality that an overly critical spirit can easily destroy. All around us, in recent years, we have seen an environment more hospitable to fantasy and color and rhythm and chant. On soup can labels and billboards, on record jackets and astrological posters, we have rediscovered a sense of color and exuberance that in our too exclusive concern with high culture we had lost. Looking back over what culture used to mean in our programs and textbooks, we find that too often it meant something genteel, refined, subdued. Aiming at excellence, thinking of Chartres and Emerson, we often in fact created a cultural environment too dry, too sober, too grey, too dull. Aiming at clarity, precision, logic, we did battle against redundant words, farfetched analogies, extravagant and mixed metaphors, colloquial language and slang. In the process, we drained off the color, drama, and whimsy in our students' speech and writing, and in our own as well.

Years ago, W. K. Wimsatt, Jr. noted that the color and vitality that teachers were successfully subduing in academic prose flourished in the **mass media**, in popular journalism. He commented on the "wild flair for metaphor" of the sportswriter, that "popular narrator of heroic conflict," quoting as examples the epithets applied to Joe Louis and Primo Carnera after their fight in 1935. Carnera was the "ambling Alp," the "Italian mastodon," the "rudderless mammoth," the "robot of the racketeers." Louis was the "brown bomber," the "dark destroyer," the "black blizzard," the "dark dynamiter," the "tan terror," the "dusky Detroiter," the "dark detonator," the "killer from the cotton fields":

> The *frozen-faced, sloe-eyed Negro's* defeat of Carnera was enacted before 57,000 pairs of eyes red with blood lust. [Carnera] lacked only one thing— natural fighting ability, of which the *black Beowulf* had more than an abundance. The *imperturbable brown bear* . . . had whanged away under Carnera's guard . . . until the *jittery giant* had become very weary indeed. . . . the *lad with the petrified puss* was upon Carnera as he rose as wobbly as a punch-drunk fighter on stilts. . . . Crack, crack! went the right and left of this *calmly savage Ethiopian* to the head of the *battered derelict*. . . . He reeled along the rig ropes, obviously begging that someone stop this *brown mechanism* that was so surely destroying him. . . . He feinted with his hands and the *vast Venetian* threw up his hands widely as his wits scattered.[12]

This may not be deathless prose, but it is not dull. If we turn for instructive contrast to the more dutiful kind of student writing, we are struck by its grey, drab quality. It is as if our insistence on understatement and cautious generalization had by and large had an overkill effect.

It is as if the natural spirit and boisterousness of our students had been covered with a large wet blanket. They have too often been told to hold in rather than let go. Part of every English teacher's job is to *un*inhibit his students, to break the ice, to recover the child's unspoilt delight in words as words.

POPULAR CULTURE AND THE NATIVE TRADITION

Once we see it as our job to help restore a natural vitality to our students' use of language, we are struck by an encouraging fact: Much of our native literary tradition is at the *opposite* pole from caution, understatement, and dry facetiousness. Many of our classics demonstrate the native American tendency toward "putting it on thick," toward pulling out the stops. Among the most authentic native literary forms are the **tall tale**, the **Gothic tale** of horror, the chanting **free-verse** lyrical poem. Thus, we open our literature anthology to a short story by Edgar Allan Poe, and we are carried away by the rich prose of a writer intoxicated with language:

> I started hourly from dreams of unutterable fear to find the hot breath of *the thing* upon my face, and its vast weight—an incarnate nightmare that I had no power to shake off—incumbent eternally upon my *heart*! . . .

> No sooner had the reverberation of my blows sunk into silence, than I was answered by a voice from within the tomb!—by a cry, at first muffled and broken, like the sobbing of a child, and then quickly swelling into one long, loud, and continuous scream, utterly anomalous and inhuman—a howl—a wailing shriek, half of horror and half of triumph, such as might have arisen only out of hell, conjointly from the throats of the damned in their agony and of the demons that exult in the damnation.

Incarnate, incumbent, reverberation, anomalous—how Poe loves "big words"! We read a short story by Bret Harte, and we recognize at once an unmistakably native quality in the oratorical flourish, the rhetorical swagger of his sentences:

> *Pulseless and cold,*
> *with a Derringer by his side and bullet in his heart,*
> *though still calm as in life,*
> *beneath the snow*
>   lay he
>   *who was at once the strongest and yet the*
>   *weakest of the outcasts of Poker Flat.*

The most authentic native form of humor is the whopper; the authentic image of the American humorist is Mark Twain delivering the most outrageous exaggerations in the most matter-of-fact, deadpan manner:

> The station buildings were long, low huts, made of sundried, mud-colored bricks, laid up without mortar (*adobes*, the Spaniards call these bricks, and Americans shorten it to *'dobies*). The roofs, which had no slant to them worth speaking of, were thatched and then sodded or covered with a thick layer of earth, and from this sprung a pretty rank growth of weeds and grass. It was the first time we had ever seen a man's front yard on top of his house.

> I thought of the anecdote (a very, very old one, even at that day) of the traveler who sat down to a table which had nothing on it but a mackerel and a pot of mustard. He asked the landlord if this was all. The landlord said:
> "*All!* Why, thunder and lightning, I should think there was mackerel enough there for six."
> "But I don't like mackerel."
> "Oh—then help yourself to the mustard."

> Noise proves nothing. Often a hen who has merely laid an egg cackles as if she had laid an asteroid.

> Adam was but human—this explains it all. He did not want the apple for the apple's sake, he wanted it only because it was forbidden. The mistake was in not forbidding the serpent; then he would have eaten the serpent.

> There is no character, howsoever good and fine, but it can be destroyed by ridicule, howsoever poor and witless. Observe the ass, for instance: his character is about perfect, he is the choicest spirit among all the humbler animals, yet see what ridicule has brought him to. Instead of feeling complimented when we are called an ass, we are left in doubt.

The most unmistakably American of our writers are those that respond to the larger-than-life elements in the American experience. American literature is Mark Twain writing about river traffic on the Mississippi, Carl Sandburg chanting the steel-and-concrete landscape of the big city, Walt Whitman creating the myths and the pageantry of popular democracy. When Mark Twain writes about life on the Mississippi, the words that hint at the deeper vital meaning of the great river are not synonyms of subtlety and restraint but words like *rough, coarse, reckless, profane, prodigal, barbaric, prodigious*:

> In time this commerce . . . gave employment to hordes of rough and hardy men; rude, uneducated, brave, . . . heavy drinkers, coarse frolickers in moral sites like the Natchez-under-the-hill of that day, heavy fighters, reckless

fellows, ... elephantinely jolly, foul-witted, profane, prodigal of their money, bankrupt at the end of the trip, fond of barbaric finery, prodigious braggarts; yet, in the main, honest, trustworthy, faithful to promises and duty, and often picturesquely magnanimous.

When Carl Sandburg writes about Chicago, his theme is not idyllic retreat but the harsh beauty and surging power of a technology that awes and at the same time intoxicates us, that is man-made and yet larger than man:

> Lay me on an anvil, O God.
> Beat me and hammer me into a steel spike.
> Drive me into the girders that hold a skyscraper together.
>
> Take red-hot rivets and fasten me into the central girders.
> Let me be the great nail holding a skyscraper through blue
>   nights into white stars.[13]

When Walt Whitman writes about the swirling masses of American democracy, he writes as a poet who could say, "The men and women I saw were all near to me":

> Just as you feel when you look on the river and sky, so I felt,
> Just as any of you is one of a living crowd, I was one of a crowd,
> Just as you are refresh'd by the gladness of the river and the bright
>   flow, I was refresh'd,
> Just as you stand and lean on the rail, yet hurry with the swift
>   current, I stood yet was hurried,
> Just as you look on the numberless masts of ships and the thick-
>   stemm'd pipes of steamboats, I look'd.

In the living catalogues of his poems, there is no narrow exclusiveness; they are *all* there:

> The pure contralto sings in the organ loft,
> The carpenter dresses his plank, the tongue
>   of his foreplane whistles its wild ascending lisp, ...
> The spinning girl retreats and advances to the
>   hum of the big wheel, ...
> The machinist rolls up his sleeves, the policeman
>   travels his beat, the gatekeeper marks who pass, ...
> The paving man leans on his two-handed rammer, the
>   reporter's lead flies swiftly over the notebook,
>   the sign painter is lettering with blue and gold, ...
>   the bookkeeper counts at his desk,

the shoemaker waxes his thread,
The conductor beats time for the band and all the performers
    follow him,

. . . .

The peddler sweats with his pack on his back, (the
    purchaser higgling about the odd cent;) . . .
The floor men are laying the floor, the tinners are
    tinning the roof, the masons are calling for mortar,
In single file each shouldering his hod pass onward
    the laborers . . .

When Whitman celebrates the great individuals that emerge from the masses, he writes about people who are an organic part of a larger drama. When he chants the grief of the nation over its chosen leader, he creates a stage on which personal loyalties and aspirations and antagonisms are projected and magnified a millionfold:

Coffin that passes through lanes and streets,
Through day and night with the great cloud darkening the land,
With the pomp of the inloop'd flags with the cities draped in black,
With the show of the States themselves as of crepe-veil'd women
    standing,
With processions long and winding and the flambeaus of the night,

With the countless torches lit, with the silent sea of faces and the
    unbared heads,
With the waiting depot, the arriving coffin, and the sombre faces,
With dirges through the night, with the thousand voices rising
    strong and solemn,
With all the mournful voices of the dirges pour'd around the
    coffin,
The dim-lit churches and the shuddering organs—where amid
    these you journey,
With the tolling tolling bells' perpetual clang,
Here, coffin that slowly passes,
I give you my sprig of lilac.

If we look for a native American cultural tradition, here are some of its roots. It is in fact this strand in our cultural tradition that the cultural revolution of the young has rediscovered, leading in our national life to a resurgence of color, chant, rhythm, drama, extravagant humor, and boisterous irreverence. If we want to deal with culture as an authentic, living thing, these are some of the roots, and these are some of the elements, to which we must be able to relate. Culture cannot be a Sunday suit worn only in English classes. It must have roots in the authentic native experience of a people.

MULTIETHNIC AMERICA

As we try to identify some of the native, authentically American elements in our culture, we at the same time become more aware of the elements that are *not* native. American English and American culture have constantly been enriched by nonnative influences. Names like Einstein, Oppenheimer, and Teller in American science; Rubinstein and Horovitz in American music; Tarantino, Alioto, and Scoma in American restaurants constantly remind us of the strong **bilingual, bicultural** strand in American life. From the linguist's point of view, one of the most striking things about American life is that *millions of Americans are, and have always been, bilingual.* While administrators required English teachers in the Bronx to speak with a Boston accent, and while textbook authors wrote exercise sentences about William Shakespeare's son and Sir Philip Sidney's death in battle, millions of Americans spoke English as a second language. They developed a life-style in which echoes of Old Country speech and adaptations of Old Country ways served as a constant leavening and enriching influence in the mainstream culture.

The basic fact about American English is that it has served as the common medium for people from a great diversity of linguistic backgrounds. The basic fact about American culture is that it is a rich new synthesis with many varied elements in various stages of interaction and assimilation. If our teaching of English is going to do justice to these facts, we must obviously break out of any remnants of a narrow, one-track WASP parochialism. We must learn to deal with American English and American life as a many-splendored thing.

Everyday work with language offers us many opportunities to develop the student's sense of our linguistic and cultural pluralism. Wherever we touch upon **linguistic geography**, for instance, we encounter traces of the languages other than English that have played a role in the American experience. Studying the place names of the West and Southwest, we find *San Francisco*—"the city of St. Francis"; *Los Angeles*—"the city of Our Lady of the Angels"; *Santa Fe*—"the city of the Holy Faith"; *Santa Cruz*—"the city of the Holy Cross"; *Los Gatos*—"the place of the wildcats"; *Palo Alto*—"the place of the tall tree"; *Las Vegas*—"the city of the plains." *Colorado, Nevada, Sacramento, Rio Grande*—these are all *Spanish* names; the very words for sierra, canyon, and mesa, for manzanita and lariat and rodeo, are Spanish. We are constantly reminded that the first European explorers in these areas spoke Spanish or Portuguese, that the mission churches were built by Spanish-speaking priests. Nor is the Spanish influence a matter of a distant, romanticized past: Restaurants in small towns have names like El Rebozo and La Cantina; the students in English classes read about characters named

Caulfield and Finn and Twist, but their own names are just as likely to be Gonzales and Garcia and Ramirez.

As we turn the page of our imaginary sociolinguistic atlas to the other end of the country, we cannot talk for long about the cultural patterns of New York City, for instance, without commenting on another prominent linguistic and cultural strain: Many New Yorkers echo in their speech and gestures, in their patterns of ingratiation and exasperation, the **Yiddish** that their grandparents brought from the ghettos of Eastern Europe. Somewhere in their background they have had contact with Jewish cooking and Jewish mothers; part of their growing up has been to absorb, to reject, or to make their peace with the kind of world that provides the background for Malamud's *The Assistant*, Saul Bellow's *Herzog*, as well as the fiction of half a dozen other prominent contemporary American writers. We can study with our students the inversions, intonation patterns, and rhetorical questions illustrated in sentences like the following:

> Him you call a philosopher?
> You have maybe relatives in New York?
> Last month I spent on doctors and medicines forty-five dollars.
> "I didn't know you were there." "What then? I was maybe in the White House?"
> A raise I should ask him for?
> Take another cookie. Who's counting?

We can discuss the role of Yiddish terms—*shmaltz, shnozzle, shnook*—in American slang. We can explain what a *mensh* is; we can explain what a *shlemiel* is, drawing for help on Leo Rosten's *The Joys of Yiddish*:

> A shlemiel takes a bath and forgets to wash his face.
>
> The shlemiel falls on his back and breaks his nose.
>
> A shlemiel came to his rabbi, distraught. "Rabbi, you've got to advise me. Every year my wife brings forth a baby. I have nine children already, and barely enough money to feed them—Rabbi, what can I do?"
> The sage thought not a moment. "Do nothing."

Outgrowing our "liberal" sensitivity to ethnic jokes, we can rediscover the whole marvelous world of Jewish humor. Here is Rosten's anecdote to illustrate the uses of *mazel tov*—"congratulations":

> Mournfully, Mr. Lefkowitz entered the offices of his burial society. "I've come to make the funeral arrangements for my dear wife." "Your wife?"

asked the astonished secretary. "But we buried her last year!" "That was my first wife," sighed lugubrious Lefkowitz. "I'm talking about my second." "Second? I didn't know you remarried. *Mazel tov!*"[14]

Almost everywhere we go in this country, we encounter ethnic and cultural strands that provide local color and regional identity. Though we find French place names in many parts of the United States, they become more noticeable and more striking as we move toward New Orleans, Baton Rouge, Lake Pontchartrain: This is Creole country, where we can study folk wisdom in proverbs translated from the Creolized colonial French.

> The ox never says thank you to the pasture.
> Every monkey thinks its little one is pretty.
> When you see your neighbor's beard on fire, throw water on your own.
> People who like eggs don't care if the chicken has a sore behind.
> The dog that makes a mess on the sidewalk forgets, but he who has to clean it up remembers.

As we become more fully involved in the multiethnic, multilingual character of the American past and present, we begin to see it as more than a technically demographic and linguistic phenomenon. We rediscover the immigrant's America—America as sanctuary, the *goldeneh medina*, the distant golden shore, the second chance. Millions of "New Americans" discovered the meaning of what one refugee from Hitler's fascism called the most profoundly significant of all American idioms: "to start all over again." This is what America means in the title of Elia Kazan's *America, America*: the sudden surging hope that it is possible to get out from under, the growing conviction that oppression is not man's natural state, the deeply ingrained knowledge that however time may have tarnished it there is a profound and special meaning in the American experience for mankind. As S. N. Behrman said in his introduction to Kazan's book,

> When I saw, early in Mr. Kazan's manuscript, the Turkish soldiers setting fire to the church in which the terrified Greeks and Armenians are huddled praying for salvation against the flames that were about to devour their Sanctuary, I knew what my own parents must have felt. . . . For Stavros' people, as for my own, America represented a sanctuary to which no Overlord would set the torch. This exigency of choice has been a primary motive in the many waves of European emigration here. It constitutes a living tissue in the fabric of this country's life, in a vast web of mingled racial memory.[15]

This is the true American myth—a myth built not around generals, and glorious leaders, or demigods. It is a myth built around people like

the Armenians, Assyrians, and Japanese in the stories of William Saroyan
—people who "are of the stuff that is eternal in man," who represent the
part of man "that cannot be destroyed, the part that massacre does not
destroy, the part that earthquake and war and famine and madness and
everything else cannot destroy."[16]

The New American sees America as an *alternative*. Much that to
others has become platitude is to him lived experience. For generations,
the assimilated American intellectual has measured American reality
against its professed ideals and found it wanting. The immigrant, the
refugee, measures American reality against past experience. He marvels
at the commonplace; he finds inspiration in things that others take for
granted. Thus, Alice Herdan-Zuckmayer, in *The Farm in the Green
Mountains*, describes her first trip to an American college library:

> There are the Romans and the Greeks . . . the geographers . . . the bi-
> ographies. . . . There are the Russians—the anarchists and the believers,
> the Christians and the terrorists, the quietists and the revolutionaries,
> down to the newest Soviet comedies and serious plays. . . . The books are
> all there—the Americans, the French, the Scandinavians, the Dutch and
> the Italians, the literature of India, China, and Spain—the nations in litera-
> ture and history, through the ages, with their religions, jurisprudence, music,
> folklore, science, agriculture . . . all the material is there, arranged in order,
> but not abridged by anybody, or sifted by anybody. The students themselves
> . . . are supposed to search, to choose, to sift.

She describes her first involvement in the public affairs of a small-town
citizenry:

> People get excited over unsatisfactory conditions . . . they talk about mis-
> takes and blunders; they criticize and are dissatisfied with things as they
> are, but the general slant, the general drift of these conversations is new and
> unusual. For behind each criticism there is always the assumption that it
> is possible to *change* things for the better—through a kind of change not
> resulting from things in general, or from the government, or from historical
> trends, but through change initiated by individuals. After such conversa-
> tions, I suddenly felt a personal responsibility, not merely for my own fate,
> but as part of that force that generates change and motion.[17]

Looking at his adopted country from this perspective, the New
American often represents a kind of "Americanism" that owes little to
conventional patriotic oratory. The apparent chauvinism of the first-
generation and second-generation American reflects a pride in the hard-
won ability to communicate in an at first radically alien language and culture, a pride in by and large making it in one's new environment on his

own, a pride in having acquired full citizenship without surrender of identity.

Conventional academic training has generally not made it easy for English teachers to relate to the multiethnic dimension of American life. To acquire culture and education often meant leaving one's ethnic background behind—shedding the "bad English" of parents and aunts and uncles. To acquire literary culture often meant following Henry James's New Englanders in pursuit of Old World sophistication, or William Faulkner's Southerners in pursuit of a baroque rural past—rather than following the odysseys of Upton Sinclair's Lithuanians and Nelson Algren's Poles through the asphalt jungles of Detroit and Chicago. For all his alleged sympathy with the "people" and the "masses," the established academic liberal is often narrowly élitist in his cultural and literary sympathies. In doing so, he often cuts himself off from the sources of folk poetry and folk wisdom and folk humor in America's ethnic traditions. He thus deprives himself and his students of some of the possible counterweights to the sense of emotional aridity, the pervading sense of alienation and impotence, that dominates much modern literature.

How do we counteract our students' feeling that modern literature is always gloomy and portentous? How do we leaven its pervading pessimism—its Waste Land psychology, its Kafkaesque sense of horror, its cult of the Absurd? One place we can turn to is a short story like Bernard Malamud's "The Magic Barrel," the story of Leon Finkle, a rabbinical student at Yeshiva University, and his dealings with Pinye Salzman, the Jewish marriage broker. Students who have seen love treated in literature only through the eyes of J. Alfred Prufrock will appreciate how Leo, after many pathetic and futile initiatives, finally finds true love through a picture left accidentally among the matchmaker's euphemistic dossiers:

> Salzman put down his glass and said expectantly, "You found maybe somebody you like?"
>
> "Not among these."
>
> The marriage broker turned sad eyes away.
>
> "Here's the one I like." Leo held forth the snapshot.
>
> Salzman slipped on his glasses and took the picture into his trembling hand. He turned ghastly and let out a miserable groan.
>
> "What's the matter?" cried Leo.
>
> "Excuse me. Was an accident this picture. She is not for you."
>
> Salzman frantically shoved the manila packet into his portfolio. He thrust the snapshot into his pocket and fled down the stairs.
>
> Leo, after momentary paralysis, gave chase and cornered the marriage broker in the vestibule. The landlady made hysterical outcries, but neither of them listened.

"Give me back the picture, Salzman."

"No." The pain in his eyes was terrible.

"Tell me where she is then."

"This I can't tell you. Excuse me."

He made to depart, but Leo, forgetting himself, seized the matchmaker by his tight coat and shook him frenziedly.

"Please," sighed Salzman. "*Please*."

Leo ashamedly let him go. "Tell me who she is," he begged. "It's very important for me to know."

"She is not for you. She is a wild one—wild, without shame. This is not a bride for a rabbi."

"What do you mean wild?"

"Like an animal. Like a dog. For her to be poor was a sin. This is why she is dead now."

"In God's name, what do you mean?"

"Her I can't introduce to you," Salzman cried.

"Why are you so excited?"

"Why he asks," Salzman said, bursting into tears. "This is my baby, my Stella, she should burn in hell." [18]

What kind of literature do we turn to when we try to respond to W. H. Auden's plea: "In the desert of the heart/ Let the healing fountain start"? One place we can go to is William Saroyan's story of the almost-blind Armenian gardener Dikran, who tried to breathe life back into the hummingbird he had found half-frozen in the dead of winter:

The old man claimed the hummingbird lived through that winter, but I never knew for sure. I saw hummingbirds again when summer came, but I couldn't tell one from the other.

One day in the summer I asked the old man.

"Did it live?"

"The little bird?" he said.

"Yes," I said. "That we gave the honey to. You remember. The little bird that was dying in the winter. Did it live?"

"Look about you," the old man said. "Do you see the bird?"

"I see hummingbirds," I said.

"Each of them is our bird," the old man said. "Each of them, each of them," he said swiftly and gently. [19]

Where do we go for the kind of earthy humor that can serve as an antidote to our modern neuroses and frustrations? One place we turn to is the traditional folk humor of generations of peasants and proletarians, the kind of humor that is part of the strength of Bertolt Brecht's *Mother Courage*, the kind of humor that outlasts glorious victories and heroic disasters. Thus, when Elia Kazan's hero discovers he cannot earn the money to go to America by hard work, he decides to marry the rich Thomna, whose appearance, regrettably, is marred by a very long nose. His aunt, looking at the photograph of the bride which the hero has sent, says, "They say that a long nose is a sign of virtue." To which the uncle replies: "With a nose like that, virtue is inevitable."

Through much of their history, an overriding goal of American schools has been assimilation, Americanization. Operating on the "melting pot" theory, the schools helped the descendants of numerous waves of immigrants become fully integrated and self-sustaining members of a new nation. Only in recent years have critics begun to feel that the process of standardization may have been *too* efficient, that it may have leveled too thoroughly the kind of diversity that provides a safeguard against a narrow conformity. The presence of earlier linguistic minorities and the constant influx of new immigrants have helped give American life its breadth and comprehensiveness. The ethnic American who retains ties to the past, who is still in some way close to his roots, is among the least interchangeable of Americans.

THE CULTURE OF MINORITIES

Our renewed emphasis on authentic native traditions close to popular culture, and the recognition of the multilingual, multiethnic strands in American life, contribute to a common effect. They both help bring about a return to the roots, a recognition of diversity, a narrowing of the gap between academic culture and the life of the people. The same is true for the third major strand in our current redefinition of American culture: the recognition of *authentic native subcultures*, of cultural minorities for whom the melting pot theory has worked badly or not at all. Basically,

> the people for whom assimilation worked were Europeans. An Italian immigrant, for example, would lean on his family, on the Italo-American club, or other Italo-American institutions until he felt secure enough to slip into the American mainstream. But the melting pot theory has no validity for black people who are former slaves and are poor through historical accident. Nor does it apply to Mexican-Americans, who come over the border to get work, nor to Puerto Ricans, nor to American Indians. . . . These are highly visible minority groups who have to survive in a society that is basically white.[20]

A very basic shift has taken place in the last few decades as the most eloquent spokesmen of these cultural minorities have abandoned or modified the rhetoric of assimilation and moved toward a new rhetoric of self-respect. Thus, in the black community, an earlier generation had aimed at full integration by emulating white standards in speech, manners, dress, food, education, and attitudes toward success. As Ernece B. Kelly has pointed out, the central message that white audiences took home from plays like Lorraine Hansberry's *A Raisin in the Sun* was "that Blacks wanted very much to be like them."[21] The movement toward black identity and black pride made a new generation scornful of their elders who dreamed of "waking up white." As LeRoi Jones says in *Home,*

> the abandonment of one's local (*i.e.,* place or group) emotional attachments in favor of the abstract emotional response of what is called "the general public" (which is notoriously white and middle class) has always been the great diluter of any Negro culture. "You're acting like a nigger," was the standard disparagement. I remember being chastised severely for daring to eat a piece of watermelon on the Howard campus. "Do you realize you're sitting near the highway?" is what the man said. "This is the capstone of Negro education." And it is too, in the sense that it teaches the Negro how to make out in the white society, using the agonizing overcompensation of pretending he's also white. . . . Any reference to the Negro-ness of the American Negro has always been frowned upon by the black middle class in their frenzied dash toward the precipice of the American mainstream.[22]

A new generation has found in the separateness of the American Negro's experience a source of solidarity, of strength, of vitality, and of insight. It has experienced the liberating, bracing effect of putting an end to self-deception and obsequiousness, of people accepting who and what they are. Nat Hentoff quotes the young girl from Birmingham who says, "I'm tired of going to church and listening to teen-agers giggle and laugh when the old songs are sung. I want to know what the old songs are. I want to know that my parents were working for fifteen cents a day. I want to know what made me."[23]

The movement toward black solidarity and black pride has forcibly reminded teachers, and English teachers in particular, that education cannot be simply the dispensing of aseptically packaged "subject matter." Education takes place in an inescapable, larger social context, and it is directed at human beings with powerful aspirations and confusions of their own. This new kind of awareness has made us take a second look at much of what we do, at much of what we imply by the choices we make and the routines we follow. Bill Cosby in an interview once described the kind of situation that puts the comprehensiveness of the teacher's sympathies to the test:

> I remember when I was in junior high school at Christmas time, and we'd been allowed to bring records in. I never owned any, but a couple of colored

girls brought Mahalia Jackson's version of *Silent Night*, while the white kids brought things like the Mormon Tabernacle Choir singing *Hallelujah* and Bing Crosby's *White Christmas*. Well, the black treatment of a Christmas carol was something the white kids snickered at, because of their own ignorance; and, at the same time, we were embarrassed because it wasn't white. Mahalia just didn't sound like the Mormon Tabernacle Choir, and Clara Ward didn't sound like Bing Crosby.

Whatever our definition of American culture, we have to recognize in the singing of a Mahalia Jackson, as in much black music and religion, something deeply rooted in the American experience: the strength of spirit of an oppressed people refusing to be crushed by adversity; the power of joy that has triumphed over suffering. Education remains shallow without experiences like hearing a singer like Mahalia Jackson sing

I am tired, I am weary, take my hand, O Lord, lead me on;

or hearing her sing

Let the children shout about the goodness of the Lord;

or hearing her sing

We shall overcome,
We are not afraid.

The time has passed when teachers could come to the black community from the outside with the assumption that they were bringing culture to the culturally deprived. Everywhere black people are beginning to feel that "blacks have a valid culture of their own, separate from and, in some respects, superior to white culture."[24] The most basic need of the American Negro is for *respect*. The most basic need of the black citizen, as of every other citizen, is for recognition of his worth as a human being. One way teachers can show respect is by relating to the sources of strength and inspiration in the black experience.

Recognition of black culture, and involvement in the black experience, in several major ways have a bracing effect on the English teacher's work with language and literature. One very basic thing happens inevitably when we take the work of authentic black writers into the classroom: We become more strongly aware of what *honesty* means in the use of language. We introduce a heightened *sense of reality* into our work with literature. We reopen for our students the basic question of how the word relates to the world. When we read writers who talk with integrity about the lives of black Americans, our euphemisms, our reassuring platitudes, and our alibis give way and we come face to face with the truth. We come to deal with the kind of bitter truth that is ultimately stronger than halfhearted lies. We learn something about ourselves, about the society we live in, about what people are capable of. When we take into the classroom a poem like Langston Hughes' "Ballad of the Landlord," we may not know how to make it the object of sophisticated critical games, but we and our students know that it is truth-telling time:

> Landlord, landlord,
> My roof has sprung a leak.
> Don't you 'member I told you about it
> Way last week?
>
> Landlord, landlord,
> These steps is broken down.
> When you come up yourself
> It's a wonder you don't fall down.
>
> Ten bucks you say I owe you?
> Ten bucks you say is due?
> Well, that's ten bucks more'n I'll pay you
> Till you fix this house up new.
>
> What? You gonna get eviction orders?
> You gonna cut off my heat?
> You gonna take my furniture and
> Throw it in the street?
>
> Um-huh! You talking high and mighty.
> Talk on—till you get through.
> You ain't gonna be able to say a word
> If I land my fist on you.
>
> Police! Police!
> Come and get this man!
> He's trying to ruin the government
> And overturn the land!
>
> Copper's whistle!
> Patrol bell!
> Arrest.

Precinct station.
Iron cell.
Headlines in press:

MAN THREATENS LANDLORD

TENANT HELD NO BAIL

JUDGE GIVES NEGRO 90 DAYS IN COUNTY JAIL[25]

Jonathan Kozol says about this poem in *Death at an Early Age,*

> This poem may not satisfy the taste of every critic, and I am not making
> any claims to immortality for a poem just because I happen to like it a great
> deal. But the reason this poem did have so much value and meaning for me
> and, I believe, for many of my students, is that it not only seems moving
> in an obvious and immediate human way but that it *finds* its emotion in
> something ordinary. It is a poem which really does allow both heroism and
> pathos to poor people, sees strength in awkwardness and attributes to a
> poor person standing on the stoop of his slum house every bit as much
> significance as William Wordsworth saw in daffodils, waterfalls and clouds.[26]

This poem may not in any superficial way "accentuate the positive"
or "tell us of something hopeful." But it does something more educational: It reminds us that our actions speak louder than our professed
ideals. It reminds us that our idealism cannot be all beautiful words.

The first great virtue of using materials from black literature and
black culture is that our students learn what it means to "tell it like it is."
The second great virtue of using such materials is that they compel
imaginative identification with an order of experience outside that of the
affluent majority. The black writer asks the student from the complacent
mainstream to "walk a mile in my shoes." One of the most basic uses of
imagination is to help us put ourselves *in someone else's place.* It helps
us break out of our own constricted little world; it makes us learn and
grow by teaching us to see and feel in new and unsuspected ways. Thus,
when our students read Richard Wright's *Black Boy,* we can ask them to
write (or talk) about questions like the following. Each question asks them
to put themselves in the place of the boy in Wright's book:

> 1.   Your father left your mother for another woman and won't pay a
> dime to support you. Your mother and you go to him to ask for money to
> leave the state. He won't give your mother any, but he offers you a nickel.
> What would you do? What would you say?

2. You are in grade school and are accused of eating nuts in class and dropping the shells on the floor. It was the boy in front of you, and you know it. The teacher is going to whip you with a switch. The boy in front of you says nothing. What would you say and do?

3. You are a Negro and work for a white man whose mean dog bites you hard on the thigh. The white man won't get a doctor and just says, "A dog bite can't hurt a nigger." What would you do or say?

4. You are young and your grandmother keeps after you to have faith in God. You are in church and whisper that you'll have faith when you see an angel. Your grandmother hears wrong and tells the minister that you actually saw an angel. The minister comes up to you. What would you say to him?

5. You are out in the country, a Negro, and some white boys offer you a ride on the running board of their car into town. You hop on. They offer you a drink and you say, "No," but you forget to add, "sir." The boys crack you on the head so that you fall onto the road. They then stop the car and threaten you. What would you do? How would you feel?

6. You are a Southern Negro and thin and hungry. One day you deliver a package to a white man from the North. He asks you if you are hungry. What would you say to him? He offers you a dollar. Would you take it? Why or why not?[27]

Books like Richard Wright's *Black Boy* and Ralph Ellison's *Invisible Man* are "social documents" in the best sense of the word: They contribute powerfully to our sense of what it means to be American at this point in history. They illuminate what and where we are. But these books are not "sociology": They make available to us authentic human experience —for us to share, to become involved in, to re-enact imaginatively. When they make patterns and meanings emerge from the experience, those patterns take shape in the full context of imagery, thought, and feeling.

The third great virtue of teaching black literature is that it helps us examine the nature and sources of *eloquence*. It helps our students sense the power of words to move, to give voice to what is deeply felt. Some of the most eloquent voices in America's present and its past are the voices of black people talking about what it means to be black in white America.

The words of Frederick Douglass and of W. E. B. DuBois command our attention because these men have something to say. When our students have been fed too much pap, when they have listened to too many speeches that were mere tired ritual, it is a revelation for them to see language used as if everything were at stake. Here is Frederick Douglass, in his Fourth of July speech delivered in 1852, speaking as a former slave about the moral implications of slavery:

What to the American slave is your Fourth of July? I answer: a day that reveals to him, more than all other days in the year, the gross injustice and cruelty to which he is the constant victim. To him your celebration is a sham; your boasted liberty, an unholy licence; your national greatness, swelling vanity; your sounds of rejoicing are empty and heartless; your denunciation of tyrants, brass-fronted impudence; your shouts of liberty and equality, hollow mockery; your prayers and hymns, your sermons and thanksgivings, with all your religious parade and solemnity, are, to him, more bombast, fraud, deception, impiety and hypocrisy—a thin veil to cover up crimes which would disgrace a nation of savages.[28]

Here is W. E. Burghardt DuBois, writing in *The Souls of Black Folk* in 1903:

Around us the history of the land has centered for thrice a hundred years; out of the nation's heart we have called all that was best to throttle and subdue all that was worst; fire and blood, prayer and sacrifice, have billowed over this people, and they have found peace only in the altars of the God of Right. Nor has our gift of the Spirit been merely passive. Actively we have woven ourselves with the very warp and woof of this nation,—we fought their battles, shared their sorrow, mingled our blood with theirs, and generation after generation have pleaded with a headstrong, careless people to despise not Justice, Mercy, and Truth, lest the nation be smitten with a curse. Our song, our toil, our cheer, and warning have been given to this nation in blood-brotherhood. Are not these gifts worth the giving? Is not this work and striving? Would America have been America without her Negro people?

Even so is the hope that sang in the songs of my fathers well sung. If somewhere in this whirl and chaos of things there dwells Eternal Good, pitiful yet masterful, then anon in his good time America shall rend the Veil and the prisoned shall go free.[29]

As teachers respond to the power and beauty of black culture and black literature, they become aware of the inadequacy of an earlier model of cultural integration, which assumed "that salvation for the black lay in merging with the white, in denigrating all that made him different."[30] We are slowly moving toward a new definition of integration founded in genuine partnership and mutual respect. While this movement toward a strong group identity within a larger pluralistic framework is strongest in the black community, the same general trend is emerging among the millions of Spanish-speaking Americans—the Mexican-American Chicanos of the Southwest and the Puerto Rican and Cuban minorities of the East and Southeast. In the words of Armando Rodriguez,

Cultural and language diversities are no shackles that must be stripped off before a full partnership in the American society can be attained. Mexican-Americans are "advantaged" peoples because they possess the richness of differences that will bring to the United States what the whole American Dream is all about—a free, democratic, and pluralistic United States of America. Whether it be the poorest, most illiterate "barrio" dweller or the most sophisticated Mexicano, the determination is equally deep to retain and strengthen his identity as an American in the true sense of the word. This means a retention and a practicing respect for his cultural heritage and its role in creating in the United States a dominating attitude that difference is strength and not destruction, that difference is what life is all about.[31]

English teachers are beginning to realize that it is futile to transpose a conventional Eastern prep school curriculum in English to classrooms where a third or half of the students have Spanish surnames. It is discriminatory to use testing instruments ignoring the fact that the student is using English as a second language. More positively, teachers are learning how to draw on the resources of the bilingual and bicultural student in order to leaven and enrich their own teaching. They are learning how to tap the rich reservoir of Mexican-American and Indian folklore. They are learning how to use comparison and contrast with Spanish to heighten the student's awareness and understanding of characteristic features of English. They are helping their students escape from a narrow cultural parochialism by introducing them to the grandeur of Mexican architecture, from the Indian past through the colonial interval to the aggressively modern present; by introducing them to the great painters like Rivera; by introducing them to the color and life of Latin American folkways.

In the past, American education has too often failed students who were economically disadvantaged and culturally isolated. Whatever the historical reasons or our collective alibis, the schools have often failed to tap the resources of these children, to engage their interest, to instill in them feelings of hope and pride. In the past, we have often blamed these failures on forces outside our control. The time has come to examine our own definitions of excellence and achievement and culture for their share of the blame. Our own one-sidedness and exclusiveness may be at least partly to blame for "the waste of years, the loss of chances, the closing of avenues, the end of hopes."[32]

FOOTNOTES

[1]Richard Hoggart, "Schools of English and Contemporary Society," *American Scholar* (Spring 1964), p. 247.

[2]Susan Sontag, *Against Interpretation* (New York: Dell Publishing Co., Inc., 1966), pp. 286–287, 303.

[3]Sontag, *Against Interpretation*, p. 291.

[4]Hoggart, "Schools of English and Contemporary Society," p. 254.

[5]Al Capp, *The World of L'il Abner* (New York: Ballantine Books, Inc., 1952), p. v.

[6]Isaac Asimov and Groff Conklin, *Fifty Short Science Fiction Tales* (New York: Collier Books, The Macmillan Company, 1963), p. 13.

[7]Arthur Feldman, "The Mathematicians," in Asimov and Conklin, *Fifty Short Science Fiction Tales*, p. 80.

[8]Ray Bradbury, *The Martian Chronicles* (New York: Harold Matson, 1958).

[9]Sontag, *Against Interpretation*, p. 213.

[10]Ibid., p. 215.

[11]Frederic Jameson, "Metacommentary." *PMLA*, 86 (January 1971), 17.

[12]W. K. Wimsatt, Jr., *The Verbal Icon: Studies in the Meaning of Poetry* (New York: The Noonday Press, a division of Farrar, Straus & Giroux, Inc., 1958), pp. 192–193.

[13]Carl Sandburg, "Prayers of Steel," *Cornhuskers* (New York: Holt, Rinehart and Winston, Inc., 1918), p. 65.

[14]Leo Rosten, *The Joys of Yiddish* (New York: McGraw-Hill Book Company, 1968), pp. 343–346, 224–226.

[15]Elia Kazan, *America, America* (New York: Popular Library Inc., 1964), pp. 10–11.

[16]William Saroyan, "Seventy Thousand Assyrians," in Charlotte Brooks, ed., *The Outnumbered: Stories, Essays and Poems About Minority Groups* (New York: Dell Publishing Co., 1967), pp. 100–101.

[17]Alice Herdan-Zuckmayer, *Die Farm in den Grünen Bergen* (Frankfurt am Main: Fischer Bücherei, 1956), pp. 190–191, 179–180.

[18]Bernard Malamud, *The Magic Barrel* (New York: Farrar, Straus & Giroux, Inc., 1958), pp. 211–212.

[19]William Saroyan, *My Kind of Crazy, Wonderful People* (New York: Harcourt, Brace & World, Inc., 1944).

[20]"An Interview with Topper Carew," *Saturday Review*, July 18, 1970, pp. 46–48.

[21]Ernece B. Kelly, Review of *New Plays from the Black Theatre*, in *College Composition and Communication*, 21 (February 1970), 93.

[22]LeRoi Jones, *Home: Social Essays* (New York: William Morrow & Company, Inc., 1966), pp. 108–109.

[23]Nat Hentoff, "The Other Side of the Blues," in Herbert Hill, ed., *Anger, and Beyond: The Negro Writer in the United States* (New York: Harper & Row, Publishers, Incorporated, 1968), p. 80.

[24]James Cass, "Can the University Survive the Black Challenge?" *Saturday Review*, June 21, 1969, p. 70.

[25]Langston Hughes, "Ballad of the Landlord," *The Langston Hughes Reader* (New York: George Braziller, Inc., 1958), pp. 101–102.

[26]Jonathan Kozol, *Death at an Early Age: The Destruction of the Hearts and Minds of Negro Children in the Boston Public Schools* (New York: Bantam Books, Inc., 1968), pp. 195–196.

[27]Marcia Pitcole, "*Black Boy* and Role Playing," *English Journal*, 57 (November 1968), 1140–1142.

[28]Quoted in Eldridge Cleaver, *Soul on Ice* (New York: McGraw-Hill Book Company, 1968), pp. 75–76.

[29]W. E. Burghardt DuBois, *The Souls of Black Folk* (New York: Fawcett World Library, 1961), p. 190.

[30]Bardwell L. Smith, "Educational Trends in the Seventies," *AAUP Bulletin* (Summer 1970), p. 131.

[31]Armando Rodriguez, "The Mexican-American—Disadvantaged? Ya Basta!" *The Florida FL Reporter* (Spring/Summer 1969), 35–36.

[32]Kozol, *Death at an Early Age*, p. 50.

FOR FURTHER STUDY

A.   It is often said that today's adolescents live in a world of their own, poorly understood by their parents and teachers. The following poems and song lyrics reflect some of the themes and attitudes of today's youth culture. Which of these do you recognize? How would you explain the feelings and attitudes here expressed? How representative do you think they are of the way young people today think and feel?

Tim Reynolds
A Hell of a Day

> This was a day of fumbling and petty accidents,
> as though the population had grown all thumbs
> at once. Watering her chrysanthemums,
> Mrs. Kamei was surprised to see the plants
> blacken, water turn to steam. Both Dote and Michiko
> noted the other's absence but not her own.
> Mr. Kime lifted his hat, but his head was gone.
> Mr. Watanable rolled a double zero.
> Photographing her son by the river bridge
> Mrs. Ume pressed the shutter and overexposed her film.
> Her son's yawn swallowed him. And everything turned on
> when pretty Miss Mihara snapped the light switch.
> Then old Mr. Ekahomo struck a match
> to light his pipe, and the town caught, and dissolved in flame.

Tim Buckley
Goodbye and Hello

> The antique people are down in the dungeons
>   Run by machines and afraid of the tax
> Their heads in the grave and their hands on their eyes
>   Hauling their hearts around circular tracks
> Pretending forever their masquerade towers
>   Are not really riddled with widening cracks
>   And I wave goodbye to iron
>   And smile hello to the air

> O the new children dance   I am young
> All around the balloons   I will live
> Swaying by chance   I am strong
> To the breeze from the moon   I can give
> Painting the sky   You the strange
> With the colors of sun   Seed of day
> Freely they fly   Feel the change
> As all become one   Know the Way

The velocity addicts explode on the highways
    Ignoring the journey and moving so fast
Their nerves fall apart and they gasp but can't breathe
    They run from the cops of the skeleton past
Petrified by tradition in a nightmare they stagger
    Into nowhere at all and then look up aghast
        And I wave goodbye to speed
        And smile hello to a rose

O the new children play	I am young
Under juniper trees	I will live
Sky blue or grey	I am strong
They continue at ease	I can give
Moving so slow	You the strange
That serenely they can	Seed of day
Gracefully grow	Feel the change
And yes still understand	Know the Way

The king and the queen in their castle of billboards
    Sleepwalk down the hallways dragging behind
All their possessions and transient treasures
    As they go to worship the electronic shrine
On which is playing the late late commercial
    In that hollowest house of the opulent blind
        And I wave goodbye to Mammon
        And smile hello to a stream

O the new children buy	I am young
All the world for a song	I will live
Without a dime	I am strong
To which they belong	I can give
Nobody owns	You the strange
Anything anywhere	Seed of day
Everyone's grown	Feel the change
Up so big they can share	Know the Way

The vaudeville generals cavort on the stage
    And shatter their audience with submachine guns
And Freedom and Violence the acrobat clowns
    Do a balancing act on the graves of our sons
While the tapdancing Emperor sings "War is peace"
    And Love the Magician disappears in the fun
        And I wave goodbye to murder
        And smile hello to the rain

O the new children can't	I am young
Tell a foe from a friend	I will live
Quick to enchant	I am strong
And so glad to extend	I can give
Handfuls of dawn	You the strange
To kaleidoscope men	Seed of day
Come from beyond	Feel the change
The Great Wall of Skin	Know the Way

The bloodless husbands are jesters who listen
    Like sheep to the shrieks and commands of their wives
And the men who aren't men leave the women alone
    See them all faking love on a bed made of knives
Afraid to discover or trust in their bodies
    And in secret divorce they will never survive
        And I wave goodbye to ashes
        And smile hello to a girl

O the new children kiss	I am young
They are so proud to learn	I will live
Womanhood bliss	I am strong
And the manfire that burns	I can give
Knowing no fear	You the strange
They take off their clothes	Seed of day
Honest and clear	Feel the change
As a river that flows	Know the Way

The antique people are fading out slowly
    Like newspapers flaming in mind suicide
Godless and sexless directionless loons
    Their sham sandcastles dissolve in the tide
They put on their deathmasks and compromise daily
    The new children will live for the elders have died
        And I wave goodbye to America
        And smile hello to the world

Bob Kaufman
Benediction

Pale brown Moses went down to Egypt land
To let somebody's people go.
Keep him out of Florida, no UN there:
The poor governor is all alone,
With six hundred thousand illiterates.

America, I forgive you . . . I forgive you
Nailing black Jesus to an imported cross
Every six weeks in Dawson, Georgia.
America, I forgive you . . . I forgive you
Eating black children, I know your hunger.
America, I forgive you . . . I forgive you
Burning Japanese babies defensively—
I realize how necessary it was.
Your ancestor had beautiful thoughts in his brain.
His descendants are experts in real estate.
Your generals have mushrooming visions.
Every day your people get more and more
Cars, televisions, sickness, death dreams.
You must have been great
Alive.

Edwin Brock
Five Ways to Kill a Man

There are many cumbersome ways to kill a man:
you can make him carry a plank of wood
to the top of a hill and nail him to it. To do this
properly you require a crowd of people
wearing sandals, a cock that crows, a cloak
to dissect, a sponge, some vinegar and one
man to hammer the nails home.

Or you can take a length of steel,
shaped and chased in a traditional way,
and attempt to pierce the metal cage he wears.
But for this you need white horses,
English trees, men with bows and arrows,
at least two flags, a prince and a
castle to hold your banquet in.

Dispensing with nobility, you may, if the wind
allows, blow gas at him. But then you need
a mile of mud sliced through with ditches,
not to mention black boots, bomb craters,
more mud, a plague of rats, a dozen songs
and some round hats made of steel.

In an age of aeroplanes, you may fly
miles above your victim and dispose of him by
pressing one small switch. All you then
require is an ocean to separate you, two
systems of government, a nation's scientists,
several factories, a psychopath and
land that no one needs for several years.

These are, as I began, cumbersome ways
to kill a man. Simpler, direct, and much more neat
is to see that he is living somewhere in the middle
of the twentieth century, and leave him there.

B. In an article entitled "The English Language Is My Enemy," Ossie Davis described "the enormous trap of racial prejudgment that works on any child who is born into the English language. . . . Any creature, good or bad, white or black, Jew or Gentile, who uses the English language for the purposes of communication is willing to force the Negro child into 60 ways to despise himself" (*American Teacher*, April 1967). How true is it, for instance, that the connotation of the words *black* and *white* reinforce notions of racial superiority? What could or should English teachers do about it? Study the following sample list for evidence—add examples of your own:

give someone a black eye, blacklist, black sheep, knight on a white charger, black-and-white contrast, White House, a government white paper, white lie, the devil is not as black as he is painted, whitewash, black market, blackhearted, that's very white of you, white plague, lily white, white as a sheet, a black mark, a black-tie affair, a news blackout, white hope, black magic, blacken a reputation, operate in the black, bleed the peasants white, white elephant, Black Shirt, white sale, white flag.

C. The following poems are by black writers ranging from Langston Hughes to contemporary young militants. How do these poems reflect some of the major themes of the black experience? What light do they throw on the rhetoric and the realities of race relations in contemporary America? How do you personally react to each poem?

Langston Hughes
Bound No'th Blues

> Goin' down the road, Lawd,
> Goin' down the road.
> Down the road, Lawd,
> Way, way down the road.
> Got to find somebody
> To help me carry this load.
>
> Road's in front o' me,
> Nothin' to do but walk.
> Road's in front o' me,
> Walk . . . an' walk . . . an' walk.
> I'd like to meet a good friend
> To come along an' talk.
>
> Hates to be lonely,
> Lawd, I hates to be sad.
> Says I hates to be lonely,
> Hates to be lonely an' sad,
> But ever' friend you finds seems
> Like they try to do you bad.
>
> Road, road, road, O!
> Road, road . . . road . . . road, road!
> Road, road, road, O!
> On the no'thern road.
> These Mississippi towns ain't
> Fit fer a hoppin' toad.

Sterling A. Brown
Sister Lou

> Honey
> When de man
> Calls out de las' train
> You're gonna ride,
> Tell him howdy.

Gather up yo' basket
An' yo' knittin' an' yo' things,
An' go on up an' visit
Wid frien' Jesus fo' a spell.

Show Marfa
How to make yo' greengrape jellies,
An' give po' Lazarus
A passel of them Golden Biscuits.

Scald some meal
Fo' some rightdown good spoonbread
Fo' li'l box-plunkin' David.

An' sit aroun'
An' tell them Hebrew Chillen
All yo' stories. . . .

Honey
Don't be feared of them pearly gates,
Don't go 'round to de back,
No mo' dataway
Not evah no mo'.

Let Michael tote yo' burden
An' yo' pocketbook an' evah thing
'Cept yo' Bible,
While Gabriel blows somp'n
Solemn but loudsome
On dat horn of his'n.

Honey
Go Straight on to de Big House,
An' speak to yo' God
Widout no fear an' tremblin'.

Then sit down
An' pass de time of day awhile.

Give a good talkin' to
To yo' favorite 'postle Peter,
An' rub the po' head
Of mixed-up Judas,
An' joke awhile wid Jonah.

Then, when you gits de chance,
Always rememberin' yo' raisin',
Let 'em know youse tired
Jest a mite tired.

Jesus will find yo' bed fo' you
Won't no servant evah bother wid yo' room.
Jesus will lead you

To a room wid windows
Openin' on cherry trees an' plum trees
Bloomin' everlastin'.

An' dat will be yours
Fo' keeps.
Den take yo' time. . . .
Honey, take yo' bressed time.

Robert Hayden
Frederick Douglass

When it is finally ours, this freedom, this liberty, this
     beautiful
and terrible thing, needful to man as air,
usable as earth; when it belongs at last to all,
when it is truly instinct, brain matter, diastole, systole,
reflex action; when it is finally won; when it is more
than the gaudy mumbo jumbo of politicians:
this man, this Douglass, this former slave, this Negro
beaten to his knees, exiled, visioning a world
where none is lonely, none hunted, alien,
this man, superb in love and logic, this man
shall be remembered. Oh, not with statues' rhetoric,
not with legends and poems and wreaths of bronze alone,
but with the lives grown out of his life, the lives
fleshing his dream of the beautiful, needful thing.

Sam Cornish
One Eyed Black Man in Nebraska

The skin quickens to noises.
The ground beneath a black man opens.

His wife in her nightgown
hears horses and men in her husband's
deathbed.

White horses move through the fields
lifting men out of darkness.

In the pillows, she keeps
a rifle and twenty two,
for hunting rabbits and keeping alive.

Still he dies,
one eye closed on the ground.

D.   The following articles deal in various ways with the gap between *academic and popular culture* and the "democratization of the curriculum." Select one, or a more recent article on the same basic topic. Discuss and evaluate the author's stand on one major issue affecting the future of English as a school subject.

Herbert F. Ostrach, "It's My Mind, and I'll Think What I Want," *English Journal*, 56 (March 1967), 443–446, 489;

G. Robert Carlsen, "English Below the Salt," *English Journal*, 58 (March 1969), 363–367;

Maxine Greene, "Against Invisibility," *College English*, 30 (March 1969), 430–436.

E.   The articles below help English teachers relate to *minority students* and minority culture. Choose one of these, or a more recent article on a similar topic. What major themes emerge from the article? How does the article confirm or modify your own views?

Dorothy Sterling, "The Soul of Learning," *English Journal*, 57 (February 1968), 166–180;

Nancy, L. Arnez, "Racial Understanding Through Literature," *English Journal*, 58 (January 1969), 56–61;

Armando Rodriguez, "The Mexican-American—Disadvantaged? Ya Basta!" *The Florida FL Reporter* (Spring/Summer 1969), pp. 35–36, 160;

Richard A. Ross, "Filling the Void: The Black in American Literature," *English Journal*, 59 (January 1970), 31–33;

Ernece B. Kelly, Review of *New Plays from the Black Theater*, *College Composition and Communication*, 21 (February 1970), 93–96;

Kenneth Kinnamon, "Afro-American Literature, the Black Revolution, and Ghetto High Schools," *English Journal*, 59 (February 1970), 189–194;

Geneva Silverman, "English Teacher, why you be doing the thangs you don't do?" *English Journal*, 61 (January 1972), 59–65.

F.   Read Jonathan Kozol's discussion of middle-class values and racial biases in textbooks assigned to black children in a Boston public school: Chapter Eight of *Death at an Early Age* (Bantam, 1968). Then study *reading materials* currently used in local schools in the light of Kozol's observations.

Index

Index